A BEGINNERS
GUIDE TO
LIVING KABBALAH

A
Beginners Guide
to
Living Kabbalah

William G. Gray

THE SANGREAL SODALITY PRESS
Johannesburg, Gauteng, South Africa

First edition, 2009
First printing, 2009

Published by The Sangreal Sodality Press
74 Twelfth Street
Parkmore 2196
Gauteng
South Africa
Email: jacobsang@gmail.com

ISBN 978-0-620-42887-3

Contents

1. The Simplified Guide to the Holy Tree of Life **1**
   A. Introduction 1
   B. The Holy Tree of Life 3

2. Simple Guide to the Paths on the Holy Tree of Life ... **31**

3. Purpose and Use of Magical Images **53**
   A. Preface by Jacobus G. Swart 53
   B. Magical Images 54

4. The Novena of the Tree of Life **91**
   A. Preface by Jacobus G. Swart 91
   B. Introduction 93
   C. The Orisons 100
   D. Epilogue 107

5. The Office of the Holy Tree of Life **111**
   A. Introduction 111
   B. The Office of the Holy Tree of Life 115
   C. Notes—Prayers—Meditations 162
       1. The Blessings of the *Sephirot* 162
       2. The "I Am" Formula 163
       3. The Qabalistic Rule 164
       4. The Qabalistic Creed 164
       5. Qabalistic Prayer 165
       6. Qabalistic Thanksgiving 166
       7. Images and the Tree of Life 166
       8. The Stations of the Tree of Life 169
       9. The Qabalistic Rosary 173

6. Language of the Gods **175**
   A. The Power of Names 175
   B. The Talking Tree of Life 191
   C. Thotols: Keywording the Tree of Life 200
   D. Vowels and Life Elements 219
   E. The Tree Alphabet, Tarot Trumps and Pathworking .. 232
   F. Questing for Definite Objectives 245
   G. Thotolese: Conversing With "Gods" 282
   H. Terminals for "Inner Intelligence" 299

Illustrations

Page 16 . . . . Tree of Life
Page 34 . . . . Numbered Paths of the Tree of Life
Page 41 . . . . The Lightning Flash
Page 41 . . . . The Serpent Path
Page 43 . . . . Pillars, *Paroketh* and *Kesheth*
Page 49 . . . . The Letter Tree of Life
Page 81 . . . . *Kether:* Holy Head
Page 82 . . . . *Chokmah:* Faithful Father
Page 83 . . . . *Binah:* Mature Mother
Page 84 . . . . *Chesed:* Kindly King
Page 85 . . . . *Geburah:* Stern Soldier
Page 86 . . . . *Tiphereth:* Magnificent Mediator
Page 87 . . . . *Netzach:* Lovely Lady
Page 88 . . . . *Hod:* Perceptive Person
Page 89 . . . . *Yesod:* Fertile Figure
Page 90 . . . . *Malkuth:* Mysterious Mate
Page 114 . . . . Complete Tree of Life
Page 163 . . . . The "I Am" Tree
Page 238 . . . . The Tarot Tree

Chapter 1
THE SIMPLIFIED GUIDE
TO THE
HOLY TREE OF LIFE

A. Introduction

Many years ago, a wealthy Texan, one Carr P Collins of Dallas took an interest in my Qabalistic work when Israel Regardie showed him a script I had written purely for private perusal. He insisted on being allowed to back its publication and it duly appeared under the title "Ladder of Lights," and indeed is still in print under the same name. When it came to discussing its subject matter with him however I found him almost incredibly unaware of its actual nature and structural significance.

The man was a millionaire, a graduate of Harvard Business School, had received a very good education, was an earnest Christian of a nonconformist type, a highly intelligent and sensitive individual, and yet could be amazingly naive and surprisingly uninformed in areas many people could have covered quite comfortably. His undoubted attraction to the Western Inner Tradition was purely instinctive, and he could not explain it other than saying that the entire field held a peculiar fascination for him beyond his understanding.

As a fellow man and friend, Carr was a delightful soul I shall never forget, but as a student he was liable to be extremely disconcerting. I would casually mention something I considered quite normal or commonplace, only to be stopped by his interjection "Now just what was that you said? Could you put that more simply, so that I can understand it please ?" He once floored me by asking; "Just what is a nebula?" To my amazement that simple word was a strange one in his undoubtedly adequate vocabulary. Eventually his repeated requests for simplification became so frequent that eventually I said jokingly; "What you need

1

Carr is a 'Child's Simple Guide to the Tree of Life'" to which he enthusiastically agreed "I certainly do, and so do a lot of us, so why don't you write one?" Put that way, what else could I do except pick up the challenge? There was certainly nothing of that nature in publication that anyone had ever heard of. It wouldpositively be a first of its kind in the field.

In point of fact the project proved a lot more difficult than I would ever have believed, but I learned a great deal from the enterprise. Maybe the best thing I learned is that there is no particular virtue in obscurity, and trying to conceal fundamental principles behind a barrier of muddled metaphor and sheer verbiage. In dealing with important matters the vital thing is to communicate them between different minds in mutually comprehensible terms. All too often when dealing with esoteric topics we find that this is far from being the case and frequently by deliberate design. There are many classics written on the topic of the "Holy Tree of Life" which are rich in detail and full of sophisticated comments, yet how many convey simply and plainly enough the central fact that the whole Concept is for practical use in making direct relationships with deity itself. That was what I had been asked to do in such a way that an intelligent child would grasp the idea. What I should more or less say must amount to "My child, this is a good way to get in touch with God and here is how to work it for yourself." So that is what I have tried to accomplish.

Looking back at this little work nearly twenty years later [introduction written 1989], it still seems to have an engaging freshness and vitality so often absent from scholarly learned treatises. Possibly on account of its sheer simplicity and sincerity, and also because it was motivated by quite genuine friendship and sincerity. Carr Collins said it had helped him grasp the tree as nothing else had, and it is my earnest hope that it might do the same for others in a similar position. Perhaps it might lay the ground in some minds which might later be covered with the help of much more advanced textbooks. Who Knows? Anyway, may I wish this further edition an even greater range and effect than the first.

Wm. G. Gray.
United Kingdom. Spring 1989

B. The Holy Tree of Life

Who is the most important individual alive? (This is a "catch" question.) The real answer is—God. Why? Because God is actually the One Life in Whom all other lives, including ours, exist.. Not only here in this world, but everywhere else too. God is with the Sun, Moon, stars, and all the emptiness in between them. Nobody knows, or may ever know exactly what God is, so we have to use words we do understand if we mean to talk or think about God at all. We often say "He," as if God were a Father. Some people say "She," and make God a Mother. Others say "It," or "That," because they don't like to think about God in any ordinary way. Our English word "God," by the way, means "what is worshipped as Divine," so it is not really a name, but a description, which is rather different. All we actually know about God is that It, He, She, That, or whatever You like to say. is the Spirit of all Life forever. Which makes a very big Being indeed.

Now let's look the other way. If everybody and everything is a part of God, then God must also be in all the little bits of Life, like animals, plants, stones, anything you can think of. Look around you and pick up something small, it doesn't matter what. Hold it in your hands and examine it carefully. Can you see any signs of God within it? Not with your ordinary eyes of course, they won't show anything except the outside. So shut your eyes and try and *feel* God with your "inside touching." Reach down into yourself as deep as you can. Forget about what you are holding, and try to find God living in *you*. Not only *in* you, but *as* you, if you can see the difference.

You'll have to keep very still and quiet for a little while when you try this. Don't go on for too long; a minute or so will do to begin with. Breathe very slowly and regularly. You can speak to God in your mind if you like, it's quite easy. Just say something like "God, this is me." (Give your own name here or a "pet name" if you have one.) "I'm calling You, God. I know You are there somewhere. Do You know I am here?" Don't say that aloud of course, but say it as a secret inside you. Then keep very quiet and still. Make as if you were listening for the tiniest whisper. Hold this a few seconds, then just stop it and be ordinary again.

Don't expect to hear any replies from God in human words,

English or otherwise. God doesn't answer that way directly. If you do happen to hear any actual words inside yourself, the chances are you make these yourself out of whatever you got, and might easily have made a mistake. So how are you to know about God? Either you feel God for yourself, or you don't. How do you know about the Sun? You feel its warmth, but the Sun doesn't talk. You know a flower is beautiful, but the flower hasn't said a word. Nature doesn't have to talk. Neither does God, who is all Nature *and* everything else. There was a time when you didn't talk either, yet your parents knew what you needed, and gave it to you. Talk with words is only one way for humans to arrange their thoughts by. There are other ways, as you will learn later, if you have not found some of them for yourself by now.

Anyhow, did you try that idea of going inside yourself to look for God? What *did* you find? Never mind if you thought you found nothing. God can live in Nothing very well indeed, which is more than we can. So if you had any impressions of "Nothing," that was God all right, Who is everything, everyone, and also Nothing and No-one. You can't get away from God in the end, however far you wander around in Him, or It. The question to ask yourself is this: do you want to know about your relationship with God and do something practical about this, or don't you care? If you really and truly don't care about God and you aren't interested in your own relationship to Him, Her, It or That, then you might as well stop reading this any more. If, on the other hand, you would like to hear about one way of living along with God, which not many other people know about, do please read on. It could help you a lot later on.

*

* *

Now then, where were we? Oh yes. If we can agree about God living in you, and everything else, then there has to be some kind of a connection linking it all together, so to speak. So if we could figure out some practical way fo finding just how God joins up with us all, and what Life is really about, this would surely be a great help for the rest of our lives wouldn't it? That would be something like the instructions that come with an assembly kit of anything, which enables us to build the bits up into whatever it is meant to be. Just stop to think what an assembly kit would be like without those precious instructions! Crazy? Well, that's like Life without any rules for guidance. In a way, Life is a sort of assembly kit, made up of endless bits and pieces that we have to put together as we go along. The point is, do we put them together properly or not? If we assemble them correctly we might get a good working model, but if not, then all we shall have will be some silly mess. And messes usually have to be cleaned up afterwards, don't they? If we want to avoid this dreary chore of mess-clearing, we ought to remember the "Golden Rule" of every assembler "Read and understand the instructions carefully *first*. Then follow them out faithfully." Read and *understand,* mark you. So where are we to find our instruction leaflet and working diagrams telling us how to put the pieces of our lives together and make something good of them? Yes, that is the million dollar question isn't it?

As you might expect, all kinds of people came up with all sorts of answers. In the end however, everyone has to find out for themselves whatever suits them best. Now here we are going to look at one very practical scheme for relating God. Man, and everything else by what was called the "HOLY TREE OF LIFE" system. It got worked out some few hundred years ago by a few people who believed they had found a simple scheme for relating with God by means of ordinary numbers and letters of the alphabet, which they put together into patterns something like the way you make models with assembly kits. All the numbers and letters stood for different things we suppose connect us with God and each other. Qualities like Kindness, Generosity, Love, Patience, and so on. Whatever makes us even in the least little bit like God as we believe Him or It to be. If God can be gracious and generous, so can we in our much lesser ways. If we think God should be loving and merciful, then so ought we to find those qualities in ourselves. Really it is rather wonderful to think we can be anything like God at all. At least that should give us some encouragement to find out more about a system suggesting such a possibility.

In the first place, it was called the "Tree of Life" for many reasons. Actual trees are living things which grow up from Earth towards "Heaven" or the starry spaces where all lives outside this world exist. We are supposed to grow up from this Earth towards a "Heaven" where we shall live as spirits in a state of perfection beyond anyting we might imagine. In fact, trees, ourselves, and all we associate with God are a lot alike in a number of ways. For instance, a tree grows from a seed as we do, and our notions of God grow from original ideas that get planted in our minds something like seeds being planted in good soil. Then, also, trees have roots, and we speak of our "roots" when we mean our connections with families, nations, or whatever we grew from originally. Since all life grows from God, we might truly say that our deepest roots reached as far as God, and they can't go any further than that.

Trees also have big trunks or bodies which hold the greatest part of their lives. So do we. It is interesting here perhaps to notice that all collections of beliefs in God have what is called a "main body" or "corpus" in Latin, which is rather like the trunk of a Tree out of which all the side branches or different ideas grow in various directions. So do trees have branches or limbs corning out of their main trunk as our limbs stick out of our bodies. Our ideas about God and Life branch out from our central stems of belief also. On a real tree, branches get finer and finer until they turn into twigs. So do our ideas become more and more defined as they multiply, until we are surrounded by a multitude of little ideas sticking out round us like the twigs and branches of a tree in winter. The older we grow, the more twigs we are likely to have. Yes, we are very like trees that way.

Trees also have leaves which fall off and get replaced from time to time. Those are like our thoughts which cover us up on the outside, yet we have to keep replacing them one by one as they wear out. Just as a tree relates itself with the rest of the world through its leaves so do we relate ourselves with others through our thoughts. This shows we can join up with God on the outside of ourselves by thinking, once we learn how and what to think about. Besides all this, trees produce some kind of fruit we can either eat to keep our own lives going, or save to plant the seeds and grow more of the same type of tree. It takes quite a time for trees to produce fruit, and even then there may not be much of it. Everything depends on how well the tree was cultivated and how good its natural conditions were.

Life is like that with us too. We speak of "fruitful" periods, where everything seems to develop into something well worth having, or so-called "fruitless" times when we just go on growing quite quietly without anything very much to notice. So it is with ourselves and God. We may go on growing for a very long time together before any special sort of "fruits" seem to appear on the "tree" we are making between us. Nevertheless, all the time we are growing up in this world among other human beings, so are we "growing up" in a different and spiritual sense with God in a secret "world" inside ourselves. Since this inner growth and development has so much in common with the way a tree comes up, we might quite truthfully call it our 'Tree of Life," because we and God are both living beings together. Just to make it sound something very special, we could call it the *Holy* Tree of Life.

Of course, there are other sorts of "Trees" than those growing in gardens. "Family Trees" for instance. Those are collections of peoples names all drawn into patterns, starting with very remote ancestors and continuing right up to the present times. They show who married whom, any children they had (or none), and how each generation was related to those before and after its times. A sort of "people-plan" on paper, so that anyone can see how all those folk are connected as one family no matter where, how, or when, they were born. If only we could do something like this out of our own relationship with the Living God or Life-Spirit, we ought to get some very good ideas about how we stand with God, and what our special relationship amounts to.

Once we start making patterns out of things they begin to make sense to us because our minds start following the pattern around. Look at a jigsaw puzzle all mixed up in its box. As soon as we commence fitting the pieces together so that some definite pattern appears, we can see there is a purpose and a meaning connecting the bits with each other. If we are guided by the picture on the box showing the whole design, we only need care and patience for putting the complete puzzle together. Now suppose we had a sort of "guide-picture" which showed how we ought to put our lives together so as to make the best possible pattern? Wouldn't that help us to live properly? Of course it could. Well, that is what the "Holy Tree of Life" picture is supposed to show. A Pattern for proper living. So let's try and learn how to make it up and put it together.

Here we shall need paper and a pen, pencil, or crayon. A scribbling pad will do nicely. Got it? Start by writing "GOD" at the top middle of the sheet, and "I AM..... (whatever your name is)" at the very bottom. Then draw a straight line by ruler or freehand from top to bottom in the middle connecting you and God. This may not look like much, but it says more than any words could. It means that you and God are joined to each other by some kind of a link, but it doesn't say just what sort of a link or anything else about it. Simply that you and God are somehow tied together. So what joins you in particular with God that you both share with everybody else? Why "LIFE" of course! We are all alive, and God most alive of all. So we call this middle line "LIFE." We can write it from bottom to top, the other way, or both ways together so that we can read it either way we look at it. Like Figure 1.

GOD

L	E
I	F
F	I
E	L

**I AM
(NAME)**

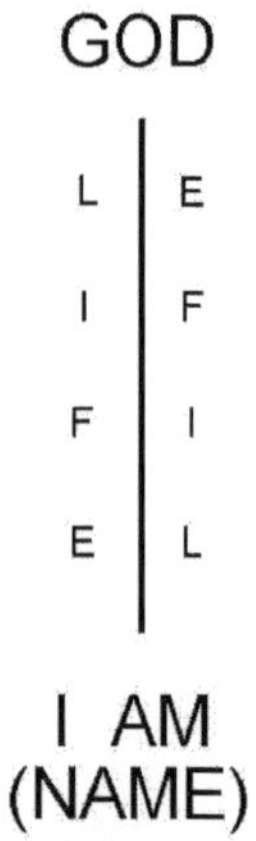

Figure 1

Suppose we simply keep looking at this very elementary pattern and think about it to see what it suggests. If we go on doing this for a while, it is surprising what ideas will come along by themselves. Try it. Then try it again, and this time attempt to put something of the ideas into words of your own, either spoken or written. You find this hard? Well of course, but wasn't it worth the effort? What did it suggest anyway? It might have hinted that we ought to live up to God while God lives down towards us. Suppose the center-line was actually the edge of a circle or hoop turned sideways to us? If we kept following that around, it would show us how life continues from us to God and from God back to us again. If this went on for as long as God lives, that would be Eternity, which is usually shown or represented by a plain circle, but sometimes like a circle on its side bent into a figure eight: ∞. That is because a circle has no special point of beginning or ending, and neither has God that we know of. We do begin and end. God begins us, and we are supposed to end in God sometime as humans, and live as spirits with Him, It, or That forever. So when we draw a circle to represent our own lives, we can imagine it starting with God, coming through whatever we are now, and then finally going back to God for connection with its beginning again. This might even make the old saying: "As it was in the beginning, is now, and ever shall be, world without end. *AMEN*", mean a bit more than it does to most people. All those are ideas coming out of the design we have just drawn, and there are plenty left. Look for some of them on your own.

*

*   *

By this time, it may have occurred to some bright minds that our simple little sketch is really a primitive Tree of Life. God above, a human being below, and Life between them branching out equally each side. That's how Life-trees are made up. However complicated they may look, there is always this simple truth behind them. God, You (or whoever else it may be), and whatever pattern of Life gets woven between both you and God. Always look for this arrangement, and the most puzzling types of Life-Trees are bound to sort themselves out sooner or later.

When we want to put a little more meaning "into our present Tree-pattern, we might try making the letters of the word "LIFE" each stand for another word signifying some other factor which also relates us with God. What about:

L	for	LOVE
I	for	INTELLIGENCE
F	for	FAITH
E	for	EFFORT

Those aren't the only words which might have been chosen, but they certainly add to our ideas about the Tree we are making. We need Love to join us with God and all other living creatures. We should have Intelligence to know what we are doing and where we are going. Without some kind of Faith we cannot get anywhere at all, and if we make no Efforts we shan't get any place in particular that matters much. So this one word "LIFE" has given us four more that show us something about how to live. Those four words could be opened up again to get new ideas, and so we might go on for as long as we like. That is how Life-Trees work. They provide us with the few basic ideas out of which every conceivable sort of consciousness can he built up. That is an idea in itself we ought to examine here.

There are not a lot of ideas in existence really. If we have to be exact there is only One Idea altogether, and that is God thinking everything through everybody. However, we certainly can't work that way, or are ever likely to. We need to put ideas together one by one, so that they will make up others in our minds. Or rather, we have to take little bits of the One Big Idea, and see what we can do with those. Our minds are not at all large when compared with God, so we have to do the best we can with what we've got. Nobody can do more than that, and few seem to do as much.

What we have to find out is this: What are the least number of distinct and different ideas we could work with and still make anything we want out of them? Furthermore, what are those ideas in themselves? Given that knowledge, we might do a lot with it. Think of things this way. How many letters of the alphabet is all this being written with? Only twenty-six. What about the millions and millions of books all over the world written with nothing but twenty-six letters of an alphabet? Almost incredible, yet true. Then what about numbers? How many of those are there? Only ten really, all the rest being just repetitions or divisions. Ten prime numbers to account for all the figures everywhere. We could write them this way in a circle like Figure 2, and they would go on around themselves forever.

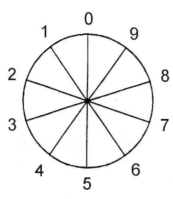

Figure 2

We have to remember always that 0, or Zero, is the starting point from which all numbers begin. This is very important, as we shall discover later. One (1) comes out of Nothing, (0), but there has to be a Nothing in the first place for One to come out of. So Zero is really of the greatest value, because without it, there wouldn't be any numbers at all. Odd, isn't it? Try thinking about it and see where you get.

So there we are. Just ten numbers which can be made up into any amount by arranging them any way we want, and only twenty-six letters that will spell all the words we shall ever use in this world. Now what about music? How many distinct notes are there to play all the tunes we shall ever hear? We generally, accept only eight actual notes, and everything else builds out of their fractional pieces and combination higher and lower. All our music made up out of only eight true notes pushed around by composers to suite their purposes. It is the same with colours. Just three primary colours of red, yellow, and blue, plus white for light and black for dark. Out of those come all our pictures everywhere. So much out of so apparently little!

By now. you can probably see where we are getting to. If all mathematics can come out of ten numbers, all writing and literature be made up from twenty-six letters, music be composed from eight notes and pictures from three colours, then, (this is so important it will have to be in capitals) WHY SHOULDN'T ALL THE MAGIC OF OUR LIVES COME OUT OF JUST A FEW ELEMENTARY IDEAS? Well, why ever not? In fact, those who accept the Holy Tree of Life pattern believe this to be true. Furthermore, they think that they have recognised and identified those few ideas in terms we can grasp and put into ordinary human words. How? Like this.

They did it in a very simple way, by reducing the ideas to only ten, so as to correspond with our original or "primal" set of numbers. Then they related these ten numbered ideas together by junctions represented by the letters of the alphabet. There were only twenty-two Of these join-ups, because they were using the letters of the Hebrew alphabet which has no real vowels, and so has only twenty-two letters. Altogether, this produced a pattern which combined all the basics of conscious life connected with each other into a Tree of Life shape. Everything in one, so to speak. By means of figures, we can work out the laws of Life. By means of letters, we can communicate intelligently about what we learn in Life. By means of our deep-down beliefs and ideas, we can relate ourselves with the Living Spirit we call God. That is what the Tree of Life should mean for us, and that is why it is called "Holy." It is a pattern for perfecting ourselves.

The pattern begins easily enough, by doing what we have just done with God at the top, Man, (which means all of us including the girls!), at the bottom, and a central up and down connecting line between both. This time however, the line gets divided into ten spaces like Figure 3.

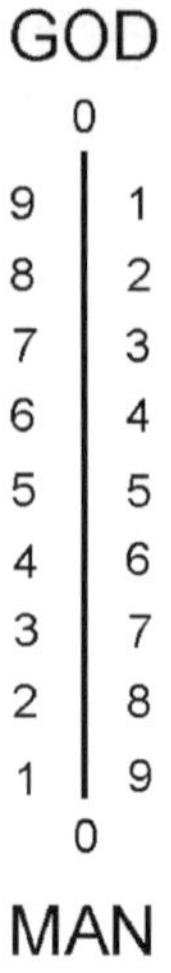

GOD

0

9   1

8   2

7   3

6   4

5   5

4   6

3   7

2   8

1   9

0

MAN

Figure 3

See how it starts and finishes with Zero so the numbers can keep going round forever as they add up to 10, then 20, then 30, getting bigger all the time? Work it the other way, and they would get smaller and smaller of course. Note how they make a pattern. Taken straight across in pairs, they add up to 10 every time. See how they "hinge" in the middle on number 5?

We could make a lot of meanings out of this, but for now we have to go on looking for patterns. There will he plenty of time to think things over when we see it all laid out. So where do we go from here?

Well, since this is supposed to be a Tree, how does an ordinary tree grow out of the ground? First of all, it sends up one small straight stem which then branches out into two little leaves. Then it grows the middle stem up a bit higher and divides into another two leaves. Then it does the same thing again, and goes on repeating the same pattern more and more in all directions getting bigger every year. Why not follow the same idea for our Life-Tree? One stem up, then divide in two, and so on. We should get something like an upside down Christmas Tree in Figure 4:

HEAVEN

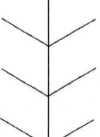

EARTH

Figure 4

The only snag with this, is that if we want to number the ends of the branches and where they cross the middle line, we shall get eleven points, but we only want ten. By leaving one out, we can work the numbers beautifully, but which one should we omit? Certainly not the outside ends, because that would unbalance the Tree hopelessly. Then which middle one has the least to support? The top one surely, because there is only a short center-stem there. Let that be the one we don't number. If we then count up to ten from the bottom, (remembering to start from Zero of course) we shall get something like Figure 5.

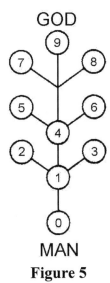

Figure 5

This is the Tree, looking up from Earth to Heaven, so it represents Man looking for God. Now what happens if we think the other way around, or arrange the numbers to show God reaching towards man? We shall have to imagine the Tree growing downwards from Heaven to Earth, and see it like Figure 6.

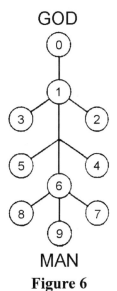

Figure 6

If we now put these two versions of our Tree together we shall get a very interesting picture indeed like Figure 7.

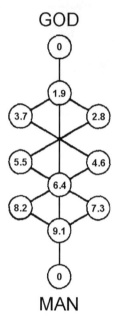

Figure 7

There it is. Everything adds up to 10 everywhere. Both God and Man match up together to make a single number at each stage. So it looks as if our design is going to make a good picture of God and Man coming together as a single One Life.

Now then, there comes another important point. How shall we make sure we are getting the proportions of our picture right? Whether we make our Tree big or little to look at, it still has to have the same proportions. The secret is very simple really. Follow this carefully. Draw a straight line of any length to represent a connection between God and Man. Divide this in half to show a willingness of meeting half way. Then halve the halves to make quarters. Now take a compass with pencil attached, and make circles from each point on the line. There will be four circles altogether. Where the circles cross each other is where the outer points of the Tree have to go. This is the right way of setting up the Tree of Life. No matter how large or small we make it, the Tree has to be correct every time. Try it on some scrap paper. Like Figure 8.

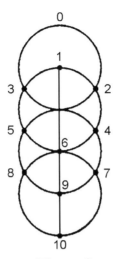

Figure 8

For the sake of calling them something, the ten points on our Tree of Life are termed "Spheres." That is to say any sort of area where definite things or activities of the same class belong together. We talk about "the sphere of music,"or "the sphere of sport." The "Sphere" of anything at all, is when we mean associating every-thing of one species in a common category. A "sphere" doesn't have to be a physical area, it can be in our minds or souls, anywhere at all, because it isn't a *thing*, but an *idea* of bringing things or other ideas together. It just means that similar sorts of things, people, thoughts, everything alike in fact, tend to link up with each other for company somehow, and however they do that makes their particular "sphere."

So that is what is meant by "Spheres" on the Tree of Life. Ten special areas, wherein ten different sorts of affairs linking us up somehow with God can be classified. They have numbers attached to them so that we shall follow them easily like the pages of an encyclopedia. Just as we find all the different subjects of a book by their numbered sections, so can we consider whatever belongs to each separate sphere of the Life-Tree, once we have firmly associated its number with those things in our minds. For the sake of simplicity again, the numbers of the Spheres are taken to be those of "God looking down at Man." This avoids confusion and misunderstandings so far as possible. We know the numbers upwards are equally good, but we may take these for granted as belonging with those normally used.

To fill the design in, and give some ideas of "Branches" usually associated with trees, the Spheres are joined up with each other by twenty-two lines or "Paths," one for each letter of the Hebrew alphabet. Most of the experts disagree about exactly which letter should go on which Path, but the general idea is to start the alphabet at the top and finish up at the bottom. Anyway there is no argument about the Spheres, and everyone agrees how the letter-lines ought to be drawn on the Tree. They go as in Figure 9.

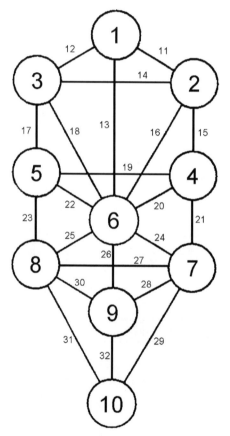

Figure 9

There we are at last. Ten Spheres, and twenty-two "Paths" between the Spheres. Thirty-two things to tink about, once we decide what they all mean. It works out that after counting up the Spheres to ten, we call the first Path eleven, and go on from there. The Paths are numbered in their particular way for this reason. The first join is between Spheres 1 and 2, so it will be "Path ten-plus-one" or Eleven. The second join is between Spheres 1 and 3, or "ten-plus-two" making Path 12. The only Path left from Sphere 1 now joins up with Sphere 6 in the middle, so this has to be "Path ten-plus-three" 13. Then we have to move on to Sphere 2, and work out its Paths in order. So we keep going down the Tree till we come to the end which joins Sphere 9 with Sphere 10 by Path 32.

*
* *

Now we ought to start thinking about what the ten Spheres might mean, apart from just numbers with rings around them arranged in a peculiar pattern. All we know at the moment is that they have to mean ten different but connectible ideas which will link us up with God and Life in general. Long ago many people did a lot of thinking and working along these lines and they certainly asked God, or the Life-Spirit to help them find some kind of an answer. It came out this way.

Life itself taught them that what are called "Qualities" make the best basic ideas on the Tree. So ten of these were chosen. Qualities are not an easy word-meaning to explain. A "quality" of anything or anyone means something it is in itself because that happens to be its own nature. For instance, someone may be a kind person, and "Kindness" is a quality. Somebody else could he cruel, and cruelty is a quality too..... unfortunately. There are good and bad qualities, but we only want the very best on our Tree of Life. If we do have any bad qualities, then we need to get rid of them or change them into better ones. So the Qualities of the Spheres on the Tree of Life should be the finest we can think of which connect us with Life and the Divine Spirit thereof. If we think of the Spheres on the Tree as being rather like fruit, while the Paths are the branches they grow on, this might help a little.

 At the bottom of the Tree, as you might have expected, is the Sphere of all the ordinary affairs that happen among us in this world. The old-time people named it "*MALKUTH*," a Hebrew word meaning "a Kingdom." That meant a lot of folk and their families associating together, who needed some kind of rules for helping them live properly. In those days a King was supposed to be somebody special who was capable of making rules for peoples' benefit, and also making sure they actually lived by those rules, so far as possible. That was why he got called a "ruler." We know that few if any Kings were ever as good as that, but it was an idea worth trying all the same.

If a really perfect Kingdom is ever possible on this Earth, everybody would be their own King. We should all make ourselves abide by rules we know are good and true so that everyone lives happily and wonderfully together. Even if we haven't got anything quite like that yet, we might as well hope for it. One day it could come true. So Sphere 10 on our Tree of Life represents the sort of Kingdom we should want to have happen here if it could. Remember the saying: "Thy Kingdom come"? Well, that's the type of Kingdom it meant. Everybody ruling themselves properly, with God as the "King of Kings" above all. Who knows. It might come us humans yet, even of it won't be very soon.

 The next Sphere up the Tree, number 9 on our list, was called "*YESOD*," meaning "a Foundation," or something built on. Now a great difficulty with so many Hebrew words was that they had so many various meanings, one inside another so to speak. This makes it rather difficult to decide which meaning might be the right one. On the other hand, it does give us a great deal of choice in finding meanings we shall understand and be able to make sense from. That is why the names describing the Spheres on the Tree have the widest possible range of meaning. What can we make the word "Foundation" mean? A Foundation is firstly a base on which anything gets built. A house has foundations, and so in a sense has a car, radio, or whatever else we build. Since Life can be considered as a structure, and we are talking about the Tree of Life, it seems obvious that what is meant here is a good Foundation for living on. What might this be?

We hear of people "founding" families, "founding" Kingdoms; Nations, Societies, or almost anything. There are charitable and other "Foundations" everywhere. It meant some people based all their ideas and hopes on whatever arrangement they built up together, and called this a "Foundation." That is the kind of thinking we should associate with this particular Sphere.

Whatever we base our beliefs in Life on. Really deep-down matters. So solid and dependable that we can build up structures and ideas high enough to reach God. No matter what we do in Life it is best to begin with as good a base as we can. In this Sphere we hope to find the best base for everything. Hence its name. We shan't stop here to enquire what all those basics might he, but just remember where to look for them when we want them Now let's see what comes next.

Here the Tree-trunk divides into two, and there is a Sphere like a fruit at the end of each branch. If we take the one marked 8 first, its proper name is "*HOD*," meaning "Glory, Splendour, or Honour." These are incentives for living which are common to most of us. We all like feeling splendid, being gloriously happy, or being honoured in someway. That is only natural. On the other hand, we ought to glorify God, and be honourable people who are happy to be well thought of by God and our fellow humans. We want to be appreciated and told how good we are. It is a very human quality, though not exactly the finest or best we have.

On the Tree of Life, we shall find that the most God-like qualities are at the top, while the more human ones are right at the bottom, our end of the Tree as it were. Here in this Sphere 8, our need for glorious honours and splendour may not he very high as qualities go, but it does at least do one thing for us. It gets us "off the ground" and starts us meaning to make something better of ourselves all the time. Providing we are guided by higher qualities still, this could be quite a good thing for us, so let's see what is next.

This is Sphere 7, named "*NETZACH*" or "Victory" in the sense of achieving something. Not a victory where somebody gets beaten down, or even beaten at all. Just the accomplishment of something done successfully. As, for instance, anyone might be victorious in learning a lesson, or conquering a fault in themselves. It means actually achieving or doing what God intends to do in you. Your own special "thing" that you were meant to do in particular. That really would be an accomplishment. Life is full of problems and difficulties to be solved successfully, and here is the Sphere of all such conquests. A victory in Life might be as small as remembering to clean finger nails, or as big as winning the Nobel Peace Prize, or anything you can think of. Its place on the Tree is right here in Sphere 7. It may not be very good or noble to want nothing but victories out of Life, but it is nice to be on the winning side sometimes, and it does encourage us to look a little higher up on the Tree.

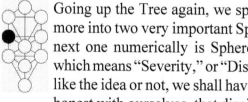

That brings us to Sphere 6, in the middle again. It is called "*TIPHARETH*" or "Harmonious Beauty." Not exactly an easy meaning to explain, since Beauty means so many different things for everyone. Here it really means a point where everything is so perfectly balanced and poised that it simply has to be beautiful because it couldn't be anything else? It may not come very often in Life, but when it does, you can't possibly mistake it. Everything and everyone seems just as it should be in relation to yourself. Nothing feels too much or too little, and it all seems somehow to *balance* equally and harmoniously. This is because you feel exactly in the middle of it all, and so you can balance everything around you. That is more or less what "*TIPHARETH*" means in Sphere 6. The quality of being beautifully balanced.

We say of really capable people: "How beautifully they behave." Here, in Sphere 6 on the Tree of Life, is that wonderful quality we can share with God of being in balanced harmony with Life. No wonder this Sphere is right in the middle of the Tree. It couldn't be anywhere else. We may not reach it very often during our lives, but at least if we know about its possibilities, it will help us closer to the top eventually. Besides, we might manage some good imitations of it one way or another, and that could be quite useful to us.

Going up the Tree again, we split from side to side once more into two very important Spheres of Life indeed. The next one numerically is Sphere 5, called "*GEVURAH*" which means "Severity," or "Discipline." Now whether we like the idea or not, we shall have to admit, if we are really honest with ourselves, that discipline and self-control are something we truly do need in Life. Nobody is going to pretend this is pleasant, but everyone knows it happens to be necessary. Without any discipline or self-control, Life would be sheer Hell for us all. Yes it would!

Imagine everyone behaving without the slightest feeling for anyone else, or ever caring what became of themselves. Think what it would be like on anv motorway if everybody drove their cars as they liked without any regard for the rules of the road. Most people would soon be killed or horribly injured. It is entirely a sense of discipline and self-control that makes people drive properly. The same sense, taken from Sphere 5 on the Tree of Life can make them *live* properly, and that is why it has such importance. Gain that Sphere, and we shall really get something worth having from the Tree. Anybody can drive and control a car, but to drive and control ourselves is very much greater in Life, and much more difficult than controlling a mere motor. Many folk never quite seem to learn the secrets of Sphere 5. Yet we shall all have to discover and practice at least some of it before we shall be fit to tackle the next Sphere.

This Sphere is Number 4, named "*CHESED*," meaning "Mercy" or "Compassion." If ever people Mercy, we humans living in t his world do! But what right have we to expect Mercy from God if we are not merciful to each other? However, if God were not Merciful, none of us would be left alive on Earth to behave the way we do. What is mercy anyway? It is mainly a loving forgiveness of people's faults, and a sincere desire to help them become better by their own efforts. It also indicates the qualities of tolerance, kindness, and generosity.

There is one very important thing to remember about Mercy. It is a quality which can only be shown to those weaker than whoever is being Merciful. For instance, no human could possibly be merciful to God. God is more powerful than all of us will ever be as humans. Yet God can be merciful to us, and we should be merciful to others in God's name. It takes a really strong soul to be truly merciful, and we should have made ourselves strong by self-discipline from Sphere 5. That is why we need it before Sphere 4. Strong people should always be merciful to weak ones, helping them to correct their faults and become better in every way. That is why we say in the Lord's Prayer: "Forgive our faults as we forgive those of others." In that way we shall be passing on God's forgiveness and Mercy to us along towards our fellow humans, which is good for everyone alike. True mercy is never a weakness, but always a very great spiritual strength which we have to gain from this Sphere 4 on our Tree of Life. The more merciful we become to those weaker than we are, the closer we may climb toward God. Let us see where we have got so far.

We have actually come to rather an interesting place. The mid-Tree crossing we decided not to number in the first instance. Remember? Can we make it mean something special? Yes, we can indeed. We might make it mean the space or gap between ourselves and all the perfection we ever hope to gain of God by our own efforts. None of us are anywhere near as good or developed enough to get very close to God. We just aren't that perfect yet. Some time in the future we do want to reach such a state, but in the meantime we have a lot more "Bridges to cross." So let this place on the Tree stand for whatever separates us from close contact with God. In fact it has already been called "The Abyss" for that very reason. An Abyss is a very deep cleft in the Earth. So deep, that we can't see the bottom, but not very wide. Maybe only a few yards or feet across. Think of the Grand Canyon with its sides much closer, and that might give you an idea.

An Abyss can be bridged of course. The Bridge imagined here is believed to be so narrow that we have to be very careful indeed while we cross it. This signifies the care we have to take in Life as we try and walk safely between its many dangers. This is not meant to be frightening, but only cautionary. Like only crossing a road at the traffic-lights, and waiting for the right signal to go. No danger unless we are silly enough to ignore the safety rules. This Bridge on our Tree has a name. Because an Abyss stands for Ignorance among other things, the Bridge is called *"DAATH"* (pronounced almost like "DOTH"), which means Knowledge or Experience.

When we come to think of it, Knowledge and experience of Life or anything to do with living, is the only thing we dare depend on far getting us safely across all the difficulties and problems we have to deal with. To live properly, we have to know how. To gain knowledge of any kind. we have to have experience. Given the right knowledge and experience, we may do almost anything, like getting to the Moon for example. Yet we did this in the end, and that is just the beginning of much bigger adventures to come.

How much knowledge and experience shall we need to

reach God? Nobody on Earth can answer that question, but we can still keep trying. Here on our Trees of Life, is where we have to make those Magic Bridges of Knowledge which will lead us safely across the abysmal depths of our ignorance toward higher and firmer levels of Life still closer to God. As we live, so should we also *learn.*

To represent the Abyss, a couple of wavy lines are sometimes drawn lightly across the Tree here, and occasionally *DAATH* is shown as sort of dotted circle in the middle. *DAATH,* or Knowledge, is not a separate Sphere at all really, but a space which would make a perfect place for our world if only we had enough Knowledge and Experience of Life for coming this close to God. Supposing we did cross the Abyss safely, what should we find on the other side?

Our immediate contact would be with Sphere 3, named "*BINAH*" or "Understanding." What a difficult word to explain. It means knowing all about things and people because of an ability to share their lives so completely that we can see Life from their viewpoints, and consequently understand what it signifies for them in particular. You might say that God understands you, because God alone knows exactly what Life and everything else seems like according to your own experience of it. You may not ever be right about anything, but God still knows how you deal with Life in your individual way. Therefore God understands you. This gives God an advantage, because you aren't able to understand God. Even trying to understand other human beings is difficult enough in this world.

To understand the slightest thing about anyone or anything, we have to sort of "get inside" it or them so far as we can, and thus gain a shared experience of Life together. People only understand each other to the extent that they are able to appreciate and experience each others kinds of living. This ability of Understanding is one of the finest qualities we can achieve. That is why it is so high up on the Tree. To try and really understand Life and its people properly, brings us about as close to God as a human being may reach from this world. Still, we can climb our Tree a little further yet and explore its opposite branch.

This takes us to Sphere 2, on the level of our last Sphere

3, and is called *"CHOKMAH"* meaning "Wisdom." About as difficult to explain as "Understanding." Wisdom is a very special quality indeed. It isn't simply being clever, or knowing a great deal of information, or being smarter than somebody else. Real Wisdom is an ability of dealing with Life in the best possible way for all concerned. Which means everybody from you to God. We might say it was the ability to live as if God were living through us individually and advising all our actions.

That is what makes Wisdom essentially good. A bad or wicked person may be very clever and intelligent indeed. They often are. But they are never Wise. If they were, they would not be bad. Wisdom is something which keeps us very closely in touch with God, but we have to "grow into it," so to speak. Wisdom is usually the last quality we develop in Life, and so it is shown here nearly at the top of the Tree. As a rule we tend to gain Wisdom slowly as we go along. We steadily *become* Wise if we really care what God means to do and he through us. As the Tree shows, the way to both Understanding and Wisdom is over the Bridge of Knowledge.

We must be prepared to wait and work for genuine Wisdom. Like all the other qualities of the Tree, it comes by degrees if we sincerely seek it in order to grow near God. Trees take time to grow up, and a Life-Tree will take a whole lifetime. We can't be Wise all at once, but only gradually. Nevertheless if we don't cultivate Wisdom while we are still at the bottom of the Tree, it won't be there to help us climb up to the top. If ever we *did* get right up there, what might we expect to find?

The top or apex of the Life-Tree, is simply called *"KETHER,"* which means a "Crown" in the sense of being a summit or absolute top of anything. As we might say "the crown of his head," for instance. From our point of view, this means the very closest we can ever get to God and still stay ourselves. We are very unlikely to reach this Sphere 1 while we are yet only human beings, but we should think and know about it if we intend ever getting there at all.

Whatever this "Crown of Life" may be, it is certainly the highest and finest point that any living being will ever reach. No one can say for sure what it amounts to, because none of us in this world is good enough to exist in such a state. However, we can all climb as high as we can up our individual Trees, and we could call that reaching the Crown of a lifetime in a way. To that degree, *Kether* the Crown does mean getting as close to God as we can during our lives. What really matters is that we should try and get there quite steadily and naturally, just like a tree grows. Trees don't jump wildly around. They simply go on extending and unfolding themselves from inside quietly and normally. As we ought to.

If ever we got to the top of the Life-Tree in fact, we should be just as God originally meant us to become. We can't say for certain exactly how wonderful this would be, but it most certainly would be far above anything we are able to imagine here and now. As we progress through Life, we keep outgrowing and outliving all sorts of things. We outlive baby toys and clothes, our tastes change, outlooks alter, and so we go on. Now try to imagine, if you can, outliving and outgrowing everything else in Life except God, Whom nobody can ever outgrow. You can't imagine this? Well never mind, nobody else can either.

To reach the real top of a Life-Tree, would mean that there is nothing else in Life for that highly placed individual to live any more. There would be no more need for learning Life the hard way as a human being. Nobody in their right minds would pretend that human life is the best there might be, and anybody claiming this world is perfect must be clean crazy. There just *has* to be some better way of living than as human beings in bodies that die among all the muddles that Mankind makes with this world. Nevertheless, we cannot get away from being human until we have worked our way up to the very top of the Holy Tree of Life. When, and if we ever get so high we need *Nothing* whatever except God, then, and only then, shall we have reached the very top of the Life-Tree. What, if anything, happens after that?

We simply cannot know. All that may be said is that if ever we reached the top of the Tree, we might go from there straight into God and live forever as God does. Because we know Nothing of this at all, the sign of Nothing, or zero is taken to mean the final step off the Tree altogether into God. Only God knows what Nothing is, because God lives in what looks like Nothing to us. Out of that Nothing, God makes everything. This is usually shown on the Tree by drawing a Zero-circle (0) and adding a few lines to represent Light-rays.

Why rays of light? Because in the Universe we can see around us. Light happens to be what is called the "Constant," or the one thing that stays unchanged while everything else alters. Strictly speaking it is the actual speed of Light which stays put, as you may or may not have already learnt. In a Universe like ours, where everything is in a perpetual state of change, it is good to know of just one thing we can depend on to remain as it is constantly. What Light does in the Universe we know about, so God does in the unseen state of life behind everything which we sometimes call "Spirit," God, being Perfect, does not change, and therefore is the Constant of what we might think of as the "Spiritual Universe."So we accept Light as being a good symbol for God.

The old-time designers of the Tree we have been considering, realised the difficulty of imagining Nothing. So they tried reaching it by three stages. Immediately after quitting the top of the Tree, there was Light. Nothing else. It just shone from Nowhere. Light in Hebrew is "*AUR.*" Behind this mysterious Light came a condition they called just "The End" ("*SOPH*" in Hebrew). That meant: "The End where Nothing Begins." As if we had come to the end of something and were just meeting empty space. After that of course there was only Nothing. "*AIN*" in Hebrew. Running these three words together, we get *AIN-SOPH-AUR*, or "Light ending in Nothing."

It is rather interesting to think what happens if we go through this the other way. Starting from "Nothing," we come to "The End," then "Light," and after that "Something." Try a sort of little experiment to get the feel of this. Take an electric torch in your left hand, put out all the lights, or go into an already dark room with the torch unlit. Turn around several times so that you aren't sure which way you are facing. Reach out carefully with the forefinger of the right hand into the dark. If you touch nothing, that will symbolise the zero of the Tree. Push forward gently with your finger moving slowly until you touch something very lightly. Don't try and recognise what you have touched. Just realise you have come to the end of Nothing, and started to know about Something.

Now switch on your torch and find out what you have touched. If that doesn't give you some ideas about the *AIN-SOPH-AUR* above the Tree of Life, then it ought to have done. Try it again and see what you can learn.

*

*   *

Well, that's it. There's the whole main structure of the famous "Holy Tree of Life" for you to look at and think about. Of course there is a great deal more to the Tree than what we have been talking about. Apart from Qualities, each Sphere has other attachments in keeping with its nature. Different Names of God, for example, to show how God related specially with every Sphere. Then every Sphere had its own Archangel, or "God's assistant" to sort of supervise the work done by the ordinary Angels, or "agents" who were like "spiritual specialists" in whatever activity was special to that Sphere. Not only that, but each Sphere has been linked up with some planet of our Solar System which seems to fit in with its peculiarities. All this of course, takes a lot of learning and working out which is far more than a little text like this can fairly tackle. However, it may as well be mentioned here for the sake of arousing interest.

In addition too, there are all the Paths to study, if you ever want to go more deeply into the Tree. As you know now, each Path has a letter of the alphabet, and letters put together make words, and words eventually make sense. The Paths will tell their own story, once you become able to combine them rightly. Originally of course the letters were Hebrew ones, but a much more modern version using English letters has been devised. Also each Path is capable of being translated into a picture-card from what is known as the Tarot pack. This is like an ordinary pack of cards in some ways, but has an extra twenty-two pictures called "Trumps" which can be made to mean all kinds of things about Life in general. There are several ways these fascinating cards can be arranged around the Paths or "branches" of the Tree. Then by combining the meanings of different cards, a great variety of mental pictures can be made which tell us a lot about living and how to get on with God and other humans. Naturally it takes a lot of time and effort to learn things like this but quite a few people think it well worth while.

Before we leave the Tree at the end of this trip, it might be an idea to mention the so-called "Four Worlds" which are bound to baffle you if you come across then for the first time in any of the "classical" books about the Holy Tree of Life. They are really quite simple once you know what they mean, which amounts to this: We take it for granted that God makes things out of Nothing, but even then, there must be some easier way of looking at this from our end. Something like the way we looked at the *AIN-SOPH-AUR* problem. If we try it by stages, it might sound more sensible. So first of all we shall suppose God *originates* anything, or *begins* making whatever it is. There has to be a start of everything somewhere. The Hebrews called that stage of Creation proceedings "*ATZILUTH*," so that is what the word means when you meet it. Next came the creative construction of anything, or making it into whatever material it is meant to be. With God of course, this means natural materials. Stone, metal, wood, Air, Fire, Water, Earth, anything at all. No more than that as yet. That part of the process they named "*BRIAH*," so now you know what that means.

Next on the list comes the formation of everything into definite shapes and sizes. Everything has to be sorted out in proper forms so that it differs from other things according to its nature. This necessary Formation got called "*YETZIRAH*," so don't let that word bother you again. Now all this Originating, Creating, and Forming takes place purely in the mind of God as a kind of "spiritual thinking." It still has to "materialise," or be turned into our sort of solids if that is what God wants to do with it. That makes the last stage, when what God has been thinking about "comes true" in our world. By making the products of His or Its mind into our kind of matter, God projects these into physical dimensions. This last part of the process is called "*ASSIAH*."

Each of these four so-called "Worlds" (a most confusing title) is really but a quarter-part of the same system which converts pure consciousness into anything concrete. ("Concrete" means something solid and substantial). At any rate, that was how the designers of the Tree of Life reckoned God made solids from pure Spirit. The idea helps people grasp how things come out of thinking, and thinking can be suggested by things. Which comes in quite useful in Magical practice.

This is about a s far as we can go with such a small book. Don't undervalue it on that account though. If you have been following along up the Holy Tree of Life as we climbed it, you should now know a good deal more about it than many people it has puzzled and perplexed for many years. Plenty get very interested in the Holy Tree of Life, but very few are able to work it out for themselves as deeply as we have here. It does need rather special sorts of people to realise just what the Tree means, and actually do something about it on their own. If you are one of those people, then you will want to know more about this Tree, and find out for yourself from all the information available elsewhere. If you aren't, then you won't. Things are as simple as that. Whatever happens, and whether you go on studying the Tree and its associated subjects or not, now that you know something about it, a lot more knowledge is bound to come your way. One Magic makes another magic everywhere in Life.

Those who try and live according to the Tree system, hope that they and also you will get to the top some time. Then we can all live in God together perfectly. Nobody knows what that sort of life might be like, but we can safely guess three things about it. It will be PERFECT, it will be PEACEFUL, and it is sure to be very, very DEEP indeed. So we might sum it all up as *PERFECT PEACE PROFOUND*. That is the traditional greeting which those who deal with this Tree wish themselves and everyone else. It is meant as the greatest possible blessing on all that lives. So may you also live to become so blessed in *PERFECT PEACE PROFOUND*. It was fine to have you climbing up the Tree of Life with us for a while. Maybe we can meet again some time and swing around its interesting branches a bit more. Till then..... Bless you whoever you are!

Chapter 2
SIMPLE GUIDE TO THE PATHS
ON THE
HOLY TREE OF LIFE

The Paths or Channels as they are sometimes called on the Holy Tree, can be very puzzling to many people, and liable to put them off studying the subject maybe for many years. Which is a pity, because there is so much to learn from them and gain by experiencing those mysterious Lifeways at first hand. What we need to know straight away is how those Paths got to be where they are, and for this purpose, apart from pencils and paper, we shall require a compass, representing the work of God since it produces circles, and a square or ruler, because with its aid the work of Man may be shown. In fact you might almost say that God made the Spheres of the Tree, while Man has to progress its Paths. If you want to study this process for yourself, take the compass and trace an ordinary circle. So:

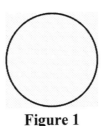

Figure 1

After which you reverse the compass, place its point on the perimeter of the circle and trace another circle of the same size. (Fig. 2), then take each intersection as a centre point and do another two circles, one to the right and another to the left, or Figure 3.

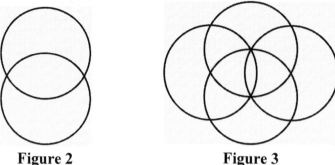

Figure 2   **Figure 3**

Now do you realise what you have done? With four interlinking circles you have represented the Great Name of God—*YHVH*, and we shall need six more to produce the ten claimed for the "Pattern of Creation." So repeat the circles of the intersections and we shall obtain Figure 4, which if the centres were all joined up would make a pattern as per Figure 5, which seems rather too perfect to be true.

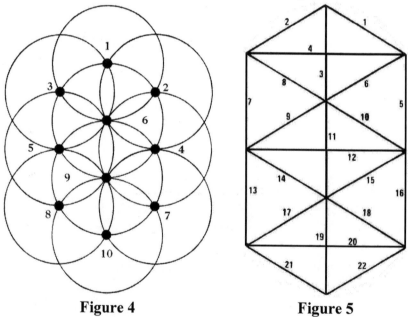

Figure 4   **Figure 5**

Incidentally, the reason we are numbering from right to left, was because the original Hebrew who designed our Tree in the first place, always worked that way, so we will do the same in their memory. We have here to bear in mind the reputed "Fall" from Heaven by which we became mortals, and since this calls for representation as well, we show it by moving the lower three circles in the centre a full half downwards, which now presents a slightly different pattern that ought to be far more familiar to us, and if we link all the centres together by straight lines which can now more properly be called "Paths," we can see the picture building up to become as we now know it.

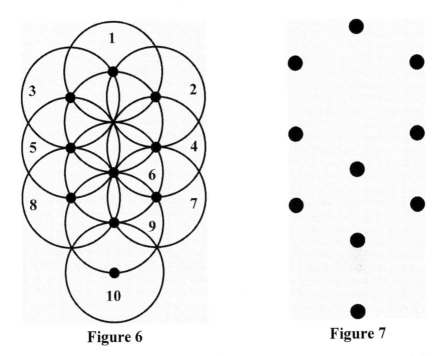

Figure 6 **Figure 7**

This should be a lot more evident at Figures 6, 7 above and 8 below. As you will see, if we take the Spheres as a basis, and then join them up in numerical order, we shall then obtain the following linkage:

Sphere 1 joins Sphere 2, making Path 11
Sphere 1 joins Sphere 3, making Path 12
Sphere 1 joins Sphere 6, making Path 13
Sphere 2 joins Sphere 3, making Path 14
Sphere 2 joins Sphere 4, making Path 15
Sphere 2 joins Sphere 5, making Path 16
Sphere 3 joins Sphere 5, making Path 17
Sphere 3 joins Sphere 6, making Path 18
Sphere 4 joins Sphere 5, making Path 19
Sphere 4 joins Sphere 6, making Path 20

Sphere 4 joins Sphere 7, making Path 21
Sphere 5 joins Sphere 6, making Path 22
Sphere 5 joins Sphere 8, making Path 23
Sphere 6 joins Sphere 7, making Path 24
Sphere 6 joins Sphere 8, making Path 25
Sphere 6 joins Sphere 9, making Path 26
Sphere 7 joins Sphere 8, making Path 27
Sphere 7 joins Sphere 9, making Path 28
Sphere 7 joins Sphere 10, making Path 29
Sphere 8 joins Sphere 9, making Path 30
Sphere 8 joins Sphere 10, making Path 31
Sphere 9 joins Sphere 10, making Path 32

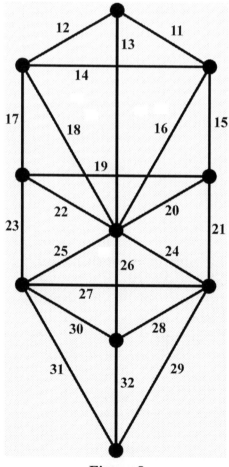

Figure 8

So there we are. The twenty-two Paths of the Holy Tree which, together with the ten Spheres, make up thirty-two in all. Once we are clear about what the Spheres mean, it shouldn't be too difficult to calculate what the various Paths outline, if we consider the effect of one Sphere upon another and think of this as being a two-way process, each modifying and somewhat altering the other. If we like to imagine the Paths as being similar to a dual carriage way with the traffic or force-flows going in opposite directions at the same time, that would be perfectly permissible. Providing we always remember three divisions from top to bottom of our Holy Tree, as with most things, Left Right and Centre. In this case we are calling our left hand three Spheres The Female and Black Pillar, the right hand three our Male and White one, while the Central four is the Neutral and Golden Pillar connecting us all with God. Now let us look at the nature of the Paths starting from their beginning, or at Path 11.

 Path 11: The Crown [1] meets Wisdom [2]. Here we might expect to find the best and finest type of consciousness in all Creation from a Masculine viewpoint. Positive and dominant exhibiting a faculty of active awareness and intentional involvement.

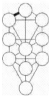 **Path 12:** The Crown [1] meets Understanding [3], this the complementary type of consciousness from the Female angle. Here it is negative and passive achieving itself through intuition and sheer absorption of presented energies.

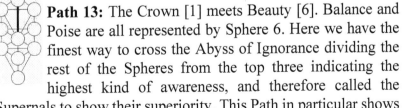 **Path 13:** The Crown [1] meets Beauty [6]. Balance and Poise are all represented by Sphere 6. Here we have the finest way to cross the Abyss of Ignorance dividing the rest of the Spheres from the top three indicating the highest kind of awareness, and therefore called the Supernals to show their superiority. This Path in particular shows the direct connection between God and Man, while emphasizing the difficulties and dangers we may expect thereon.

Path 14: Pure Wisdom [2] meets with Pure Understanding [3]. This shows an ideal mixture of Male and Female Awareness at its very best. Since it is above the Abyss, it is superior and free to flow in the best possible way so as to obtain optimum results.

Path 15: Wisdom [2] meets with Mercy [4]. This is an Abyss crosser and shows what happens when we are guided by a superior instinct to be intelligently tolerant and well meaning toward our fellow creatures. Otherwise making allowances for others who may be different from ourselves, thus avoiding arguments and dissensions.

Path 16: Wisdom [2] meets with Harmony [6]. Another Abyss crosser showing us the type of qualities we ought to develop when we are wise enough to seek an ideal balance between everything we encounter during our lifetimes. That takes a lot of experience and learning, usually resulting in Knowledge which eventually crosses all chasms in consciousness.

Path 17: Understanding [3] meets Severity [5]. This is where we can see the need for discipline and learn how to apply it properly, so that we can be clever without being cruel. This Abyss crosser shows how a mother should control her children capably, or how God teaches us by and through necessary experience.

Path 18: Understanding [3] meets Harmony [6]. The last Abyss crosser showing what happens when Female Intuition encounters the best of a beautifully balanced and properly poised life. It shows direct guidance by God to look for harmony and beauty in every experience, however unlike that may seem at first.

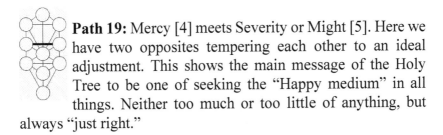

Path 19: Mercy [4] meets Severity or Might [5]. Here we have two opposites tempering each other to an ideal adjustment. This shows the main message of the Holy Tree to be one of seeking the "Happy medium" in all things. Neither too much or too little of anything, but always "just right."

Path 20: Mercy [4] meets Harmony [6]. There have to be times in life when everything seems wonderfully happy, or as we sometimes say "Too good to be true." Otherwise we might never know there was anything worth living for. This is one such Path on the Plan. An encourager, or the carrot in front of the donkey.

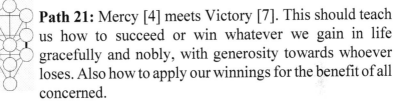

Path 21: Mercy [4] meets Victory [7]. This should teach us how to succeed or win whatever we gain in life gracefully and nobly, with generosity towards whoever loses. Also how to apply our winnings for the benefit of all concerned.

Path 22: Severity [5] meets Beauty [6]. As we know, there are many upsets and difficulties to be dealt with in life, and this is where we encounter these, but also discover the reason for them and how to get any good from the situations if possible.

Path 23: Severity [5] meets Glory [8]. Life can sometimes be a shameful and inglorious affair, so here is where we encounter those unpleasant experiences, but also learn not only how to cope with them, but also the best ways of turning them to advantage and benefit.

Path 24: Beauty [6] meets Victory [7]. This is where we larn how to make the most out of all we gain in the best possible, and most balanced, way for our spiritual progress. That may not always be the happiest of fates to follow, but it will certainly bring out the nicest side of our natures.

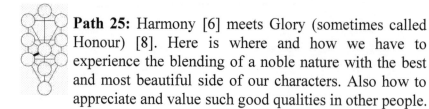

Path 25: Harmony [6] meets Glory (sometimes called Honour) [8]. Here is where and how we have to experience the blending of a noble nature with the best and most beautiful side of our characters. Also how to appreciate and value such good qualities in other people.

Path 26: Beauty [6] meets Foundation (also called Basis of Belief) [9]. This is where and how we collect all our basic ideas and beliefs out of which we construct the world of consciousness in which we live, and connect them with a central spiritual sense of Harmony and Beauty which gives the whole of our lives any real meaning or purpose.

Path 27: Victory [7] meets Glory and Honour [8]. This is where we have experiences which teach how to win honourably and fairly through life, in addition to granting others the merit they deserve as well.

Path 28: Victory [7] meets Foundation [9]. Here we must learn how and what to select for the best ideas in life, and what will enable us to find what we need to make us successful in our undertakings. Putting our dreams into practical use.

Path 29: Victory [7] meets the Kingdom [10]. Here we have to apply all our inner abilities to the outer world in order to live with reasonable success, and also apply our outer experiences to our inner Selves so as to obtain the best results with our characters.

Path 30: Glory [8] meets the Foundation [9]. On this Path we have to find out which are the most honourable beliefs and ideas to choose from those we hold in mind, so that we may follow these faithfully through Life with spiritual satisfaction.

Path 31: Glory [8] meets the Kingdom [10]. Our chosen ideas and beliefs have to to applied to Life as we know it, and the ideas we learn in this world have to be "fed back" into our inner selves, so as to encourage the characteristics and qualities we need most to develop.

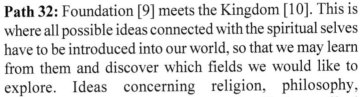 **Path 32:** Foundation [9] meets the Kingdom [10]. This is where all possible ideas connected with the spiritual selves have to be introduced into our world, so that we may learn from them and discover which fields we would like to explore. Ideas concerning religion, philosophy, psychology, metaphysics and the like. Anything likely to afford adventure and experience, exchange of ideology, or construction of character.

So that is what the Paths are. All different areas of experience, or kinds of consciousness, which we should not only know about, but actually put into practices for ourselves, so that we might eventually evolve into something better than ordinary human beings. In other words, each separate Path is a way of life which is calculated to improve our individualities and bring us nearer to God. If the Spheres represent pure Qualities, then the Paths are a blend of both and that will always be the story of the Holy Tree. Seeking for ways to combine both ends of everything, and then trying to follow the control line between them. That is why the Spheres are arranged the way they are in groups of three, Right, Left and Centre. This is how we were built ourselves.

In one sense our Holy Tree is not unlike a Christmas tree which people hang present and gifts on, so that friends and families may collect them at will. Old time philosophers once attached a variety of meanings to all the separate Paths where were presumed to correspond and link up with each other, so as to make a combination of ideas in the minds of those who understand the language. That is to say, if a letter of the Hebrew language alphabet were attributed to each Path and you know how to spell, then all you had to do was combine the Paths to make words which you could then interpret along entirely different lines. This made a kind of "mind-code" very difficult to understand unless you know the secret. Yet in a way it was no more difficult than being familiar with the Morse code and knowing that if you heard three short sounds followed by three long ones and then three short ones again, you would have heard the international distress signal of the well known S.O.S. standing for Save Our Ship, or Save our Souls, whichever interpretation you preferred.

Similarly if you heard the Hebrew Name of God *YHVH*, you recognised it Qabalistically as Beauty-Mercy, Beauty-Wisdom, Mercy-Wisdom and Beauty-Wisdom, because the Hebrew letters were placed on those particular Paths. For a real expert there was an extra secret meaning also. The physical form of the first letter *Yod* [׳] was like a male seed, and that of the second letter *Heh* [ה] like an empty womb. The third letter *Vav* [ו] presented an erect phallus, while the final *Heh*, with the little dot or *dagesh* in the middle [ה], represented a human womb with a male seed inside it, or a pregnant female. In other words, when looking at the Holy Name of God in Hebrew you were seeing a sacred sign of the sex-act. No wonder the old Jews respected the name of their God and kept it holy, saying "Thou shalt not take the Name of the Lord thy God in vain."

So the complete Holy Tree, spheres, Paths, and symbols together, was supposed to be a basic and universal framework on which could be hung all the necessary factors connected with our spiritual "salvation," in the sense of making us worthwhile and well integrated individuals. Just as at one time the planets and signs of the Zodiac all had particular things attributed to each, so that they would form a kind of reference frame whereby people could classify themselves, the Holy Tree might be considered as a more advanced type of spiritual filing system. Whatever could not be associated with any of the Spheres, would probably fit quite well under some Path heading, or with one of the special symbols.

For example, there are two special ways for connecting the

highest heavenly top of the Tree with its very lowest and basic bottom. One is a fast lightening flash like figure 9, said to represent the "Fall" of Lucifer as an Archangel from heaven to earth in a split second, and the other is believed to be his slow and serpentine crawl back again, transversing every single Path of the Tree as in Figure 10. Here they are:

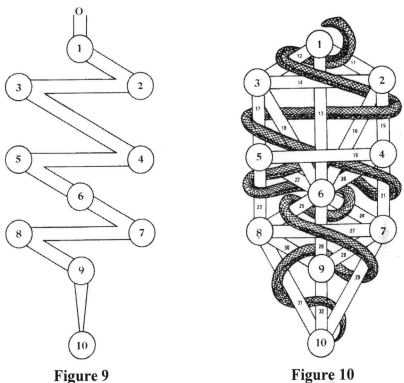

Figure 9   **Figure 10**

We could of course take these as meaning our own arrival on Earth as the seed of *homo sapiens*, and our subsequent crawl up the Ladder of Life step by step via the long hard climb of Evolution. We do however have an option of choice between what are called the "Three Paths of Progress." The emotional Path of Feeling on the right, the thinking and intellectual Path on the left, and the devotional Deistic Path in the centre. These are called the "Orphic Path," because of the music and dancing and gaiety on the first one; the "Hermetic Path," because of the ritualism, intelligence and science necessary for the second, and the "Mystical" for the central Path on account of its ascension by prayer and meditation alone.

This ideal Middle Way is regarded as the most difficult of the three to follow. These three Ways correspond with the principles of Mind (Hermetic), Soul (Orphic), and Spirit (Mystical), though of course it would be possible to combine them, but it is reputed that the best way for the average Westerner to follow in general is the Hermetic, since it includes elements of both the others.

Usually this triple vertical division of the Tree is known as its Three Pillars, the Black left one being called the "Pillar of Severity," the White right one named the "Pillar of Mercy," and of course the "Middle Pillar of Mildness" has to be Gold. Those can be topped with silver for the White Pillar, copper for the Black one, and again gold for the Middle Pillar. If need be, these could be considered in terms of our old money values to decide the order of importance. Yet in addition to those three upright Pillars, there are also three crosswise or horizontal factors to estimate as well.

The first of these is the "Abyss of Ignorance" and everything separating us from the nature of God, hence appearing just below the Supernal Three at the top of the Tree., It also forms a very convenient "Space Gap" down which God can get rid of all the rubbish he doesn't want cluttering up his consciousness. A kind of spiritual sewer as it were. The second division is named *Paroketh,* or a curtain veil normally before a sanctuary. It is usually shown as being just before Spheres 4 and 5, but it actually represents the limits of perception up the Tree which factually might be anywhere between top and bottom, so the position of *Paroketh* depends entirely on individuals. The third and final division is shown as a Bow (*Qesheth* in Hebrew) and an arrow (*Chetz*), which is normally placed just below Spheres 7 and 8. This signifies the aim and intention of whoever is dealing with the Tree. Given accuracy of aim and sufficient strength of will, anything available could be hit. It may be of interest to note that the colossal impudence of a Jewish beggar is called Chutzpah, and failure to hit the mark is termed *"hamartia"* in Greek, normally translated as "sin," or an offence against God because it missed its target. The original meaning seems more apt than the usual interpretation doesn't it? At any rate the completed Holy Tree looks like this.

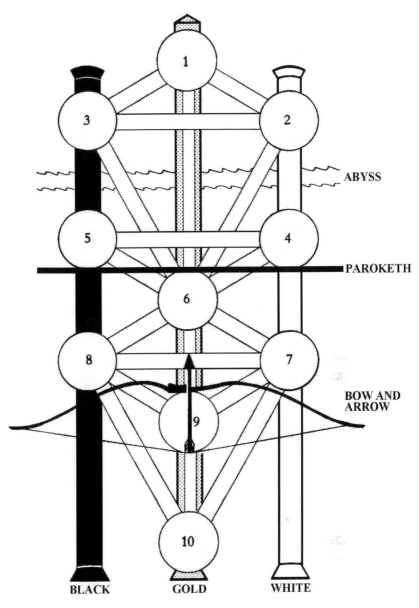

Figure 11

It should always be kept in mind however, that ur ideal aim in life should be the restoration of the Tree back to its original pattern or pre-Fall position, which would mean "lifting" the levels of our living away from Matter altogether, and replacing it at its primal point of importance in our Sacred Scheme. Perhaps you may have noticed that this Middle Pillar, which seems to need pushing up or raising to its proper level with the outer two, might be called the "Pillar of Light" since its planetary attributions are the Sun at Sphere 6, the Moon at Sphere 9, and the Stars at Sphere 1. This means that when we have been sufficiently "illuminated" (or enlightened as the saying goes in mystic circles), we shall be able to "cross the chasm" of the Abyss via the restored Sphere now to be entitled "Knowledge" or *Daath* in Hebrew. Tradition says that this will be done by means of a Sword-bridge, so strait and narrow is the Way between extremities. It also signifies the exceptional care and caution which would be needed to cross it successfully. In other words, once we have gained sufficient knowledge and experience from Life itself, we shall be able to bridge the gap between God and ourselves. Be it specially noted that although the ultimate Sphere of the Crown could be approached by the conscious Paths of Understanding at one end of the Abyss and Wisdom at the other, the only Power sufficiently strong to bridge that vital gulf in the middle by the Mystic Path, is pure LOVE which is willing to sacrifice itself in order to gain the God-Grail it seeks. Therefore it must also be synonymous with an ultimate of Faith and Hope as well, thus making the famous triplicity of FAITH, HOPE AND CHARITY, the latter term coming from the Latin "*caritas*" or love, and so signifying the conclusion of a final self-conquest.

Just as the Spheres of the Holy Tree were supposed to tell us of the character qualities we needed in order to reach its top eventually, so the Paths are there to inform us about the types and conditions of life we must encounter with them so as to live most effectively. For this reason the Tarots have frequently been attached to the Paths of the Tree as symbolic significators. However, there are really three classes of Tarot cards. First the ordinary deck of pips repeated in four suits, then the Court cards, four to each suit, and lastly the unique Trumps or "Triumphs," being a set of twenty-two Concepts or Ideas connected with living in this world.

There can scarcely be any argument about the "pip" cards, since these obviously go with the numbered Spheres, four to each one. The Court cards equally obviously signify the types of people being dealt with, male or female, junior or senior according to suit. When it comes to the Trumps however there are differences of opinion in all directions. In the end it seems best to ignore their numberings which might have come from anywhere, and place the cards where they seem most appropriate from the idealistic viewpoint. Supposing we erect a framework first which appears mos likely. Starting from our world, the closest Cosmic contact would be the *MOON*, between Spheres 10 and 9, Path 32, followed by the *SUN* at Path 26, then the *STAR* at Path 13 between Spheres 6 and 1.

This gives us our Pillar of Light, and links our solar system with all others in this universe. Now we must cross them three times too. *JUDGEMENT* goes best between Wisdom and Understanding, Spheres 2 and 3, Path 13, Neptune-Saturn. *JUSTICE* looks good between Mercy and Severity, Spheres 4 and 5, Jupiter-Mars, Path 16, while the *WHEEL OF FORTUNE* (or just plain "luck") goes well at Path 27 between Spheres 7 and 8, Victory and Glory, Venus-Mercury. This gives us the cross bars of the Tree on three levels of Fatal action. Now we have to do the circuit around them. Starting from the top again, we begin with:

The *HIEROPHANT* between Spheres 1 and 2, Crown and Wisdom, Path 11, Uranus-Neptune, than the *HERMIT* at Path 12, Uranus-Saturn, Spheres 1 and 3. This symbolises externalising and internalising awareness, or male and female types of consciousness.

DEATH between Understanding and Severity at Path 17, Spheres 3 and 5, Saturn-Mars. This is an Abyss-crosser. Then the *DEVIL* or Tempter between Spheres 5 and 8, Severity and Glory, Path 23, Mars-Mercury. This is the Misleader.

HANGED MAN between Spheres 3 and 6, Understanding and Beauty, Duty and Karmic debts accepted, Path 18, Saturn-Sun. Then *TEMPERANCE*, or Path 16 between Spheres 2 and 6, Wisdom and Beauty, Neptune-Sun. Intelligent dealing with all presented energies.

EMPEROR. Benevolent ruler of awareness, between Spheres 2 and 4, Wisdom and Mercy, Path 15, Neptune-Jupiter. Then the *EMPRESS*, or benevolent rule of feelings, on Path 21 between Spheres 4 and 7, Mercy and Victory, Jupiter-Venus.

TOWER. Energetic breakdown or katalysis, Spheres 5 and 6, Path 22, Severity and Beauty, Mars-Sun. *STRENGTH*. Energetic build up or analysis, Spheres 4 and 6, Mercy and Beauty, Path 20,

Jupiter-Sun.

CHARIOT. Travel and discovery. Adventure between Spheres 6 and 8, Beauty and Glory, Path 25, Sun-Mercury. Then the *LOVERS*, attraction, the Life urge, and finding truth in others, between Beauty and Victory, Spheres 6 and 7, Path 24, Sun-Venus.

The *MAGICIAN* (or Priest). Hermetic type of initiate and work. Rationalism and science, Path 30 between Spheres 8 and 9, Mercury-Moon. *PRIESTESS*, the Oprhic type of initiate. Emotion and art on Path 28 between Spheres 7 and 9, Victory and Foundation, Venus-Moon.

FOOL (or Innocent). At the bottom of the Tree the "common man" or at top the Emancipated Ego. This card could change places with the *WORLD*, or general living conditions amongst humans here. Respectively between Spheres 8 and 10 and between 7 and 10, Mercury-Earth and Venus-Earth, Paths 29 and 31.

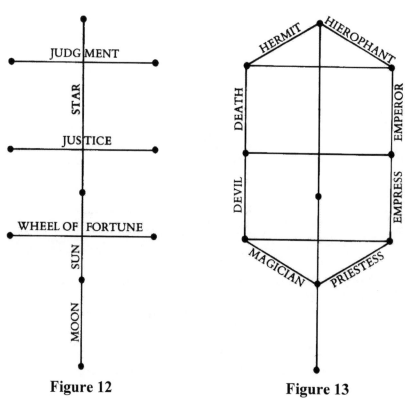

Figure 12   **Figure 13**

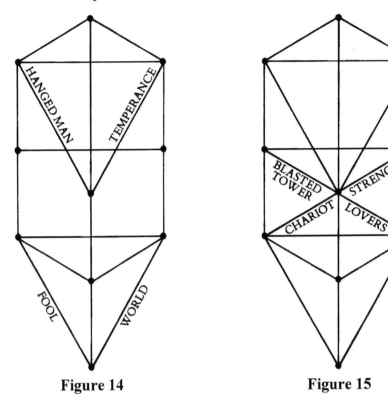

Figure 14   **Figure 15**

Did you notice how the cards got paired off to match each other after the initial Triple Cross framework was set up? Also that there were three types of light: Moonlight, Sunlight, and Starlight divided by three classes of consciousness control, the highest one being the Faculty of Judgement at the top, the central or poising one being the Principle of Justice which seeks to equalize everything, while the lowest is just that of Luck, or the way things work out circumstantially or according to Fortune. Nevertheless, despite this very reasonable attribution of the Tarot Trumps to the most probable Paths of the Holy Tree, it takes considerable skill and experience to read them rightly for any particular reason, so it is best to leave them in the hands of professional people, who have developed such abilities by the required amount of practice.

It is a common practice amongst those who follow this "Path Process" closely, to put themselves through meditational experiences confined to each particular Path either sequentially or by selection. This has become known as "Pathworking" and deals exclusively with whatever types of people, places, things or thoughts, which we might expect to find solely or especially on that

Path alone. Sometimes the associated Tarot Trump is taken as a guide and its Figure strongly imagined, conversed with, or experienced in whatever way seems likely to the thinker. Or else there might be lists made of the most probable circumstances to encounter on every Path, and once a choice of any Path had been made, the whole conscious attention is confined to those topics entirely. The whole idea of such exercises of course is to gain conscious control of thinking and willing, two vital integers of Mind and Magic. Without any abilities in those two vital areas, nothing much could ever be accomplished. A quote from "*Concepts of Qabalah*" (Weisers 1984 - republished "*Qabalistic Concepts*") would not be out of place here:

"Always bear in mind the aim of this work you are doing with the Tree; to align every part of your consciousness, whether objective or otherwise, to focus on your own ultimate identity in union with Divinity. Not just a scattered thought here or there, but *all* of yourself on every level of existence. Think of the analogy of a huge airliner with several hundred passengers and crew on board. When the small auto-control compass is set to a bearing, the entire ship with every soul on it is pointing in the same direction relative to this world, regardless of which way they may be facing on board. So you should set your Tree so that every bit of you is pointing the same way inwardly no matter how you are angled otherwise. The Tree *is* a compass in one important sense. Wherever you are in this world, it will always indicate the same direction—the most direct line between you and Deity."

Therefore understanding the purpose and practise of the Paths is just as important as appreciating the significance of the Spheres. To that end a complete "*Office of the Holy Tree*," has been compiled by the author of this short "Simple Guide." It is recommended reading for anyone needing to dig somewhat deeper into the Tree theme for a better comprehension of its complications. This "Office," previously published as a separate text and later reprinted in "*Sangreal Ceremonies and Rituals*" (Weisers 1986), has been incorporated as Chapter 5 of this book. Apart from being a complete prayer session by itself, it is a metrical capitulation of all the various attributions and ideologies associated with the Spheres and Paths of the entire Tree. As such alone it is both inspirational and informative.

The Hebrew alphabet of twenty-two letters can be distributed among the Paths of the Tree so that they might be combined so as to make sensible messages, so also can our Latin alphabet with a little adaption. All we need to do is omit the vowels, as with Hebrew, and add a single letter from the Anglo-Saxon alphabet—*Eth* or *Th*. The vowels will all go together at Spheres 1 and 10, where they can be called from as may be necessary to make understandable words from combinations of consonants. We shall then obtain a letter-Tree looking like this:

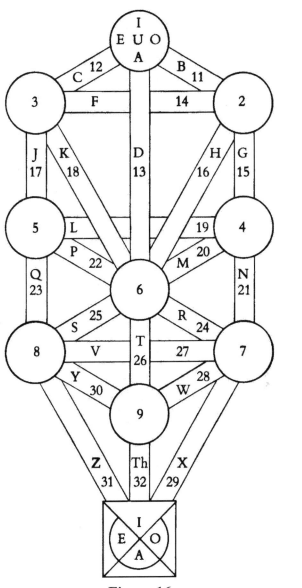

Figure 16

This Tree is capable of conveying messages in English instead of Hebrew, either via the Tarot symbols or their letter-equivalents. For instance, if the letters *D-H-P-S* came up at a random draw, they could be converted into a surprising number of words by the addition of vowels. Here is a short list which might quite easily be extended by an addition of *S* to pluralise them or an *ED*. Also we should not forget that since vowels may be used without stint, those may commence a word also. So using those four letters lone coupled with, or presumably by, vowels, we would get at least the following list:

aPe, aPSe, aDD, aSH, aSP, DaD, DaSH, DeeD, DeaD, DeeP, DieD, DiP, Did, Do, DoeS, Dope, DuD, DuDe, DueS, DuPeS, eaSeS, HaD, HaS, HaSP, Ha, HeaD, HeeD, HiD, HiDeS, HiP, Ho, HoD, HoP, HoPe, HoeD, HooDeD, HooDooeD, iDeaS, iS, oH, oDDS, PaSSeD, PaiD, PaDDeD, PaSHa, PaP, PeaS, PePPeD, PeeP, PiSS, PiPe, PiP, PiPPeD, PoP, PoPe, PooPeD, PoD, PoSSeSSeSS, PuPS, PuPae, PuSheS, SaiD, SaD, SaP, Sea, SeeS, ShaPe, SHaDeS, SheDS, SHe, SHiPPeD, SiPPeD, SiDeS, SHoed, SHoeS, SoDS, SoaP, SoPPeD, SouP, Sue, So, SuDS, SHoP, uP, uS

Surely out of all these words some intelligent message can be assembled? Such as "SHOP HAS HOPES," or "DO HOPE SO," or "ODD IDEAS PAID," or perhaps "HOPES HOODOOED, SAD." Whatever it may be, the import must come from impressions made on the mind of whoever views the single letters, and obviously some experience of working with anagrams would be most useful here. It would certainly be best to keep the cards in smallish numbers, otherwise there will be risk of considerable confusion. The message should be given as the most likely which comes to the viewers mind, and classified as favourable or unfavourable. Practice at this may be gained by studying random assemblies of letters at intervals, remembering to use consonants only and fit the vowels in with ones own mind.

So in the end we can regard the Paths of the Tree as either connecting lines between the Spheres, or extensions of the Spheres themselves towards each other, the effect is just the same in any case. Fundamentally they are exchanges of energy or meetings and matings between distinct Principles of Power. Much as if two notes were struck at first singly and then together as an harmonic, or two colours were first seen apart and then blended to form a mixture which is then regarded by itself. Or for that matter, if two humans were first thought of as individual beings, and then together as another person they presented between them. The triplicity principle in practice. That will always be the Holy Tree of Life, and the Great Name of God uttered.

We are told of course that this is an unpronounceable four-letter word. *IHVH*—the first letter being male, the second female, the third male again, and the last one a pregnant mother, but there is a further factor to consider yet. The potential children within that mother's child, plus their children for the remainder of our time on this earth and beyond. The seeds within the seeds within the seeds as it were. That is why the Great Name was truly said to be unpronounceable—because we should need the whole of eternity to pronounce it, and no single human being can live that long in one form. Life is and always was an indefinitely repeatable phenomena, or theoretically so at any rate. Whether we actually do reproduce ourselves or not is beside the point, it is our potential for doing so that matters, and what can be accomplished by every generation. That is why the Tree of Life will always continue to be holy and the Great Name of God never entirely pronounced.

SO MOTE IT BE,
AMEN.

Chapter 3
PURPOSE AND USE
OF
MAGICAL IMAGES

A. Preface
by
Jacobus Swart

This text was commissioned by Carr Collins, the American sponsor of William Gray's writings. In early 1970 he got an American artist named Bruce C. Griffen to create a set of "Magical Images" to align with concepts associated with the ten spheres on the Kabbalistic Tree of Life. On quizzing William Gray about the images, he stated emphatically that he disliked them with a passion, and voiced his dismay in no uncertain terms. In fact, I found his account of the unfolding of this little work rather amusing. William Gray informed me that whilst he did the best he could with "that artist, the truth behind them is that Carr Collins had this idea about presenting his friends and relatives as images on the Tree. The first set I saw were so revolting in a '*Ycchhh*' sense I nearly blew apart." He continued that he was so horrified, that he got a young friend with some drawing talents "to outline two of my ideas for *Kether* and *Malkuth* Images. Carr got his own artist to draft these out, and shoved others at me across the Atlantic."

Apparently a kind of to-and-fro went on for a couple of years, with the artist slowly "trimming a bit at a time," until in sheer resignation and total exasperation William Gray exclaimed "Oh publish the bloody things as they are." I dare confess he was not the most patient individual on earth, to say the least. However, he did concede that "they were just about tolerable."

In discussing with him the possible republication of this work, William Gray hinted at the possibilities of getting an artist who could do "some *real* images." However, in the current instance I have settled for the original set of "Magical Images," as they have "historical value" as far as the personalities portrayed and the work of William Gray are concerned, and he agreed that the written text "applies to *any* image seen on the *Sephiroth*."

As it is Carr Collins' "Magical Images" are:

Kether:	William Gray's concept copied by the artist;
Chokmah:	Israel Regardie given long hair and a beard;
Binah:	Carr Collins' mother;
Chesed:	Carr Collins' eldest son;
Gevurah:	William Gray given a beard, and taken from a photo of him in character in a play;
Tiphereth:	Carr Collins as a young man;
Netzach:	Yvonne, Carr Collins' wife;
Hod:	Carr Collins as an older man;
Yesod:	James Hall, a Jungian psychologist; and
Malkuth:	William Gray's concept interpreted by the artist.

B. Magical Images

This might as well have been entitled "The Magical Use of Images" because all images are magical in a certain sense. Specific usage of almost any image according to methods traditionally termed magical makes that image or symbol of especial spiritual significance to the user. It is the inner employment of an image which constitutes the magic, rather than the image itself, however esoteric it might appear to the uninitiated.

The realisation that we could take absolutely any sort of a symbol or image at all and make it magical is a very highly important reachment of initiated awareness. It means that we can use all kinds of very commonplace and ordinary things around us as symbols and images which will connect our consciousness with much higher levels of life-intelligence that deal with inner areas leading up to spiritual states approaching divinity itself.

This was (and still should be) one of the main fundamentals of the Masonic craft. The craft of mystery, as it used to be called, taught relatively unsophisticated men who were skilled craftsmen how to treat the normal tools of their trade so that these became symbolic aids for their best spiritual development. Though the tools and materials in this case were limited to the building trade, the principles involved are universal and have only to be applied in any field according to its characteristics.

It is really a question of the famous "outward and visible sign of inward and spiritual grace" definition of a sacrament. That sums up the meaning of magical images very well indeed. In the Masonic practice for instance, each grade or degree of the craft had its own magical images appropriate for the particular type of inner working. With the first old grade of Entered Apprentice, the images were those of a two-foot gauge or rule and a common gavel. In the words of the ritual, candidates were told:

"The 24 inch gauge is an instrument used bit operative masons to measure and lay out but we as free and accepted Masons are taught to make use of it for the more noble and glorious purpose of dividing our time. Eight hours for the service of God and our bretheren, eight for our usual vocation and eight for refreshment and sleep. The common gavel is generally used to break off the corners of rough stones, the better to fit them for the builders use, but we as Free accepted Masons are taught to employ it for divesting our hearts and consciences from the vices and superfluities of life; thereby fitting our minds as living stones for that spiritual building not made with hands, which is eternal in the heavens."

Divested of verbal screens, this means simply that what can be done with hand-tools physically on Earth can also be done with the spiritual equivalents of those same tools and activity on purely spiritual life levels. What was of vital importance was to get this fundamental fact so deeply into the consciousness of an initiatory candidate that he would actually start doing something with it on his own account. That was and still remains the problem with magical images; how to convince people of their inner value and persuade those same folk into putting such images and symbols toward some practically beneficial purpose.

For instance, let us suppose it penetrates the mind of a newly Masonic-Entered Apprentice that an ordinary ruler and heavy gavel have important metaphysical significance for him. At the same time it seems to him that Masonic ritual appears to be mostly a series of questions and answers. If he applies a similar procedure to life in general, is it likely to help him? Having asked his own deep, initiating intelligence that question, he immediately gets his answer: "Yes, that is a good way to tackle life." Keep asking it questions until the answer turns up in oneself. The ritual has taught him how to do this, and the images have a lot more to say if he queries them.

A two foot ruler. Why two feet? Does that signify he is supposed to stand on his own two feet while facing his life-work? He thinks of all the various number associations with 24 inches. The hours of a day. Two years. Three as the only odd number dividing into it. Many intriguing ideas suggest themselves. Then comes the idea of a ruler's main purpose. It connects any two points in the most direct manner, and acts as a standard for measuring and estimating spatial proportions relatively to commonly accepted concepts. Should this tell him to act likewise in the inner dimensions of his life? That is, ought he to accept common standards of mental and spiritual measurement with which to estimate his own lines of living and apply these to spiritual situations much as he uses a ruler in physical circumstances? Does the gauge tell him to be straight and carefully measured in all he does for 24 hours a day? Does it also suggest that he ought to calculate and measure everything he attempts in life very carefully indeed before he applies any form of force thereto? Surely a combination of gauge and gavel says something like, "Think first, act later."

Then the gavel. It is a heavy and rather coarse tool for applying a force of weight to any point of a work in progress. As the ritual says, it knocks the corners off rough stones so as to prepare them for finer processes. Does not the same apply to rough humans, knocking the awkward projections off each other in this coarse world so that we shall be ready for much better treatment by the Master-Craftsman who intends our perfection? We also, have to direct enough weight and effort towards all the various points about ourselves and our living so as to prepare those same selves for higher degrees of polish by finer means. Then too, a gavel calls for attention with its traditional three knocks. We have been told, "Knock and it will be opened." If we want an answer to our enquiries about life, God, or any eternal enigma, then we shall have to learn how to knock out signals that will attract the attention of inner intelligences able to answer us. Once a straightforward question is asked with a definite rule pointed in the right direction and the issue driven home with enough effort in the proper place, our positive answer is bound to result sooner or later. The symbols of an ordinary rule and gavel should tell us that much if we use them in this magical way. They will say considerably more than that if we develop skill in their employment as true Masonic craftsmen should. The fundamentals of this important degree of Entered Apprentice amount to learning the possibilities of applying material symbols for spiritual ends, and realising that such symbols can be combined to spell out a whole programme or inner meaning, just like letters of the alphabet can be put together so as to make intellectual sense that everyone can share together. This is another magical use of images.

Of course, not only Masons used symbol-images for magic. Any operative or initiate of inner mysteries did the same thing in their own way. Eventually, it became discovered there were definite sets of symbols which could be combined from a minimum number of basics in order to achieve a maximum output of conscious arrangements and understandings; again like a few alphabetical signs making up all the languages of this world. Once enough inner experience had been gathered along these lines it became obvious that if a standard set of convenient symbols of consciousness could be agreed upon, these would serve as archetypes out of which all other awareness possible to their users would emerge. Qabalists believe such an ideal set of magical symbols exists in the Images attached to the Spheres on the Tree of Life. These so-called Spheres are really distinct and discrete inner areas of categorical consciousness, distinguished from each other by very definite characteristics and by their titles.

Other systems of inner approach to immortal identity had their own sets of symbolic images which they generally kept as sacred secrets or confidential lines of approach, leading them toward their highest beliefs in a universal life-spirit. They observed such secrecy from no mean or ignoble motives but simply from an instinctive love and respect for something they realized was too beautiful and true to deserve ill-treatment and bad handling by careless human companions insufficiently evolved to appreciate such issues. Common sense alone told advancing souls to keep good counsel about whatever linked them with their highest lines of inner light. If any undue interference cut them off from this perception of perfection, it would be a great loss to them indeed. So they learned the art of silence and discretion with these inner affairs. They still should.

Some of the pagan cults and survivals of primitive faiths

into mainly rural districts of even our modern times made use of very humble (yet quite adequate) magical symbol-images indeed. The sheer poverty of these people alone accounted for that. Their working tools, which they turned into magical use, consisted of the most elementary cottage and even hovel equipment. Sticks, pieces of string, bones, broomsticks, knives, shears, stones with holes in them, bits of wood with designs burned on them with pokers, all these pathetic little possessions were used systematically and symbolically to link up the consciousness of even the poorest human with the all-awareness of the life-spirit itself. How many moderns with their incredible collections of the wealthiest objects imaginable have a fraction of that fundamental faith in the spirit standing behind every symbol? Can people make use of their Cadillacs and other status-symbols to establish some kind of working relationship with the infinite? They could, but it is more than doubtful if they actually do.

*
*   *

Even though it is quite possible to take any kind of image at all and make magic with it, experience has shown that suitably graded and selected image-symbols, chosen with conscious care to cover from end to end our evolving life-entities, are best for magical purposes. This is exactly what happens with the Magical Images of the Qabalistic Tree of Life. A theoretical scale with decimal divisions has been drawn between man at one end, God at the other and a definite image-symbol appointed to illustrate each point. The scale has ten divisions, ten descriptive and distinctive images each typifying a spiritual state of life rising from ordinary earth-existence to the highest possible condition of cosmic identity imaginable. This really amounts to what we may be ourselves, as minimum or maximum states of living individuality. We might otherwise say it was an up and down lifescheme of the entire Universe.

The Magical Images of the Tree are simple enough in principle as concepts of consciousness common to all that lives for the sake of its own spiritual perfection. They are:

1. The most Senior state of Spiritual Selfhood.
2. An absolute Father of Wisdom.

3.   An eternal Mother of Understanding.
4.   A Majestic Mercy.
5.   A Dedicated Disciplinarian.
6.   A composite of Simplicity, Sacrifice, and Survival.
7.   Graceful Victory.
8.   Intelligent Curiosity.
9.   Vigorous Vitality.
10.   Natural Normality.

These are symbolic of the various selfstates we should assume singly, sequentially, simultaneously, in part or totally, in order to make ourselves into spiritually developed people-worthy of being considered true Children of Light, Companions of Cosmos, or any other description of humans seeking divinity. If we make the right magical use of these particular Images, they will take its from the base of our life-trees to their very tops.

The values of these concepts are that they contain all the common energies of consciousness directed into them by those employing them, whatever the life-status of such beings may be. Not only human minds make use of them. They are current also among higher-than-human life-orders and are accepted as an exchange medium of mental and spiritual energies—more or less throughout the whole of Cosmos— reachable by consciousness on any life-level. Thus, those using them magically are spiritually speaking the language of life itself, We can actually use them to communicate with higher, finer, and more advanced levels of life than those we encounter during ordinary Earth existence. True, learning to speak inwardly in such terms may take a lot of time and effort, but how many years does it normally take an average human to master the art of fluent eloquency in any tongue? Some never achieve this in a lifetime and many need quite a few of our years. If we only discover how to speak spiritually in relatively "baby talk" during a whole human lifetime, we shall be doing well. Here, the symbol-images are like the major point of life which babies have to grasp first so that they may learn later how to link up meanings between them and converse with other life-companions on their own levels.

This issue is important. When babies are first adjusting to earthlife they have to accept large and inclusive "lumps" of it as whole areas of awareness, enabling them to distinguish "this" from "that."First of course, there is an "I live" sense into which all else sums up. This is *Kether* on the Tree of Life. Then follows a father and mother realization tied up with food, warmth and safety. These are *Chokmah* and *Binah*, the next two Spheres of life. Then comes "I love this," in relation to comfortable and kind happenings, opposed by "I hate this," relatively to painful or dangerous experiences—the Spheres of *Chesed* and *Geburah*.

Assuming that everything equals out into fairly contented and harmonious conditions of life, baby feels beautiful about himself and everyone. This is *Tiphereth*. Then comes a more ambitious attitude. "How can I get my own way by cajolery?" The Victory of *Netzach*. After that, "how do I get what I want by cunning?" The Glory of gain at *Hod*. Having covered all these issues, baby realises, "If this is life, how do I get more of it?" The same way I got it myself sex and vitality. I'm a boy (or girl), "Look out Life! Here I come and I can scarcely wait to grow up!" *Yesod* on the Tree.

Lastly the clever little creature cottons on to the fact that if any of these ideas are to materialize it will have to adapt into living conditions of consciousness and circumstances but fast. Every assistance afforded by Nature has to be accepted, just as though Man were married to Matter. Baby is usually only too anxious to establish a working partnership with Nature as *Malkuth* of the Life-Tree. So, with only a few principles of awareness do we begin our actual process of living through our physical projections into these dimensions.

Unless we actually grasped such major living-concepts at first, we should never be able to extend and refine our realisations into the subsequent sophistications of coherent, conscious communion with Cosmos. Those concepts or symbolic images are the entire supply-sources from which all our later definitions and distinctions of consciousness are derived. We make up the whole of our mental processes out of and through the original set of life-symbols we adopted as we began our beings. They are as important as that. Fortunately we can modify them and develop them into very efficient energy-exchangers later in life if we really mean to. Most people seldom bother to make any such attempt or even suppose this might be possible.

It is by means of Magical Images that beneficial changes of character may be carried out. That is their best employment in the Holy Mysteries and their main purpose for being placed as they are upon the Tree of Life plan-itself the image of an ideal identity.

How are they to be used? Easy to tell in a few words, but likely to take much more of a lifetime for putting into practice. We have to deal with the Images by three progressive changes of consciousness concerning them.

First. We must be conscious of them.
Second. We must be consciousness with them.
Three. We must be conscious as them.

The whole of this process forms a magic circle of consciousness containing our lives therein.

The first stage is relatively easiest, though it calls for considerable qualities of perseverance and perceptiveness by the practitioner. Here we have to make ourselves conscious of the symbol-image concepts—not only as artists' and writers' descriptions on paper but as actualities of life, observable in other people and anywhere else we can recognise their appearance. For instance, we might notice someone behaving in a very kind-hearted and generous way. This should make us think, "That looks like the Kind King of *Chesed*." Then we might look at a group of strong healthy young folk vigorously playing around together with lots of living energy, quite normally concerned with their sexual attraction for each other. This ought to to evoke the image of Virility of *Yesod*.

Then again, we come across some person or people behaving very badly or even viciously. This is where the value of the images comes in. We should consider such nastiness and then realise that there is nothing like that on the Tree at all. Not a single image should suggest any such activity. Therefore we do not recognize the bad behaviour as belonging to the Tree of Life we are trying to grow in our inner gardens. Instead, we mentally take the unpleasantness and do the natural thing with it—drop it down the Abyss for disposal where it will be reduced to harmless and helpful "spiritual sewage," ready to come back into Cosmic life-cycles again on root or sub-levels of our Life-Trees.

All this of course, takes quite a lot of time and effort to get working. There are meditations to make on the concepts, small magical rituals to devise so as to link up with the inner intelligences connected with the concepts, recognition signals to arrange which will alert our attention to the symbols as they appear in our lives and all sorts of other routine magical procedures. The outcome of such efforts ought to be that we become steadily aware of life in terms of the Tree-concepts. We begin to realise how everything connects together so as to make up the One Consciousness in which we all live. That alone is more than worth the trouble we may have taken.

Once some degree of success comes along these lines, we can start working with the Images. Just as a craftsman assesses the needs of anything he is dealing with and selects exactly the right sort of tool for perfecting that particular work-stage, so should we learn to do the same with spiritual situations of life. After all, we have to work at life to make it liveable for ourselves. So we might as well use the right tools for the job. Those tools are the symbols with which we adapt our attitudes to life and its situations to ourselves. During our previous dealings with the Images, we just looked at them, watched others using them and learned about their functions in a theoretical way. Now the time comes when we must actually pick them up and put them into life-practice. That is the same way anybody learns how to handle anything, and here we are discovering how to handle the materials of life itself.

There is a distinct and different life-application for each Image—just like an ordinary set of bench-tools. All this has to be learned by tuition and experience. In any given life-situation, there are appropriate methods for dealing with it by means of the Magical Images, once we know which to select and how to apply them intentionally. First we have to think of them, and then act with them—the "rule and gavel" principle in practice. What is meant is that we must learn how to apply ourselves and our energies to life with will, in the manner of whatever Image may be appropriate for use at any given instant. We must learn how to employ all of them at once if we have to, or any combination whatever which may be called for. Naturally it comes easiest to handle one at a time first of all, and then develop real skill in life-- craftsmanship as we go along.

All this again takes a great deal of magical activity to achieve even moderate success. Once more there are rituals to devise which will accustom the operator to making practical use of the Images—both in inner and outer ways of living. Each Image has to be evoked and reacted with appropriately so that the practitioner becomes able to apply an intention of will to life, by means of that Image in particular. That should he the purpose behind all ritual practices. These are for conditioning our consciousness so that we live according to the lines of life we are laying down. We might otherwise think of this as steering our cosmic course toward whatever star represents the self we ought to become at the end of our entities in Ultimate Light. If we want to be very modern, we may suppose ourselves living in our own spiritual "spaceships," which have ten major controls for guiding us as we will among all the awareness of cosmic consciousness. Those controls are the Symbol-Images of life as located on the Tree thereof. The rest of the Tree-plan is the elaborate circuitry connecting us with all the points we may need to contact throughout Cosmos, in order to keep us correctly on our life-course.

We shall quite naturally make many mistakes and errors while we are trying to do things with the Images and here, once more, we need to learn how to use the Abyss for disposal of our dismal failures (which have gone too far for repairs or restoration to be practical.) Even garbage is valuable if processed properly back to basic elements, and this has to be properly planned as part of the inner economies belonging to our life system. It must never be forgotten that the Abyss is an invaluable item on the Tree of Life—once we know how to use it effectively. Though not shown. as all actual Image, the Abyss is still a symbol to be used in connection with the Images. Its most valuable function is to begin the cycle of turning our mistakes in life into ultimate successes, by reducing them to fundamental energies and presenting these eventually for further evolutionary efforts.

When we have made some degree of progress in working with the Symbol-Images, we have to start living as them. This means to say we must be able to adopt each or all of them at will as our own life-attitudes and attributes. In a certain sense, this may sound rather like the assumption of a role by a character actor, but it is not the same thing at all. An actor knows quite well that he is only simulating the characteristics required for presenting some specific theatrical part. A magical practitioner, operating as a Symbol-Image, is actually creating those cosmic characteristics in himself, as integral items of his own spiritual identity. In this way we eventually become (in ourselves) a sort of conscious compendium, containing all the Image capabilities associate with them on the Tree of Life.

*

*   *

Magical Images are successfully invoked by an identification process through which the qualities symbolized by the Images are recognised and raised in the individual invocant, so that a sense of identity is experienced with whatever archetype the idealized Image represents. This same end-effect may be achieved by quite a number of ritual practices.

The first thing to realise is that the intrinsic factor concerned is quality. This means the specific spiritual characteristics of any Image in question. All the external appearance or appurtenances connected with an Image should be for the sole purpose of suggesting or symbolizing definite qualities associated with the overall idea behind the Image. Many qualities may be contained by the same concept, and each evoked by its own suitable symbol. With each Image therefore, we have its complete concept and as many characteristics or qualities as we may discover.

The ten Archetypal Images of the Qabalistic Tree of Life are ten concepts of divinity which also cover all that mankind may ever become, collectively or individually. Every individualising human entity has fractional proportions of all those concepts and therefore traces of qualities connected therewith in themselves. These are what must be invoked in, and invoked from, those who use the Images to identify with the Infinite Intelligence behind them all.

Outside appearances of an Image are only artistic aids for reaching some degree of realisation concerning what its entire concept means to Cosmos as a whole, and the invocant as an individual item of that same Cosmos. Therefore it pays not to be over-critical of image-presentation, providing that this is really capable of calling up the actual concept itself in the consciousness of a beholder. Sometimes a few very simple lines may be much more effective for this purpose than the most elaborate and complicated affair. Clarity of concept is the spiritual superlative to be accorded priority here. How such clarity is achieved is a matter for technicians of consciousness to work out and apply according to experience. What matters is that concepts should be presented in whatever style is likely to evoke maximum empathy with the idea and a minimum of confusion as to meaning. The principles involved are of paramount importance and the way these are presented depends entirely on constructional ability.

In the case of the Tree-Images we have ten fundamental concepts, presented as personalisations through which we should seek identification with the Conceiving Intelligence. To recapitulate these, they are:

Magical Images of the Tree of Life

	Sephirah	Concept	Personalised by Image
0	*Ain Soph Aur*	Nil	Vacancy
1	*Kether*	Apex of Awareness	Holy Head
2	*Chokmah*	Wisdom	Faithful Father
3	*Binah*	Understanding	Mature Mother
4	*Chesed*	Mercy	Kindly King
5	*Geburah*	Severity	Stern Soldier
6	*Tiphareth*	Beauty (Harmony)	Magnificent Mediator
7	*Netzach*	Victory	Lovely Lady
8	*Hod*	Glory	Perceptive Person
9	*Yesod*	Foundation (of Fecundity)	Manly Male or Fertile Figure
10	*Malkuth*	Kingdom (of Nature)	Mysterious Mate

The problem now is to relate with these concept-figures so that at least one quality of each is recognised by invocants in themselves and their own divine potential may therefore be realised, to however slight a degree.

This may he accomplished by taking the Images at first one «t a time, considering each consciously and finding some quality in common which identifies the individual with the Image. Then as empathy is established, extending attentive awareness into this inner experience so that all actual sense of spiritual identification with the concept is achieved. It is important to understand that this identification is not with the Images as they stand but through them, into but through them, into and with the concept-principles they personify. That point must be made abundantly and sufficiently clear before any work with the Images is attempted. Failure to appreciate the significance of this will invalidate the whole exercise on its best inner levels.

It must also be fully realised that image-quality identification has nothing whatever to do (except very remotely) with anyone's social, sexual or any other kind of personal status. The qualities we are concerned with here are universally applicable to human and allied beings, *per se*, as spiritual entities. Everyone has at least trace-degrees of them, and the aim or our image-exercises is to contact, extend and expand these in a spiritually sane and balanced way, so that the practitioner achieves the greatest possible inner benefits. At first impression it might seem impossibly incongruous for, say, prizefighter to find common qualities with a Mother-image or a highly intelligent Hermaphrodite (to say nothing of a graceful Lady) but in point of fact this is perfectly natural and normal. Even prizefighters are born to some mother and therefore have something of her nature in them. Their actions must be swift and skilled like the Mercurial image, and the easy grace of their movements or a fondness for animals and children links them with the Lovely Lady concept. There is something for everybody in all the concepts but all must discover what is there for them by their own efforts. It is useless making a list of concept qualities and expecting people to pick what they fancy from this. The magic of the process consists of finding mutual qualities with the Magical Images and enhancing these empathically.

Suppose we follow an imaginary session with the Images in company with an average young male person seeking spiritual sections of himself, so to speak, in the Images of each Sphere. First he acknowledges his Zero potential of pre-being before birth and post-being after he ceases to be himself. These may be theoretical self-states, but they still have to be considered. Without a Zero, no numbers whatever can exist. No session is complete without recognition of the Nil-State. From this comes the Holy Head concept of pure consciousness. Just that. An awareness of "I am conscious, alive. I may be what I will," and like thoughts. A head by itself should suggest authority, comprehension, all this has to be actually felt and experienced in the participant. I n this case, he must arouse these particular feelings in himself and stay with them to the exclusion of all others during this part of the exercise. That is the secret of Living in the Spheres-using only whatever category or frequency of consciousness belonging to each Sphere, while associating with it individually. Switching from one Sphere to another, or changing a categorical type of consciousness with a different one is a Path operation. It is possible to use all the Spheres and Paths simultaneously of course, but this takes practice. Here, our young man is proceeding sensibly by single steps.

It would be a mistake for him to imagine himself like the symbolic head in its picture. The end-aim should not be to visualize himself as anything, but to experience himself as what the symbol suggests. The visual symbols have to be translated into inner actualities of awareness in terms of spiritual self-recognitions. Here, the invocant should realise and live with his own highest inner authority, deriving from divinity itself. Once the Image has helped suggest this state of inner awareness it may be faded out altogether, while the experience it has evoked is continued with consciously. At first, this will be difficult, but the knack comes with persistent practice and should be persevered with until each concept can be consistently concentrated upon for at least a whole minute at a time. Once the ability is gained, lengthening periods out becomes merely a matter of repetitive effort.

From the "I will be" stage, the Concept of Fatherhood is dealt with. Since our young man is not a physical father as yet, he must identify with father-ability in himself. He may not actually be very wise or responsible as he stands, but somewhere in him there must be even the faintest degree of wisdom and responsibility lurking. Let him realise this, and concentrate on his latent fatherhood faculties which he shares in common with the Cosmic

Father-Principle, suggested by the Image. This is in him to be as he wills. In this principle, he and God are one, however far separated otherwise. Something has actually been found whereby a little human and the highest entity have so much together in Cosmic-Life. The more such a principle is practiced the closer it will bring both beings together and this is the main objective of the entire exercise.

After the Father-Principle comes the Mother-Principle. How might a young man identify with this? In a multitude of ways his invention should discover. May he not receive seed ideas from other individuals and after gestating these in his deep subconsciousness, bring them forth again to light in new forms? What is this but the Mother-Principle working through him? Patience is a quality of this Sphere. So are understanding, and intuition. Whatever quality our invocant finds in himself, enabling him to identify somehow with the Mother-Principle suggested by the Image here, let him call this out of himself and live with it particularly for even a few moments. That is how principles are invoked and used through these Images.

It should be relatively easier to deal with the next few Images. Surely most people of average goodwill would wish to identify with the Magnanimous and Merciful Monarch Concept which follows, expressing which follows, expressing (as it does) the principle of compassion extending throughout creation. Perhaps it may not be quite so pleasing to locate the characteristics of severity and discipline in oneself (symbolized by the Soldier-symbol) but this is also a necessary duty, especially for a young man. Young women too need this Sphere just as much in their own ways. They have life-disciplines and duties to undertake as well, and may no more avoid cosmic obligations than any other sort of people.

Identifying with the principles behind the Mediator-image may be more difficult because this is a compound image taken in three stages—not three separate Images but the same one seen from different levels. It is really the Sacred King Image in a state of innocent incarnation, sacred sacrifice and resurrected redeemer. Here the young man might identify with the complete concept through his sense of innocence or harmlessness, his sacrifice of self-interests for some spiritual reason and his intention of transcending above or redeeming whatever wrongs he meets within life. There are plenty of identity points to pick up in this central sphere.

An average young man could perhaps hesitate to identify with the next Image of a beautiful woman, but there is no metaphysical necessity for this. His normal sexual inclination—to keep lovely ladies in objective relationship with his personal polarity—is perfectly correct but the principle of identification concerns grace, music, art-appreciation and very many qualities that enhance any civilized young male seeking a cultivated type of Cosmos. We might remember that love of floristry, gardening or horticulture comes in here. No shortage of identification items whatever.

The next Image of a Perceptive Person who could be either sex is mainly Hermetic in character. It positively teems with qualities the average young person, male or female, ought to recognise in themselves immediately. Curiosity, scientific spirit, humour, adroitness, intellect—an absolute flood of characteristics common to man, woman, child or almost any living creature. Anyone having any difficulties of identification with the Spirit of this Sphere must have something seriously wrong with them.

This last remark also applies to the following Sphere of Fertility and reproductive life which is the Foundation of our existence on this Earth. Not only should we be fertile physically, but much more importantly fertile in mind, soul and spirit. Our children of consciousness are as vital to Cosmos as our human descendants have validity in worldly affairs. He or she who cannot find anything of themselves in this Sphere can scarcely be a person with much hope of anything worth living for.

Lastly, we have the Mysterious Mate Image to identify through into the Natural Kingdom. The figure here suggests a feminine aspect of nature but this is a conventional connection with an old concept of nature as being capricious, changeable and unpredictable. All are qualities bestowed on women by men ever since sex began. We can afford a sympathetic smile nowadays without demanding alterations to an Image, which would also destroy concepts of her charm, desirability, fascination and eternal attraction for the whole of mankind. The idea of a divine spirit manifesting through nature as a mate or spouse for humanity applies to man or woman alike. Either we partner with nature in a workable and happy marriage, productive of many splendid offspring, or—but why accept even the possibility of ultimate failure in this all-important field? All marriages have ups and downs and there is no divorce possible with this one. Man's marriage to nature is strictly an "until death us do part" affair. It is possible for anyone of any age to find identification points through this Image at any instant of life. Our own natures, whatever these are, keep us permanently married to the principle involved here. We have only to follow where these lead—inside ourselves—and "meet our Mate of the Holy Mysteries," or what was once culled the Spouse of Spirit.

Those then, are the principles of invoking the Spirit of Life, via the Concepts of the Holy Tree, and by means of the Magical Images attached thereto. The actual practice is bound to vary according to individual abilities and availabilities but in broad outline, it largely consists of rneditational procedures in association with each Image—possibly accompanied by mimed dramatisations of the characteristics being conceived. Whatever ritual means seem likely to induce empathy between the individual and the idea with which identification is sought, may be put to this purpose. Here are some suggestions.

The collection of pictures at the conclusion of this chapter represent the ten principle Concepts of the Life-Tree. Adopt a standard formula for establishing a relationship with them. Something quite simple and straightforward is best; such as:

IN GOD I RECOGNISE.....the principle concerned.
IN ME GOD RECOGNISES.....some quality claims.
AS ONE MAY WE FOREVER BE. *AMEN.*

Instead of the word "God," whatever title or description the invocant invests the Supreme Spirit with may be used. Let each Image and idea be specifically saluted, identified with and dwelt upon one after the other up or down the whole Tree of Life. At least a minute should be given to each single Sphere in order to expect reasonable results. An "Image a day" may be done this way, and the rite be simple or elaborate according to choice.

An elaboration of this, for instance, would be to set up all the Images in a circle around the room and then progress from one to another, rather like the Christian "Stations of the Cross" practice though these would, of course, be the "Stations of the Tree." A very beautiful and satisfying experience can be arranged in this manner.

The "Office of the Holy Tree of Life" (Chapter 5 in this book) is most helpful. The invocations of tho Spheres may be selected one after the other and a circuit of the entire Tree made. Suitable Sphere-music can also be recorded and used for background effects, coloured lights and perfumes introduced or whatever is needed to build the Rite into impressive proportions. The Images may quite well be projected as colour-slides if this is possible. It cannot be overemphasised however, that no matter how expensive or elaborate any rite may be, nothing will ever substitute for or supplant the individual efforts and adjustments made by anyone for and in themselves as a direct act of relationship with Divinity.

Essentially the invocatory exercise must boil down to one formula. Addressing himself to Infinite Awareness, by whatever term best conveys truth to the individual concerned, he says, and must mean with all his heart,

> "I SEE THIS IN THEE
> LOOK AT THIS IN ME
> BY THIS INDEED MAY WE
> RELATED EVER BE."

A good exercise, for those intending to work these invocations, is setting up for themselves a list of the Principles and Images then (under each heading) writing down whatever appropriate qualities of their own to fit in with each Sphere. It is very important to make an honest assessment of these and from time to time it pays to review the list and revise it where necessary.

Enlightening as it may be to discover qualities shared with Divinity, it is well to remember that human identification with divine attributes does not mean that we equate with God—or ever will. An ant has marks of identity with a human being. It eats, rests, fights, walks, lifts weights and identifies with us up to a certain point but cannot equate with us because we have qualities quite beyond its highest attainment. So have we attributes in common with God but the Life-Spirit has qualities and properties far beyond our capabilities of conception. We can only acknowledge these unknown factors through our Nil-Concept, yet this is our most important recognition. For the rest we may follow our contacts with the Tree-Concepts, which outline mankind's maximum limits of identification with divine life. If and when we learn how to use these effectively, we might be trusted with wider ranges of inner realisation.

Another helpful device along these lines is keeping, what might he called, a .score-card record of contacts. This is simply a card or paper with n heading somewhat like:

Occasion _____
Concept _____
Response _____
Degree _____
Remarks _____

_____
_____
_____
_____
_____
_____

The heading, "Occasion," allows for time-date-place details or any special locationary references.

Under "Concept," the Sphere Name or member is all that is needed to indicate the particular Sphere-Image being dealt with. These may be taken in sets, individually, or sequentially through the entire ten.

Under "Response" a single word is usually sufficient to describe the identification-quality discovered in the individual to match the Concept in question.

Under "Degree," an estimate is needed of whether the response seemed only faint, fair or reasonably marked. These might be designated by the letters A, B or C.

Lastly, under "Remarks," any very brief comment of two or

three words which may seem needed to explain or amplify the previous findings may be added.

This score-card idea is of greater value than might be supposed because it develops correct habits of consciousness with a minimum of trouble. It can be used absolutely anywhere (even in public) since it only gives an impression of someone making a few necessary private notes. For that purpose a small looseleaf notebook is ideal and it can he used at any odd occasion whatever. Every so of ten it is advisable to look through the completed pages and discover what sort of a pattern is building up among them. This will provide a. lot of helpful information to the persons concerned about their progress and peculiarities.

With the aid of the same note-book, concept-identification may be worked on very light levels almost like a rather enjoyable game. It is always good to find pleasing delight in spiritual practices because frequently we achieve with a single touch of fun what cannot be obtained after hours of solemn cudgelling. This particular game might be called Holy Hide-and-Seek. It consists of calling a Concept, then looking carefully around the room for something which links with or evokes discovery of that Concept inside the seekers own character. The fundamental purpose of this game is to develop a recognition of divinity in ourselves by reflection from all we encounter outwardly around us in living. It makes a very good game too. One session of it could go like this, for instance:

Concept sought	Outside me	Inside me
Justice (5)	A ruler on a desk	Sense of standards
Mercy (4)	Springs in chair	Protective instinct
Wisdom (2)	A book	Will to learn
Glory (8)	Polish on furniture	Sense of amusement
Foundation (9)	A growing plant	Rising life
Beauty (6)	Shining sun	Well-being

Victory (7)	A solved X-word	Achievement
Understanding (3)	A friends' letter	Empathy
Kingdom (10)	The desk-top	Present feelings
Crown (1)	Ceiling light	Life-aim

Where might a simpler game be found to give such a sense of Divine immanence? It can be played again and again with varied results each time. Eventually, the Concepts will begin to play games back on their own accord and pop out of the most unlikely places unexpectedly. When this starts happening and the ordinary things around us, including our fellow humans, commence revealing quite surprising spiritual contents linked with the Life-Tree Concepts, we shall know that the Living Spirit is speaking to us in its own language. Once this kind of communication opens up, we should make every effort to listen and learn what it tells us of life for this is the true Enochian speech whereby all may speak with God in their own inner tongues.

By these, and allied means, we may "Invoke the Magical Images" of the Tree-Concepts. If we achieve any degree of success with the system, a remarkable thing will happen. The Images will come-alive, and the divine concepts they represent will invoke us as images of themselves in return. That was and ever will be, the primal purpose of our first formation—to act as living agents for the Infinite Intelligence, in whose images we were made. The clearer these become to us the better use we shall be in this Universe. So may the Light of Life increase among us steadily forevermore.

*
* *

In old and new ritual practice, the idea of taking into oneself the qualities of one of the Spheres of the Tree of Life was referred to as "Assuming a God-Attitude." It meant acting as if one actually were some particular deity (or aspect of divinity) in a minor way of Life. Why not? We are constantly told to take some divine example, such as Jesus, for a model and base our behaviour upon that Being as far as we can. With the Images of the Tree we have ten distinct aspects to assume so that we may relate ourselves with life, as though we really were any or all of those aspects on a smaller scale of self. It must be remembered that, though they may appear as different beings, they are actually all parts of One Being only. So we shall simply be arranging our same selves in ten varying life-attitudes to cover every cosmic angle of approach.

It may be asked how some very masculine human might adopt the feminine aspects of the images, or an intensely feminine soul assume the masculine aspects. Apart from the evident metaphysical truth that ideal individuals should have both polarities balanced in themselves, we should bear in mind that the Images are intended to convey life-qualities which every human being ought to develop, regardless of biological bias. Should not a woman be wise, or a man understanding? May not a man be graciously successful, or a woman disciplined and strong? We all need all the qualities of the Tree, whatever physical sex our bodies may belong to. It is entirely a question of attaining and apportioning these, according to our life-needs. The Images are associated with specifically sexed symbols purely for convenience in consciously dealing with them in conformity to our customary Western attitudes. They link up with the mainstream of our inner spiritual tradition and so evoke energies out of us which might otherwise have stayed latent for a lot of our lives.

Although much of our ability to live as the Symbol-Images of the Tree will be developed by skilled use of magical ritual practice, this is mainly of value during the initiatory stages of its acquisition. In a way, a Magical Temple is a sort of Life laboratory in which the spiritual techniques and methods are initiated, tested and assembled before being extended into more ordinary areas of living. Before any ordinary commercial produce ever reaches a commodity market there has to be a very great deal of expenditure, in terms of research, trial runs, testing and all the rest of what is now generally accepted procedure, prior to releasing any manufactured item for public purchase. This ensures a relatively reasonable standard of article. If only we did the same along our spiritual lifelines of production, we should all live in a much improved world. That is where Magical Temple procedures can really help.

If we employ magical methods of ritual practice for

learning how to live as our Images and treat our Temples like laboratories and test-rooms (in which we are developing our inner productions up to a point where they may he released from the confines of our self-circles into more general cosmic circulation), this will prove the most valuable use we might make of such facilities. That is the best justification for any Temple established on Earth, whether magical or not.

Nor must we forget our faithful Abyss while learning to live as our Life-Images. So much is bound to occur which is both unworthy or inferior (in respect of the ideals our Images represent) and quite unfit for inclusion in the identity we should be building for ourselves by our attempts to live as these Symbol-Images. Therefore the best thing to do with our productions (which are impractical to improve) is abandon them down the Abyss and let them be broken back to basics for later living. This is all part of the life-process we have to learn in order to live as the Tree-Images with any degree of success.

Altogether these Image-symbols are life keys which will literally open up unimaginable areas of inner and spiritual existence far more real and enduring than the very limited and scarcely satisfactory conditions of consciousness confining us purely to this relatively small planet. The Images are integrated with life-truths on the deepest possible levels and where they are acceptable, so are those who customarily use them as a means of manifesting consciousness. They are, to that extent, almost our passports to ultimate perfection. All that lives has its own built-in "pattern of perfectibility" and the tree-plan, with its idealistic Images, is that very design imprinted into humanity by a divine hand. We have only to carry it out consciously and consistently. If we really lived the Tree Images in actuality on all life-levels, we should undoubtedly be people approaching perfection in the closest possible way.

Supposing some human individual had the qualities of wisdom, understanding, compassion, discipline, equinamity, grace, intelligence, vitality and naturalness, all combined together in good degrees to present a whole self as a spiritual entity? We should certainly believe such an unusual person was practically perfect as a human being. That is exactly what work with the Magical Images of the Tree of Life aims to produce, however long this process might take to show reasonable results. If we need to develop any or all these qualities in ourselves then we must get in touch with their archetypes by means of whatever magic we may, and effect energy-exchanges between ourselves and their symbol-spheres so that we change our states of consciousness in conformity with their characteristics.

Surprising as this may sound, it is a perfectly practical proposition. All the tree-qualities are actualities of what might be called, inner energy, available to human beings in exchange for efforts made to achieve them. They can all be developed, acquired or attained (to minor or major degrees) by even quite ordinary people, if these live persistently enough in pursuit of such aims. Let us ask ourselves one vital query here. Just what happens to all this processed inner energy? Millions of people in this one world alone are exercising these remarkable qualities every moment we live. Other life-entities associated with its are also concerned with the very same qualities, along their particular levels of living. Altogether an incalculable amount of life-energy in our own minute cosmic corner of creation is being expended universally in the exercise of the life-tree qualities. Surely there must be some means for each of us, as life-entities ourselves, to link up with this incredible "pool of power" and convert it into terms of personal progress. In other words, if we do not have enough wisdom, understanding, compassion, etc, of our own, why cannot we obtain what we need from other sources while we are growing our own life-links directly with divinity itself as the ultimate supply of all spiritual sustenance? In fact, we can and should. All living organisms evolve that way by compensating each others necessities. It is simply a question of procedure and practice.

In our case the Tree-Images are like specific call-signs, connectors, or any such equivalent means for linking us up, quite factually, with our most immediate supply of whatever type of inner energy they represent. If we need to connect ourselves with the quality of wisdom, *per se*, then we do so by making conscious use of the wisdom-symbol. True, this will only make us wiser by whatever degree we are able to respond inwardly with the contact gained, but this can always be improved by practice.

It is the principle involved which is so important. We can make ourselves as we will, according to the perfection-pattern covered by the Symbol-Images of the Tree, by drawing the required energy to do so straight from inner sources freely available to us from the forces generated all around us in our ordinary life-circumstances. Those energies are there for the taking, once we learn how to ask. This is no more remarkable in a way than working a radio-machine to use energies originating on the other side of the world, except for one vital difference. Clever as we may be with machinery of electronic design, there is one thing they will never do—live for us. Machines may and do enable us to live more comfortably and conveniently but living will always be a strictly do-it-yourself affair. We still have to live our image-ideals in order to identify and individualise as the sort of selves they stand for in spiritual dimensions.

An obvious question often asked is, why should the images be humanoid at all if they are supposed to portray divine abstract qualities? The simple answer is because we are human beings ourselves who need to develop exactly these qualities if we are ever to approach divinity. Those Images are concepts of what God would most probably be like if He were human and what we poor humans would resemble if we ever grew to any degree of Godhood—a sort of half-way meeting between the Mind of God and the minds of Men. On no account whatever should the Tree-Images ever be confused with "idols" of any kind. They are not for worshipping, but for working with. We should consider them as spiritual implements to be used for our own personal progression and as guides of our entire human destiny toward divinity. In a sense, they are God and Man imagining each other.

Without Image-Ideals of any kind, men and women are rather helpless and ineffectual creatures. They get born into this bewildering world where they are pushed around, processed and otherwise in influenced in all directions, by whatever or whoever comes in contact with them. At the end of each life they have turned into whatever sort of spiritual shape circumstances may have knocked them into—modified to some extent by their own defensive or adaptive activities. This is seldom a very attractive or remarkable life-result, however passable it might seem. It could be described as minimal mediocrity at best. Those content with such a "selfstate" should never be condemned for their choice but simply offered spiritual opportunities to change their life-courses if they so will.

In the case of others in possession of some definite set of

Image-Ideals (such as those of the Tree) things are rather different. Life knocks them around just as much as anyone else but it knocks them into the shape and nature of the Images they have adopted for exactly this purpose. However life may hit them, and whatever may happen to them in this world, they will only become built up into the interior design they have freely chosen as their spiritual selfstate and the image of their own ideal identity. In order to be as we will, we have first to know just what we will be and it is Images like those of the Tree which provide us with ideas needed for this purpose. Once we get these concepts deeply enough into our consciousness, they will shape our spiritual selfstructure according to their archetypal divine design. That is what they are for. If we choose to call the means by which we effect this inner implantation "magic," why should we not do so and admit the debt we owe to a tradition of truth which has always been behind the highest aspiration of mankind?

The Tree-Images are based on immortal and indestructible qualities of life. If we identify with them we become as eternal as they are in essence and entity. That, after all, is the sole point of our becoming created beings in the first place. With this one point in view, life means everything, but without it life has no meaning worthy of cosmic consideration whatever. The issue is as clear as that. If we have no hopes of ever being more than merely mortal, we might just as well not bother to live at all. That is the crux of our entire concern with life as individual living entities and the ultimate determining factor of our whole human destiny. Who and what are we to be? What must we not-be? That is the eternal enigma we have to solve for ourselves on spiritual life-levels. As a start toward finding our answers, we might try being what the Tree-Images represent, and not-being whatever they exclude from the "plan of perfection" they portray. That effort should get us a long way closer to the solution we are seeking.

The magic with which we accomplish this life-task has to be devised and applied by everyone for themselves. That is an essential and indispensable part of the whole procedure. It cannot he otherwise because each single self in the process of initiation is an individuant, emerging out of the average human aggregate level of life towards the ultimate truth of that single spirit whence all life originally issued. Though we may live with each other in this or any world, not one of us can ever live for another. Life is a be-it-yourself affair. The basics of magic are not really difficult to grasp and most intelligent people know them already instinctively, did they but realise that fact with their focal consciousness. The problem we all have to face is bringing these basics together into some kind of a sensible self-system that will serve our spiritual structures of life and apply to other levels also. This is positively possible for anyone with enough imagination and intentionally directed initiative. Here, we have been dealing with ten basic Images to work with, and they will tell us how to develop everything else if we approach them rightly.

Suppose we have some problem, query or other point on which we need responsive relationship with life. Depending on. the nature of this, we evoke the appropriate Image or Images concerned. Sometimes one only might serve, and othertimes they might all be needed like a Cosmic Committee of Consultants. By doing this, we not only objectify all our own capabilities of dealing with whatever it may be, but also call into contact those particular capabilities existing in other living entities on higher and finer levels of life than commonly available. This is an act of living at the Images. We then project our point at issue at the evoked Images and respond reactively to what we receive in return so that this enters our awareness cognitively. This is an act of living with the Images. Then we recall the Images back into ourselves and continue our conscious association with life, conditioned by whatever has passed between us and the Images we have used. This is an act of living as the Images. The whole process is one of living in conjunction with the Living Cosmos of God and Man, looking for Life in each other. If that is not magic in the highest and truest sense of the term, what is?

All the foregoing comments and remarks concerning Magical Images are but brief indications of the possibilities they present for those individuals with sufficient spiritual interest in life to follow them inwardly and much deeper into more detailed fields of consciousness. Nevertheless, every important point of contact has been touched on for the guidance of sincere enquirers who feel the need to know where life is leading them. May all such souls, and ultimately everyone, become in truth most faithful Images of the Living One in Whose immortal likeness Man was made.

1. UNITY FROM ZERO
KETHER
AHIH — I AM THAT I AM

Light from darkness. Life from light. Intention from inanation. Divine identity determining itself. Self starts. Cosmo-consciousness commences. Being begins. All awareness is one.

HOLY HEAD
SPIRITUAL SUMMIT OF ENTIRE EXISTENCE

2. DUALITY FROM UNITY
CHOKMAH
IHVH — I AM AS I WILL

Paternal power personified. Will with wisdom. Supernal Sapience.
Decisions of divinity. Assertion of authority. Maximal masculinity.
Impregnator of ideas. Father of force.

FAITHFUL FATHER
WISDOM AND WILL

3. TRINITY FROM DUALITY
BINAH
ELOHIM — WE ARE HE AND SHE

Maternal principle personified. Universal understanding. Acceptor of awareness. Words of will. The great gestatrix. Full femininity. Inherent intuition. Mother of form.

MATURE MOTHER
UNIVERSAL UNDERSTANDING

4. THREE + ONE
CHESED
EL — THE ME

Mercy manifest as monarchy. Concept of compassion. Benevolence and beneficence. Grandeur of generosity. Kindliness and kingliness. Merciful magnanimity. The all-accelerator.

KINDLY KING
COMPLETE COMPASSION

5. THREE + TWO
GEBURAH
ELOHIM GIBOR — GOD ALMIGHTY

Duty and discipline. Severe strictness. Concept of correction. Cleanser of corruption. Efficient economy. Stern saviour. Divine decreaser.

STERN SOLDIER
DIVINE DUTY

6. DOUBLE THREE
TIPHERETH
ELOAH VA-DAATH — GOD OMNISCIENT

Balance of being in beautiful holy harmony. Poising point of cosmic creation. The divine drama as innocent incarnation, sacred sacrifice and resurrected redeemer. The mystery of Melchizadek. Man and Maker meet. Common union of consciousness.

MAGNIFICENT MEDIATOR
BLESSED BEAUTY OF BEING

7. THREE + FOUR
NETZACH
IHVH SABAOTH — I WILL BE EVERYONE

Triumph of tenderness. Achievement of aims by affection. Enjoyment of emotions. Cultural consciousness. Artistic ability. Victorious vivacity. Graceful gentleness. Sentient soul.

LOVELY LADY
VIRTUOUS VICTORY

8. THREE + FIVE
HOD
ELOHIM SABAOTH — WE ARE EACH OTHER

Splendour of sagacity. Initiated intelligence. Mind over matter. Clever consciousness. Scientific skill. Humour and honour. Adaptable attitude. Resilient reasoning. Trained thinking.

PERCEPTIVE PERSON
GLORY OF GENIUS

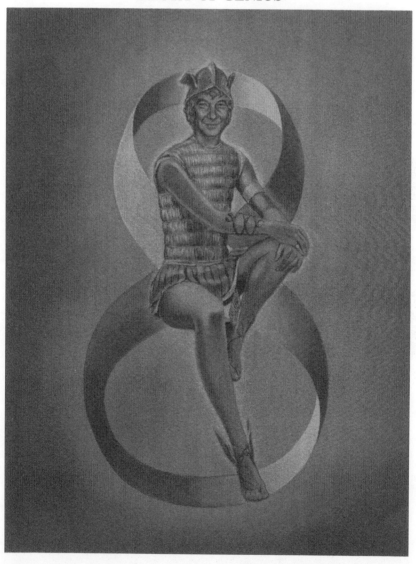

9. TRIPLE THREE
YESOD
SHADDAI EL CHAIIM — LORD OF LIVES

Foundation of families. Establishment of evolution. Virility and vigour. Sexual stability. Best biological behaviour. Good genetics. Respect for reproduction. Love of life. Fruitful fertility.

FERTILE FIGURE
FOUNDATION OF FERTILE FAITH

10. ONE — ZERO
MALKUTH
ADONAI MALAKH — NOBLE KING

Nobility of Nature. The perfect partner for material man. Mystical marriage of mankind with matter. Human hopes of earning emancipation from Earth. A blessed bride delivered by Divinity as mate to mankind. The Kingdom making all men kindred souls in search of Spirit.

MYSTERIOUS MATE
KINGDOM OF KINSHIP BETWEEN MAN
AND MANIFESTED BEING

Chapter 4
THE NOVENA
OF
THE TREE OF LIFE

A. Preface
by
Jacobus G. Swart

I n order to practice the Novena of the Tree of Life, you would
need thirteen candles of the following colours:

1.   White *Keter* (Crown)
2.   Light Grey *Chochmah* (Wisdom)
3.   Black *Binah* (Understanding)
4.   Blue *Chesed* (Mercy)
5.   Red *Gevurah* (Severity)
6.   Bright Yellow *Tiferet* (Beauty)
7.   Green *Netzach* (Victory)
8.   Orange *Hod* (Glory)
9.   Pale Yellow *Yesod* (Foundation)
10.   Four Candles of the following colours:
        Light Green
        Dark Green *Malchut* (Kingdom)
        Russet
        Dark Brown

You next need to place these candles in small, round, SAFE
candle-holders, and then arrange them according to their colours,
on a table or altar surface in the shape of the Tree of Life.
Alternatively, you may arrange them in the required pattern by
sticking them to a **METAL** tray. Your four candles in *Malchut* are
arranged in a small square, and, depending on the size of the
candles, could be placed quite close together in the following

manner:

> Light Green at the top.
> Dark Green to the left (right in the Southern Hemisphere)
> Russet at the bottom.
> Dark Brown or Black to the right (left in the Southern Hemisphere)

When you light these last four candles representing *Malchut*, you start with the Light Green candle, then the Dark Green, followed by the Russet, and finally the Dark Brown or Black candle. In this manner you will notice that you are lighting these according to the "Way of Light," i.e. the movement of the Sun in the Northern or Southern Hemisphere. This procedure should be worked in a place which is undisturbed by outside influences, such as querying, perturbed or even hostile eyes, and that this space should remain undisturbed for the entire period during which the Novena is being worked. It is also important that you understand the entire procedure of the Novena of the Tree before attempting the ceremony. Be therefore absolutely sure to read and re-read the Introduction, study the Orisons and their meaning carefully, and afterwards read the Epilogue.

Since the preparations and approaches pertaining to and discussed in the document "Working the Tree of Life," is also related here, I will again delineate them. It helps to prepare yourself beforehand, maybe by taking a bath and dressing in fresh clothing or wearing a robe, and to prepare the room or Temple by lighting perhaps a pleasant incense. The perfume of the incense is not important, since what is required is that you should feel prepared, relaxed, surrendered to your purpose, and to insure that this procedure is worked in a place which is undisturbed by outside influences for the entire duration of your Novena.

Note the importance of reading or uttering the words slowly. Try to get a "feeling appreciation" rather than a thinking one of the words, and do not allow yourself to go on "mental trips," which is to try to use reason in order to ascertain the meaning of the words. By saying them slowly, you pause on each word just long enough to "feel the word out" without losing the overall sense of the sentences. If you "feel the words" out in this manner, you will find you naturally begin to "feel the meaning" and invoke an "inner response" inside you. In this way you will practice a very intense form of meditation, while at the same time practising the "art of invocation" or calling up responses inside yourself. It is important to do these Orisons with maximum intensity of thought and feeling, and this can, for example, be achieved by imagining that you are speaking the words in your heart, or even in your Solar Plexus.

Lastly, I should explain the consecrating action entitled the "Cosmic Cross," which appears at the end of each Orison. It is effectuated in the following manner:

Touch forehead with the forefingers of your right hand, say:
IN THE NAME OF THE WISDOM,
Move the hand downwards, and touch the solar plexus, say:
AND OF THE LOVE,
Touch the right shoulder (left in the Southern Hemisphere), say:
AND OF THE JUSTICE,
Touch the left shoulder (right in the Northern Hemisphere), say:
AND THE INFINITE MERCY,
Moving the hand over the head, encircle all points, say:
OF THE ONE ETERNAL SPIRIT.
Bring both hands into prayer position, say:
AMEN

I am sure you have noticed how closely this action corresponds to the more well-known "Kabbalistic Cross," and you can use the latter in its stead if you so wish. What is important is to ensure that you are using your physical arm as well as its "spirit" counterpart at the same time. This is done in by imagining that your "spirit arm" moves first and is then followed by the physical one. This creates an incredible intensity in the practice, and "intensity" is what this entire procedure is all about!

B. Introduction

In current Christian practice is a very ancient custom which in essence must surely stem back to a time when religion and magic were virtually synonymous. This is the *Novena*, or a ninefold series of reiterated prayers at specific places for some particular purpose. The aim being to obtain, bring about, or somehow cause the objective of the novena to manifest as an actuality of our experience on earth. Its methodology consists of the regular and increasing repetition of prayers until enough momentum is set up to commence causative action in superphysical spheres. Eventually this energy is hoped to continue until the intended effort becomes factually accomplished in human terms of hopes.

The principle of this is the same as a heavy hung weight being struck a series of light blows at regular intervals. The result is that eventually the weight begins to swing, and providing the blows are struck precisely at the right instant when the amplitude is at its maximum, the swing will increase and continue doing so while the blows are repeated rhythmically. When they cease of course, the weight will continue swinging with diminishing amplitude until all the accumulated energy is exhausted when motion ceases completely. This entire phenomenon is known as a cumulative effect, or a large number of small impulses accomplishing work which would otherwise be done by a single much stronger one.

A Novena is theoretically the same well-known law being applied metaphysically. An intended effect which might possibly be achieved through the application of an enormous amount of esoteric energy, is sought for through this "little by little" scheme, in which regular and rhythmical impulses are applied with careful calculation. With the Christian system, prayers are usually addressed to some saint or Blessed Being whose interests are believed to favour the sought after request. For example, a novena made for the recovery of lost or missing objects would be addressed to Saint Anthony of Padua, or for the relief of throat troubles to Saint Roche. The agency invoked normally departmentalises the object specified, and is purely for the sake of regulating the rest of the procedure.

It may be wondered why the particular number of nine should be selected for the performance of this practice. The obvious reason is a connection with the nine months gestation needed for the production of a human being. If it takes that time for a human to appear on earth from insemination to physical birth, then a related period should be allowed for the manifestation of a mystical equivalent from inception as an idea to its expression on earth as actual energy. Usage of the Tree of Life scheme, enables the entire process to proceed quite naturally from stage to stage in normal sequence, each Sphere corresponding roughly to a month of womb-development. After the initial insemination at Zoic Zero, the first three Spheres (*Keter-Chochmah-Binah*) deal with Origination (*Atzilut*) of the idea, the second three (*Chesed-Gevurah-Tiferet*) with its Creation (*Briah*) in which its broad principles are associated with each other, the third three (*Netzach-Hod-Yesod*) finalises Formation (*Yetzirah*) where details are specified and then related with each other until everything except its projection into earth actually is accomplished. This takes place at the last Sphere of *Malchut* (the Kingdom) on the Tree of Life, and it all depends on adequate work being practised with the previous Spheres over the preceding period.

The process commences by firstly deciding on a required objective, then carefully considering whether or not a novena is justified for obtaining it. Only in the case of a positive answer being arrived at would the session begin. On the first day, only the insemination stage of Zoic Zero should be attempted. This is purely the inception of the idea *as such*, pushed with as much power as possible into the Great Unmanifest from which emerges entire existence as we understand it. On no account ought any definite specification to be made. No more than the initial impulse, but with maximum intensity of input. If required, the prayer may be said silently several times, and all that should be expressed is an almost desperate and most urgent need of fulfilment for its own sake. The sense of implantation should be orgasmic as if a real release of pent up power had been made from human to Divine levels of life. Subsequently a period of relaxed contemplation can be enjoyed. On the second day this procedure is repeated, and the first candle is lit at *Keter* (the Crown) with its appropriate prayer. Here the feeling should be one of confidence that the projection process has been positively placed on a line of life which will definitely deliver it to our world in due course. Origination (*Atzilut*) has most certainly commenced on a true Tree of Life, and all hat is needed now is the ensuing development through the other Spheres.

On the third day, after repeating stage 0 and 1, the Origination is continued at Sphere 2 (*Chochmah* - Wisdom), where this process has the positive element of consciousness brought into it. That is accomplished by concentrating solely on the masculine principle of awareness as applied to the objective. No more than that. Whatever may need consideration from the deliberate and calculated planning point of view in its broadest sense, and the most overall way. The prayer must be repeated once and the appropriate candle lit which will mean that there should now be two candles alight. These may be extinguished in reverse order at the conclusion of the ceremony. Next day, stages 0, 1 and 2 are repeated and Sphere 3 (*Binah* - Understanding) tackled. This time the Origination is dealt with from a feminine and negative aspect of consciousness involving intuition and all the softer aspects of the objective aimed at. This is to be in a most abstract sense, and at the end of the prayer candles 1, 2 and 3 should be alight.

The Creative stage(*Briah*) commences on day 5 at Sphere 4 (*Chesed* - Mercy), when prayers number 0, 1, 2 and 3 are said and their candles lit. The principle and quality of Compassionate Mercy is then applied to the objective. Whatever comes within that category by connection with it is concentrated on and considered while the prayer is being said and the candle lit. All its best aspects are thought about and brought to mind. On day 6 the opposite ideas are dealt with at Sphere 5 (*Gevurah* - Severity). Here, all possible disadvantages are considered and every correction calculated. All previous prayers are said first, candles 1, 2, 3 and 4 lit, and then the appropriate orison of the day uttered as candle 5 is kindled. Day 7 sees completion of the Creative stage, as the results of Spheres 4 and 5 are combined at Sphere 6. The objective must here be seen as balanced, corrected, and harmonious throughout all its parts in principle, having come to a point of readiness when it is fit for its next stage of Formation in which it will be defined to a degree where it will only need expression into existence in order to become a finished production. When it can be contemplated in such a condition, prayer 6 should be said and the candle lit.

The following day, when prayers and candles have been activated to Sphere 6, the process of Formation (*Yetzirah*) can be commenced at Sphere 7 which is Victory (*Netzach*). Here the objective may be considered in detail for the first time so far as its winning characteristics are concerned. Everything to do with its success possibilities should be thought about, and formulated carefully. Any ideas which might aid such success can be added here with definite details. All that of course, must be confined to purely mental levels at this stage of development. There is no reason why this should not be though about on previous occasions apart from the Tree practice. After the prayer is said and the lamp lit at Sphere 7, attention may be turned to Sphere 8 the following day. Here the Formative factor is Glory or Honour (*Hod*). This time, everything of importance in avoiding failure and dishonour due to relationships with the objective should be considered in very definite detail and concentrated upon most carefully. Again this must be mental rather than put into uttered words.

Be it noted that at each stage of Origination, Creation and Formation, a triple move is made first to the Positive White (Right Pillar), then the Negative Black (Left Pillar), and finally to the central Golden Mean (Middle Pillar), which balances both in terms of the level being dealt with. At this particular point the need is for the maintenance of favourable conditions by avoidance of any dishonesty or whatever might diminish the quality of the concept being dealt with. Having conditioned this as carefully as possible, the prayer should be said and the lamp lit. Next day the penultimate Sphere of 9 may be approached. At Sphere 9 (*Yesod* - Foundation), a finalised mental formulation is made when this objective is found to have reached its maximum potential by being nicely balanced between Victory and Honour so that any gains made will be honourable ones, untarnished by disreputable conduct or acquired Karmic indebtedness. *Yesod* is the fulfilment of dreams and visionary experiences, but it is also the immediate category of consciousness from whence we derive our materialized concepts. If our objective were an engineering project, *Yesod* would amount to the experimental workshop where plans and blueprints would be associated with each other, and assembled before being considered complete as a marketable product. The main concern here is preparation for projection into mundane conditions. Is everything imagined as it should be? Has anything important been omitted or overlooked? This is the last occasion for rectifying such oversights and every opportunity should be taken for doing so. After lighting the previous candles and saying the related prayers, the appropriate prayer of Sphere 9 is said once, and the candle lit. A sense of immanence should be felt prior to the last invocation.

At Sphere 10 (*Malchut* - Kingdom), the objective should be clearly specified in words and given the codeword of an identifying name which may be used for future communication. This exact wording needs very careful working out beforehand, which should be done some time in advance on paper, yet never pronounced aloud until the vital moment in the ceremony. The reason for this is that we cannot know for certain before a child is born, exactly what it will be like until it actually appears in this world when we may then specify the obvious detail so fits sex, colouring, general appearance, and other details. So we must describe the exact nature of the now named objective which is invited into our world as an integral item of its composition, whether concrete or conceptual. It is important here to put plenty of stress and insistence into this particular into this particular invocation at Sphere 10 (*Malchut* - the Kingdom). The prayer may be repeated several times or certain names repeated as might seem necessary. The verbal description of the objective can be written or typed, and placed prominently beside the ritual script. The code-name may be written in capitals beside the *Malchut* position on the Tree of Life, and should certainly be memorised for future use in connection with the objective, whether as yet evident on earth or otherwise. It is obvious this should have some close connection with the objective. For example, if this had been the provision of money through opportunity of earning it, the code-name of that could well be EARNOP or MAKEMON, whereas if the aim were obtaining esoteric knowledge of the Qabalah, it might be QABQUEST or LEARNLAW. Whatever will identify in the mind of its maker with its intended effect.

Once named, the quest-aim should be treated as an actuality, whether it materialises as an earth experience as intended, or takes some alternative and seldom recognised form. Responses to novenas are often unrecognised because of large time lapses or alteration of character during the production process. Sometimes it calls for considerable skill and practice to perceive that such a response has indeed occurred, though not precisely as has been hoped for, nor at the moment anticipated. There is an art in eliciting exact responses from novena activated requests of Eternal Energy, and this can only be developed by intelligent practical experiments, which constructive usage of the Holy Tree should certainly encourage. It should never be supposed that Tree novenas are an automatic short cut to fame, riches, and all the advantages of life, that humans generally crave for undeservingly, and usually fruitlessly. They can and do however, make intelligent contact with higher than normal levels of life, thus opening avenues of approach unavailable to unappreciative souls. Once such channels become clear through repeated use, many strange forces are able to flow through them and quite unexpected effects are liable to occur.

The various precautions inserted in the prayers should be properly appreciated. Mankind frequently demands favours which would not be beneficial in the least, even if appearing so to an inadequate eye. For that reason various safety clauses have been carefully inserted to protect incautious petitioners from their own ignorance or over-optimistic importunity. It should also be especially noted that any deliberate misuse of the Tree system for malicious or unjustified purposes will automatically negate any further action. For example, attempts to procure ill effects on others, or gain illegal acquisitions, would immediately invoke the cancellation clauses and close down channels of communication. The Tree of Life has been deliberately designed to disallow its employment for what could be considered evil or anti-social intentions.

It might be supposed that the symbolic ritual of accompanying the petitioners prayers by lighting flames associated with the various Spheres could be theoretically dispensed with, but in fact it could not. If the required aim is to institute something which will eventually have an action on earthlife levels, then surely there must be some material symbolic signs of such a happening while the request is being made. What could be more appropriate than the summoning of light at the point of intention in question? No reasonable practitioner would neglect this part of the proceedings.

To some hesitant sectarians it may be said that the Holy Tree of Life symbol is in no way an object of worship, or to be regarded as any kind of idol. It is no more than the physical sign of a spiritual system, and the indicator of a procedural process relating Deity and Humanity in a rational and reliable way. Its methods combine mysticism with mathematics in a scientific and sensible scheme which many intelligent people have found invaluable over the centuries. Of course those with adequate comprehension of the Tree scheme will naturally work better with it than others, but surely the best way to learn anything is to practice with its principles, and what could possibly prove more practical than a solid presentation of the Holy Tree of Life with its accompanying illuminations? So if whosoever reads these lines is thinking about asking Deity for some especial favour, and at the same time wondering how the Holy Tree of Life works, they could scarcely do better than acquire a simple yet effective apparatus for dealing with both projects simultaneously. All they will need otherwise is a small table or other surface where the Tree can be set out and remain undisturbed except for lamp lighting during the entire session.

Intending users are especially advised against treating the Tree as some device for inducing Deity to do whatever they want and whenever they demand it. It will do no such thing, but only facilitate sincere and sensible approaches made for sufficient reason at appropriate moments. It can of course, be used purely for contact or meditational purposes without any definite requests being made whenever such is felt. In which case both prayers and lights may be entirely optional at the discretion of the operator. Any amount of interesting exercises should soon suggest themselves to the enthusiastic enquirer. Those unable to think of these by themselves should make that the aim of their first novena. They could be very gratified by their results.

C. The Orisons

ZOIC ZERO
(*Said Silently*)

I invoke the Immanence of Everlasting and Eternal Energy in the Name of *OMNIL*. Be that what It will become, because of my intention intercepting Its free flow of force towards eventual expression on our Earth. I will inseminate Its wondrous Womb with this, my special Seed-Thought. Let it be an act of Love alone, as I await the working of that Will, through every separate Sphere upon our Holy Tree of Life, until it manifests as *Malchut*, and completes its cycle of Creation. Be it born of my beliefs in the beneficence that comes of Cosmic Consciousness commencing at the secret and supremely sacred Source of *Ayn Soph Aur*.

(*No Candle is lit here*)

FIRST SPHERE
(Uttered aloud)

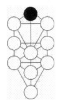

At the Apex of my Ideation I invoke the Laws of Life with perfect purity of Purpose. May Provident and Primal Power be poured into my work of will, which I here offer to Omnipotence for fateful and Divine Direction. Be this bare beginning blessed by every Energy and Emanation coming through the Sphere of *Keter*, at this origin of our most Holy Tree of Life.

(Form the Cosmic Cross)

In the Name of the Wisdom,
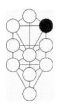And of the Love,
And of the Justice,
   And the Infinite Mercy
Of the One Eternal Spirit. *Amen*

(White candle is lit here)

SECOND SPHERE

I will work with Wisdom to obtain what I am asking for, originating from its Highest Heavenly Hands, Supreme Sagacity shall sanction it, and Infinite Intelligence inspire its institution. Who is wiser than the Lord of Life that knows our needs and deals with our demands as we deserve? So may this be with my sincere petition here presented at the Sphere of *Chochmah* on our Holy Tree of Life.

(Form the Cosmic Cross)

In the Name of the Wisdom,
And of the Love,
And of the Justice,
And the Infinite Mercy
Of the One Eternal Spirit. *Amen*

(Light grey candle is lit)

THIRD SPHERE

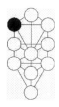

Of Understanding is originated an existence of comprehension, coming only from the Mother of our manifested universe. May She hear me as I ask for Her help with all my many aspirations, and most heartfelt hopes. Refuse not my re1uest Beloved Being, if it be possible within Thy Powers of Providence. Send sure and certain succour from the Blessed Sphere of *Binah* on our Holy Tree of Life.

(Form the Cosmic Cross)

In the Name of the Wisdom,
And of the Love,
And of the Justice,
And the Infinite Mercy
Of the One Eternal Spirit. *Amen*

(Black candle is lit)

FOURTH SPHERE

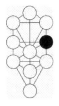

Magnanimity and Mercy be with me benignly. Cause Creative Consciousness to care for Its conceptions with Compassion and all capability. Create what must be made with character and natural nobility. Let its attributes be altogether amiable, and awaken in all human hearts a sense of spiritual sympathy. May such qualities be made available to me that ask and quest for them at *Chesed,* the Compassionate upon our Holy Tree of Life.

(Form the Cosmic Cross)

In the Name of the Wisdom,
⊕And of the Love,
And of the Justice,
      And the Infinite Mercy
Of the One Eternal Spirit. *Amen*

(Blue candle is lit)

FIFTH SPHERE

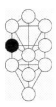

Strictness and Severity be with me strongly. Create a carefully compelling conscience in whatever will appear, because I asked it to become itself and act as Deity directed. Therefore let due Discipline be done and then accepted in the spirit of corrective conduct as a needed lesson to be learned of life alone. May I meet such Spiritual Straighteners always at this special Sphere of *Gevurah* on our Holy Tree of Life.

(*Form the Cosmic Cross*)

In the Name of the Wisdom,
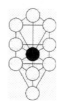And of the Love,
And of the Justice,
And the Infinite Mercy
Of the One Eternal Spirit. *Amen*

(*Red candle is lit*)

SIXTH SPHERE

Be Balanced Beauty held in Holy Harmony while occupying itself with work of overall importance. Let Creative Consciousness become concerned with the production of a perfect pattern, typifying the individual will of the identity within it. So can Concentrated Central Energy exert effective power on every particle of contact in Its compass. Be this to me the blessed touch of *Tipheret* from the poising point of our most holy Tree of Life.

(*Form the Cosmic Cross*)

In the Name of the Wisdom,
And of the Love,
And of the Justice,
And the Infinite Mercy
Of the One Eternal Spirit. *Amen*

(*Bright yellow candle is lit*)

SEVENTH SPHERE

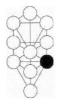

Thou Formative Forces acting on the object of my orisons, vindicate my vision with true Victory. Shape it as it should be, and project it properly into perception. Do not permit it to deceive or disappoint me, but let it become a valuable and a valid asset sent from Special Spiritual Sources. Be this blessing framed and formed from *Netzach* on our Holy Tree of Life.

(Form the Cosmic Cross)

In the Name of the Wisdom,
⊕ And of the Love,
And of the Justice,
And the Infinite Mercy
Of the One Eternal Spirit. *Amen*

(Green candle is lit)

EIGHTH SPHERE

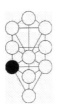

Glorious are the generous gifts of God. Are they not formed from knowledge of our needs and comprehension of our capabilities? Shall we not honour and appreciate what we are sent from Heavenly Hands? Do we not discern Divinity as it responds to our requests? Who will ask for bread and then be sent a stone to swallow? Here at *Hod* on our Most Holy Tree of Life, I beg that what is best for me will always be my answer.

(Form the Cosmic Cross)

In the Name of the Wisdom,
And of the Love,
And of the Justice,
And the Infinite Mercy
Of the One Eternal Spirit. *Amen*

(Orange candle is lit)

NINTH SPHERE

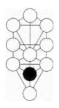

Firm Foundation of our fertile faith here finalise its formulation. Fix and focus my especial enterprise into its finest form, before it faces me as fact within my earth experience. May it not materialise until Divinity decrees and all Co-ordinates of Cosmos are agreeable. Then, at that instant, let it live an independent entitised existence, interacting with my own, because I bade it into being and so accept the onus of this obligation. At *Yesod* on the Holy Tree of Life my thoughts will turn to truths and I shall thrive.

(Form the Cosmic Cross)

In the Name of the Wisdom,
And of the Love,
And of the Justice,
And the Infinite Mercy
Of the One Eternal Spirit. *Amen*

(Pale yellow candle is lit)

TENTH SPHERE

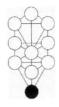

Let the Will of Heaven live to be the Word and Will of all on Earth! Come through into this Kingdom of our kind O thou the Thought-thing of my mind. Appear in this my realm of reason and reality. Be born into our world of wondering and waiting. Be concealed no longer by a cloak of abstract and arcane allusions, but be clothed with words of mine describing you in detail.....(*Here follows the description*). Also receive a recognition name from me, so that communication can be simplified. It is.....(*the name of your thought creation*), while mine is....(*your own name*), who have invoked you into earth expression. May our relationship be well with one another in this Sphere of *Malchut* on the Holy Tree of Life.

(*Form the Cosmic Cross*)

In the Name of the Wisdom,
⊕ And of the Love,
And of the Justice,
And the Infinite Mercy
Of the One Eternal Spirit. *Amen*

(*The four special Tree-coloured candles, representing the cycles on this earth, are lit. They are coloured respectively light green, dark green, russet and brown*)

D. Epilogue

Again it should be noted that the position of *Ayn Sof Aur* is shown above the diagram of the Tree of Life, while not being included in the candle representation which only indicates the actual Spheres or Ten Force-Fields of typified energy, because those are what we are dealing with in this work. So the initial invocation addressed to

Ayn Sof Aur is usually made silently with closed eyes or in darkness to the Individual Light in oneself, which is the Potential Power behind every intended action. Thus there is no need for physical illumination at this point, because contact is being sought with the pre-creative source of Supreme Spiritual Energy. This is the equivalent of a sexual impregnation, destined to develop afterwards into whatsoever may be willed. If this were a human fertilisation, such a result could only be a male or female human being.

Since we are concerned with super-physical phenomena in this particular exercise however, such subsequent development is aimed at altogether different terms of truth. So much depends on this initial impregnative act that it is difficult to advise how this should be accomplished, so here the imagination of the operator can help considerably with the structure of this essential act. There should certainly be silence and a minimum of movement made during the presentation of this point, and every repetitive procedure should be as identical as possible.

At the final Sphere, not 1 but 4 candles are lit to indicate the number of expression according to the Tree-scheme. They are in the colours of the seasons and should be lit in that order. Light green for Spring, dark green for Summer, russet for Autumn, and dark brown or black for Winter. Such are the colours of tree foliage at those times. This brings in the time element of our process and emphasizes the difference between the condition of *Malchut* and the other Spheres. For that reason it is presented as being square, to signify the acute angles of mundane life and all its curious corners with their pointed problems.

Despite the disquiet that an apparent total of 13 candles may cause, an assurance may be made here that there are really 10 lights, since the special illumination at *Malchut* is acting as a single light displayed in four modes of presentation. Thus the theoretical number of lights on our Tree remains unaltered and its symbology still accurate.

It would be well to add one final word of warning. Once a novena is commenced, it should never be abandoned short of very serious reasons such as illness or some other adversity. To break off because of boredom, or for some trivial cause, invites ill-fortune on those who treat their spiritual commitments with such casual indifference. An accidental interruption may certainly be recommenced from the very beginning, but it is always best to check up for any likelihood of interference with the prayer programme projected. The finest rules to follow are those of regularity and rhythm, coupled with a clear commitment. So should the Holy tree of life be served by those approaching it for favours.

BLESSED BE OUR HOLY TREE OF LIFE
IN ALL ITS SACRED SPHERES
AND POTENT PATHS FOREVERMORE.
AMEN

Chapter 5
THE OFFICE
OF THE
HOLY TREE OF LIFE

A. Introduction

This is a compendium of prayers, meditations, and spiritual exercises for regular use by practising Qabalists and in their daily and periodic devotions. It consists of a separate prayer section for the *Ain Soph* and all ten Spheres, plus a special Path-Invocation for each of the 22 Paths or connections between the Spheres as outlined by the Tree-Glyph itself. There are also a short series of statements and responses for relating the required Spheres and Paths together so as to make a useful devotional practice. Some additional matters have been added, such as blessing formulas, quick credos, hymns and so forth, to be used at the discretion of the practitioner.

The general plan for use of the Office is to take a single Path each day, and work steadily from top to bottom of the Tree, then back again in a continuous prayer-plan. Although the script has been very carefully arranged for ordinary Gregorian chanting as a complete short ceremony either alone or in company, it may also be read or recited in silence or aloud as required. This Office is best worked last thing before sleeping, so that the soul is able to meditate and live with that particular Path during physical repose.

It will be seen that each Sphere and Path invocation is built by associate linkage through the Four Worlds, and other connective concepts including sensory symbology of colours, scents, and various conventional attributions of God-Names, Archangels, Angels, planetary personifications, Telesmic Figures and so forth. The customary way of connecting Spheres is by their proper Paths. Therefore the general procedure is to lead in with the introductory phrases, select and read or chant the first of whichever pair of Spheres lies at the proximal end of the chosen Path, then work the Sphere at its distal end, and finally pronounce the Path invocation itself. After this, observe a few moments of meditation upon that particular Path. Whatever may be cut or curtailed in the Office, the Path meditation of the day should be regarded as obligatory, for this is the Inner contact of the Life-Spirit vivifying all our Tree-concepts. When this meditation has been completed, the valedictory chants and responses are given, and the daily Office has been duly offered up to the Living Spirit it should serve.

In ceremonial form an Office may be as simple or elaborate as demanded. Conventional costume consists of plain habit and girdle with no special ornamentation. Hoods are to be worn up as with meditational work. Lights at low level. Signals by numbered raps for the Spheres, a handclap to announce the Path, otherwise soft gong-strokes. Musical background or otherwise at will, but meditation period should be silent. The leader, who chants the statements in Gregorian style and should proclaim the Path also, is responsible for terminating the meditation time. Otherwise the Spheres are worked between everyone in chant-style or by rhythmic recitation with low resonance. It is usual to stand for the introduction, valediction, and proclamation of the Path, but be seated for the Spheres and, of course, the vital Meditation.

The true function of this, or any Office, is to open and develop in souls who use them a spiritual sense of their own existence and continuity in a state of Inner Cosmos on levels of life which extend far beyond the boundaries of manifested matter. This will certainly eventuate providing that regular and rhythmic use is made of an Office. That is the most important factor of all, which may be summed up as: Constancy in Conscious Contact with Inner Cosmos and its Concepts.

Full ritual usage of an Office is unlikely to be a practical proposition every day for many modern people. Nevertheless, the least that can be done is to carry the Office book somewhere about the person in pocket or handbag. If daily use of this consists of no more than a single opening, brief glance through even one paragraph, then returning the book to its place until next time, this constitutes an Office of a sort which is bound to lead souls lightwards. It is better to do a faithful and regular minimum, than sporadic and disjointed splurges of performance. If, say, a daily minimum and a weekly expanded effort is possible, that would be a sensible and helpful usage.

Every major faith has an Office of some description, and in offering this present Office for use by those relatively fewer souls who follow the Qabalistic System of Human-Divine associations, it is felt that a long-missing link has at last been forged in the great chain of consciousness joining God with Man in the Spirit of Eternal Life. May this be truly so indeed.

In the Name of the Wisdom,
And of the Love,
And of the Justice,
And the Infinite Mercy
Of the One Eternal Spirit. *Amen*

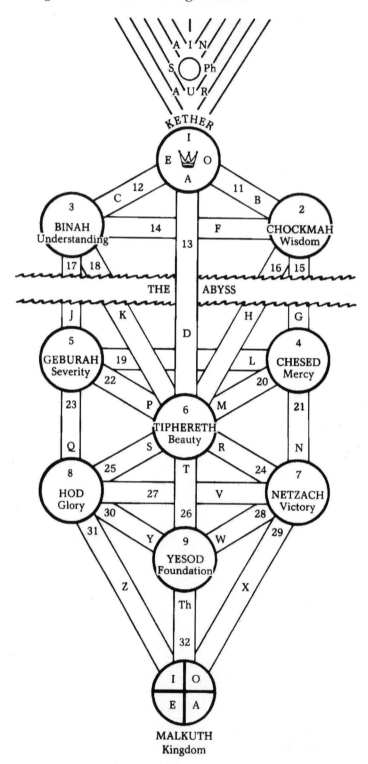

B. The Office of the Holy Tree of Life

i. The Office

[*Standing*]

In the Name of the Wisdom,
⊕ And of the Love,
And of the Justice,
And the Infinite Mercy
Of the One Eternal Spirit. *Amen*

Blessed be the light by which we learn the laws of life.

Response: Holy is the Tree thereof whose fruits fulfil for us
the faith we place in all its powers.

Blessed be the Principles and Paths throughout the Tree that
constitutes our conscious cosmos.

Response: Tenfold is the truth of our beloved Tree, while
two and twenty are the ways between its blessed
branches.

From mere mortality among mankind, our Tree leads up to
infinite extension past existence as identity in Perfect Peace
Profound.

Response: Let us therefore find and follow faithfully our
present Path upon the Holy Tree o f Life
between the Principles of.....and.....So Mote It
Be.....Amen.

(*Knocks of the starting Sphere*)   [*Seated*]

Blessed be thou unto us, O thou First Principle of.....

In the Name of the Wisdom,
⊕ And of the Love,
And of the Justice,
And the Infinite Mercy
Of the One Eternal Spirit. *Amen*

(*Invocation of the Sphere concerned*)   [*Seated*]

(*Knocks of the completing Sphere*) [Seated]

Blessed be thou unto us, O thou Last Principle of.....

> **In the Name of the Wisdom,**
> **And of the Love,**
> **And of the Justice,**
> **And the Infinite Mercy**
> **Of the One Eternal Spirit.** *Amen*

(*Invocation of the Sphere concerned*) [*Seated*]

(*Single Handclap*) [*Standing*]

Blessed be thou unto us, O welcome middle way that we must walk between extremities of our existence in this present instance.

> **In the Name of the Wisdom,**
> **And of the Love,**
> **And of the Justice,**
> **And the Infinite Mercy**
> **Of the One Eternal Spirit.** *Amen*

(*Invocation of the Path*) [Standing]

Blessed be the information and enlightenment we shall experience through mediation of this potent Path.

> **In the Name of the Wisdom,**
> **And of the Love,**
> **And of the Justice,**
> **And the Infinite Mercy**
> **Of the One Eternal Spirit.** *Amen*

(*Short Meditation*) [*Seated*]

CHANT

Glory be to the
O living one of light.
May we forever be
Upon thy path of right

Direct us from above
According to thy law,
And may thy boundless love
Be with us evermore.

Let thy sublime design
The Tree of God and Man
Both human and divine
Prove our most perfect plan. *Amen.*

Thanks be that we are better for the will which has been worked within us.

Response:　　Let us now change consciousness from inner cosmos to our normal living levels.

Because of what has happened in ourselves, may we impartt some benefit to other souls.

Response:　　Blessed be what has been done with us, and so may everyone experience divinity in whatsoever way they will.

In the Name of the Wisdom,
And of the Love,
And of the Justice,
And the Infinite Mercy
Of the One Eternal Spirit. *Amen*

ii. Invocations of the Spheres

AIN SOPH AUR
Principle of Light beyond all Being

O Perfect Peace Profound beyond all being; thou that art not what thou wilt not-be.

O Cosmic Cipher infinitely inexisting; Zero-Zenith of transcendent truth.

Unidentifiable art thou; and utterly apart from anything thou art.

Naught would exist as anything; unless thy universal nucleus of nil began its being.

Thou art pre-primal first and final factor of emerging and equating energy.

Limitless art thou that livest not; bornless and unbounded is thine unilluminated light.

We reverence in thee our whole unmanifested universe; thou art parabeing and pure potential.

We know we know thee not; and only thus we know thee.

We know no symbol for thee; nor have we any name for thee except necessity of nothing.

In gaining life we lose thee; and by our loss of life thou gainest us.

Our solitary means of recognizing thy reality is inwardly through silent stillness of our senses.

With awe do we accept thine actuality; and now await thee with due worship.

So Mote It Be. Amen.

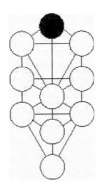

KETHER
Principle of the Summative Crown

O thou Solitary Spirit of Entire Existence; Begetter of All Being and Light of Every Life.

Thou art what thou wilt be within thyself; O Ancient of the Ancient Ones.

Concealed art thou of the concealed; thine end and origin is with thyself alone.

Thou art the source and sum of every soul; O Perfect Point of everyone and everything.

Thou first emerging entity upon the Holy Tree of Life; Crown of Consciousness and apex of awareness.

O Light of Lights we are thy separated sparks; who seek for our fulfillment in thy sacred flame.

May our searching souls arise toward thee; until we rejoin thy ruling radiance.

Most Mystical Intelligence beyond the comprehension of created beings; inspire in us a sense of thy true actuality.

So at last in striving to attain thee; we may surely come to know ourselves.

O Highest Holiness of the Originative World; thy still small voice breathes forth thy name—*Eheieh* (*Ehyeh*).

Blind us not by thy surpassing brilliance; but encourage us to live by whatsoever light enables us to recognize thine absolute reality.

Most mighty *Metatron*, thou privileged Archangel of the Only Perfect Presence; mediate for us in the creative world that power none other than thyself may deal with face to face.

Shine thou before the blessed throne of truth; like purest light outpoured in benediction.

Chaioth ha Qadesh (*Chaiot ha-Kodesh*) thou art Holy Living Creatures and the first formative angels; uphold the dignity of life before all lesser dignities.

Uplift also our hearts and take our prayers to heaven; like an offering of ambergris arising from our earthly altars.

Shine thou as a spiritual beacon; and become our welcome watchfires of the inner way.

O Primal Motion of our matter with the swirling nebulae expressed into existence; be unto us the sign of Cosmos coming forth from chaos. Let the light in darkness of thy golden sparklings set in space awaken us to look above ourselves and find illumination.

Thou Oldest One of the Vast Countenance Eternal, *Amen;* in thee is nothing left but only right remains.

Ancient of Days be thou our whole significance; and only point of our becoming separated selves within thee.

Blessed be thy symbol of the spinning cross and central stillness; around thy point of poise all powers revolve forever.

Let thy light in us reveal thy real intention with us; that by its aid we shall accomplish what thou wilt through our continuance in thee forevermore.

So Mote It Be. Amen.

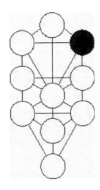

CHOCKMAH
Principle of the Eternal Wisdom

O Supernal Spirit of our Primal Procreation; Father force of Life art thou, projected into people.

Send forth the living stream of thy most sacred seed; that every soul alive proclaims thy parenthood.

May each and every one of our humanity acknowledge the authority of thy Divinity.

Thou second Sphere upon the Holy Tree of Life; praise be to thy paternal principle of wisdom.

True wisdom was brought forth before all other attributes; and its beginning lies in our perception of thee as our Supreme Patriarch.

O thou Omnipotent Omniscience; may we be wise within thee.

Intelligence of true illumination manifesting the most high magnificence; be exalted over us eternally.

Allow us to achieve immortal entity; existing with thee everlastingly. Name of Names within the world of origins; that never may be said by mortals save through substitution.

Tetragrammaton! Thou made us in thy mind; make us more mindful of thee in ourselves.

Thou art the spirit of our sapience; be thy beneficence around us like a soft blue sky.

Archangel *Ratziel*) thou herald of the Holy Wisdom throughout all creation;

Thou speakest from the summit of thy mystic mountain. Proclaim aloud to us the word we lost on earth; so that we shall remember how to regain Heaven.

Protect us with thy good grey cloak from all the perils possible upon this path.

Angel Order of the *Auphanim*, true-turning ones of the formative world; work well with us through our life cycles on the ceaseless wheel of cosmic changes.

O pearly iridescent ones take thou our thoughts into the holy presence; like the stimulating scent of musk makes meaning for our senses.

Mazloth, thou mysterious influence appearing in expression as our zodiac; be thy solar cross and circle a significance of our salvation.

Let thy soft white light so shine around us that we shall see all cosmic colors in our spiritual spectrum.

Almighty *Abba* our first father; thou hast bred us of thy being.

Sacred be to us on earth thy symbol of the standing stone; or staff erect and strong in its significance.

Thou art our most trustworthy tower of truth; set thou us at the top of it with thy straight scepter.

Take our left shoulders and direct us in the upright way; that lies along the line (if light from our unworthiness to thy Divinity.

So Mote It Be. Amen.

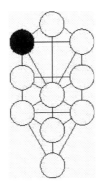

BINAH
Principle of the Omniscient Understanding

O thou Mysterious Mother from whose womb all lesser entities emerge; from thee our souls set forth as selves upon their paths of progress.

Thou art *Aima* darkly waiting impregnation by the seed of light; *Aima* art thou as it burns within thee on its way to birth.

O Spiritual Sea supporting life as space supports a universe; let us be borne in thee with utmost safety and security.

Third upon the Holy Tree of Life art thou O Understanding One; thy total comprehension covers complete Cosmos.

From thee, O Mother, we inherit intuition; and thou art the instinct of all conscious creatures.

We would consider ourselves as thy chosen children; cherish us as we have confidence and trust in thee.

O Sanctifying intelligence in whom begins primordial perception; thou art the fount of faith and foster-mother of fidelity.

Teach us to accept thee absolutely; believe in us as we have reason to rely on thee.

O Matriarch of all Mankind within the world of origins *Evoi Elohim*; thou art Mother to the greatest gods themselves.

Only thou art mistress of the mighty ones; crimson is thy clothing with the blood of all becoming.

Archangel *Tzaphkiel* who watches over every entity

from the creative world; guide and guard us through gestation and in excarnation.

May we find a blessed sanctuary beneath thy black concealing cloak; when we would hold communion with most sacred silence.

Angel Order of the *Aralim*, thou seats of sapience in the formative world; uphold us as we try to understand the meanings of the Holy Mysteries. As we sometimes send ourselves into a deep brown mood of study; so send our meanings to the universal mind as myrrh is offered in the way of worship.

Thou Sphere of Saturn in expressive terms be not to us a sign of sadness; but a symbol of stability and sensible behavior.

Thou art the counterbalance of creation; and the certain test of every truth.

May we recognize within thine ashen grey; those rosy tints that tell of an impending golden resurrection.

O Supernal Mother, we depend on thy Divinity for life and our perception of its purpose; in thee do we perceive a promise of eternal entity.

Sacred be thy symbol of a stone outspread on earth; and honored be the cup of celebration or the cauldron of a consecrated circle.

Take thou firmly and securely our right shoulders; then complete thy cosmic course with us forevermore.

So Mote It Be. Amen.

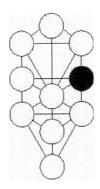

CHESED
Principle of the Perpetual Compassion

O thou Good Governor of Life with an affectionate authority; thou givest thine attention to us with a generous amusement.

Since we were created with a shout of laughter; let spiritual happiness and holiness be truly one.

We pray that we may always please thee; affording thee the highest form of any entertainment.

Fourth upon the Holy Tree of Life art thou O Kindly King of Cosmos; thy beneficence extends to every being.

Magnanimity and mercy are thine attributes; thou art concerned with care and consolation for thy creatures.

Boundless are the blessings of thy bounty; and we are comforted by thy compassion.

O thou receiver of intelligence, thou boldest all the holy powers; from thee emanates the essence of exalted virtues.

Cohesive is thy special consciousness; send thou a share of this into our souls.

Thy name is singularly simple in the world of origins; *El* alone art thou, the only one from evermore to evermore.

Violet seems to us the veil before thy face; be thou good and gracious unto us forever.

Archangel *Tzadkiel* most righteous art thou in the creative world; guide us gently in whatever way we ought to go.

Be thou forbearing of our frequent failures; and correct our courses with thy beams of brightest blue.

O Angel Order of the *Chasmalim* with thine especial gift

of cheerful speech in the formative world; welcome unto us are all thy words of faithful friendly feelings.

Bear our thoughts to heaven like the scent of cedar on a sea-born breeze; and may a pleasant place await us in the purple shadows of thy secret shades.

Thou expressive Sphere of Jupiter supply us with thy joviality; prosper us upon this planet.

Help us to earn and afterwards enjoy; the rich rewards of our endeavors on our earth.

Lead us ahead by thy deep azure light; which hints at happiness to come for every soul.

Thou art the recompenser of the righteous; may we be recognized within thy realm.

May we be glad to share thy gifts; with those who truly need them in thy name.

Blessed be thy symbol of the fourfold form; and spiritual scepter of sovereignty.

Take our left arms and guide us graciously; throughout thy path that leads toward perfection.

So Mote It Be. Amen

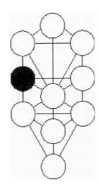

GEBURAH
Principle of the Almighty Justice

O thou Spirit of Severe Economy throughout existence; thou art the eternal enemy of evil.

In making man observe obedience of thy divine decrees; thou also makest us amenable to thine authority.

Deal not with us on purely past deserts alone; but because of what we shall become when we have learned our lessons.

Fifth upon the Holy Tree of Life art thou O Ever-Winning Warrior; thou art the certain champion of Cosmos.

Inflictions of injustice are avenged by thee; nor will wickedness prevail against thy power.

On thee do we rely for restitution of our rights; and we obey thine orders with respect and reverence.

Radical is thine intelligence, being rooted in the depth of reason; thy principles of retribution are entirely free from passion.

Sensible is thy sincere severity; may we realize its strict impartiality.

Elohim Gebor the Overcoming One art thou within the world of origins; may we be worthy of inclusion with thy holy hosts.

Let us always act with confidence and constant courage; defending our beliefs in thy Divinity beneath thine orange banner.

Archangel *Khamael* thou burning one of the creative world; cleanse corruption from us with thy torch of truth.

Free thou our souls from every filthy falsehood; by thy most faithful fire that melts our fetters with its searing scarlet flames.

O Angel Order of the Seraphim, thou Fiery Serpents of formation; burn out of us ideas of rage, revenge, or any rash behaviour.

Sterilize thou such infections of the soul like an ammoniacal antidote dispels all acid dangers; and be thy brilliant scarlet badge an honored pledge of health and purity.

Thou mighty one expressed as Mars, spare us from stupid strife; may we not waste this world with savage wars.

Let us learn instead to fight the enemies within ourselves; without inflicting injuries upon each other.

Be thine ensign of exacting red and black; our best reminder of this all-important issue.

O thou prevailing power whose symbols are the sword and scourge; be unto us a surgeon, not a slayer.

Help us realize the reasons why we must find fortitude; and face faithfully the dangers and disasters, on our Paths to peace.

Take us by our right arms and make us resolute; that we may conquer all adversities against thy cosmic cause.

So Mote It Be. Amen

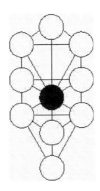

TIPHERETH
Principle of the Transcendent Beauty

O thou Central Cosmic Spirit of the Living Light; entire existence hangs upon thy perfect point of equilibrium.

May we receive thy radiance into our souls; according to our state of readiness for such intense illumination.

Let us not demand more light from thee than we may hold; with dignity and honour for thy high Divinity.

Sixth upon the Holy Tree of Life art thou O Beautiful and Blessed Being; thine image is like immolated innocence.

Priest-King and Risen Son of rightful royal blood art thou; perpetuated through thy line of light forever.

May we who sacrifice ourselves in spirit; become related with thee in reality.

Thine intelligence is interceding as a mediator; issuing influences through itself that offer inspiration to entire mankind.

Thou bringest what is best to bear on everyone; may we experience thy true enlightenment.

Thou art *Aloah Va Daath* the Knower of All Life within the world of origins; let us also be aware that we live in thee.

May we recognize thy rosy rays of rising; that the radiance of thy Divinity will surely dawn upon us.

Godlike art thou Archangel *Michael* in the creative world; we pray for thy protection.

Free us from a fiery fate; and liberate us with thy shaft of light from every evil.

Send thou thy golden ones of grace to guard and guide

us; past all the pitfalls that prevent our progress on our Paths.

Angelic Order of the *Malachim*, thou art the regulating ones of the formative world; help us rule ourselves before we seek control of others.

Correct our conduct carefully; with thy roseate reminders.

Take thou our thoughts unto the eye of Heaven; like finest frankincense arising from our earthly altars.

O Solar Center of the expressed Cosmos; thou art our oldest sign of spiritual order.

Thy seasons show our passing Paths of progress; and thou art the point round which we pivot on this planet.

Lead us by thy golden-amber light; into thy secret inner system.

Thou art the lesser countenance which hides the holy face no mortal may behold; let our waking inner vision be unclouded by a veil of willful ignorance.

Honoured be thy cross and cube together with the six-pointed star; thine is the harmony that holds the spheres together as a whole.

Let thy sacred sign of LVX shine forth; from every single living breast forever.

So Mote It Be. Amen.

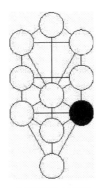

NETZACH
Principle of the Unceasing Victory

O thou Amiable Spirit of Achievement; thy truth must triumph over all in time.

Thou dost not win thy way with wicked wars; but slowly gains supremacy by gentleness of soul.

May we also come to share in thy success; conquering conditions set against attainment of thy potent peace.

Seventh on the Holy Tree of Life art thou; O Force of Feminine and Virtuous Victory.

Thou art She in whom brutalities become abated; and absorbed by thine amative sense-subduing softness.

Reform our rudeness and our bad behavior; that lust becomes in us an ardent love instead.

Hidden from humanity is thine intelligence by its concealment; courtesy and charm come to those souls who cultivate thee.

Only deepest insight will discern thee; in ecstasy alone art thou experienced.

Yahwe Tzabaoth is thy name within the world of origins; thou wilt be to every one of us as thy whole entity.

Let us realize thine ambience with every amber ray attracting our attention; and may we become aware of thee with all our spiritual senses.

Archangel *Auriel* in the creative world art thou; who like a lamp upheld on earth exemplify the light of Heaven.

Shield us safely and securely with thine emerald aegis; defend our sensitivities of soul from desecration.

O Angelic Order of the *Elohim* in the formative world;

thou art the godlike inner images mankind may look upon and live.

Be gracious to us in thy groves of golden-green; where moving music makes us glad to be alive.

Send our supplications like the scent of sandalwood to Heaven; that we may hope for happiness in earth existence.

Thou Brilliant One of dawn and dusk expressed behind the veil of Venus; shine upon us with sweet sympathy for our aspiring souls.

May thine olive-golden garments give us goodly grace; and signify a stimulating life of peaceful plenty.

O Lovely Lady of Divine Delight, thou art the deep necessity of our divided natures; satisfy our spiritual senses so that we are conscious of complete contentment.

Thou whose sacred symbols are the girdle and the lamp; lead us lightly by thy tender touch on our left loins.

Let us love thee always and show unto us thy true affection; when we come to thee for comfort, counsel, or in search of consolation.

So Mote It Be. Amen.

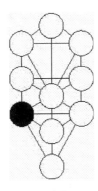

HOD
Principle of the Surpassing Glory

Thou Splendid Spirit of Sagacity and Honour; in thy hands are held the works of hidden wisdom.

Thou art the instructor of our intellects; and mentor of our mental movements.

Thy special secrets are revealed to us by reason; initiate our minds into the meaning of the Holy and Hermetic Mysteries.

Eighth upon the Holy Tree of Life art thou; O Glorious Hermaphrodite of Heaven.

Male and female talents meet in thee with clever caution; thou combinest in thyself the best of both.

At thine instigation we inquire into the laws of life; with thy willing aid do we investigate enigmas 4 existence.

Perfect is the inner path of thine intelligence; it prepares us to perceive the principles behind our beings.

Thou showest us the splendid sorts of souls we may become; we take our best encouragement from thine example.

Thou art *Elohim Tzabaoth* in the world of origins; Maker of Multitudes and Lord of Legions.

O thou who livest always in the thoughts of everyone; awake thy people's vision with thy purple-violet light.

Archangel *Raphael* art thou in the creative world; healing hurts sustained in swordlike situations.

Invest us also with the air of thine authority; and may our entire organisms be invigorated by thine orange emanations.

O Angelic Order of the *Beni Elohim* in the formative

world; thou art the descendants of Divinities.

Let thy likeness lighten up our lives; like children of our consciousness.

Send our thoughts into the spheres of spirit as an interesting scent of storax; and may we remember thee with every shade of russet-red that we shall ever see.

Thou art expressed as Hermes of the Heavens; silver speech is thine with scintillating wit.

Be thy black and yellow whipped with white; a secret sign to us of subtlety and commonsense combined.

O Thrice Great One, be our trusted teacher in thy spiritual schools and temples; make our minds achieve thy mutability and motion.

Thou whose sacred symbols are the written Rites concealed within the ancient craft-adornment of an apron; take thou and train its in the rules of ritual and magic methods.

Lead us skillfully by our right loins along the special inner lines; which we must follow for initiation sponsored by the spirit.

So Mote It Be. Amen.

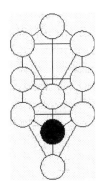

YESOD
Principle of the infallible Foundation

O thou basis of our living beings and fount of our fertility; Thou art the softly shining one of the *Shekinah*.

Thy reflection shows us safely what we dare not look directly at as mortals; thou art the link between our ignorance and true illuminations.

In thee appears the cause of our continuance as human creatures; for thou art the reality our reproduction represents.

Ninth upon the Holy Tree of Life art thou, O Vision of Virility; thou art the firm foundation of our faith in life itself.

While thy potent force prevails, we surely shall not perish from this planet.

We evolve through thee into much more than mortal entities; our inner destination lies with thy Divinity.

Thine intelligence is termed the purified; it prevents imagination from distorting or destroying thine intention.

Thou art the systematic savior of our sanity; through thee do we discern the basic truth behind our dreams.

Shaddai el Chaiim the Lord of Lives art thou in the creative world beginning every birth; of thee do we emerge into embodiment and end our days on earth.

Dark as deepest indigo is thy profundity of purpose; may thine intentions come to light among mankind.

Archangel *Gabriel* art thou in the creative world; awake us all to life on every level.

Call and awaken us across the holy water held within thy cup; that we may hear thy voice through thy thin violet veil.

O Angelic Order of the *Aishim* in the formative world; thy powers are adequate to found the families of fit and proper people.

Let us experience the taste of life enjoyably like jasmine; and protect us from its perils with thy purple panoply.

Elusive light of night art thou, expressive Moon of many meanings; may thy bright beams become a bridge for us to cross the chasms of confusion.

Let us not be lost amid thy maze nor tangled with thy thorns; but live to share the secrets of thy silver castle in its citrine-azure setting.

O thou mighty and majestic mystery; how shall our souls seek thy solution?

Deceive us not nor let us doubt unduly; may we make some sense of what we see within thy magic mirror.

Thy sacred symbols are perfumes and sandals; when employed for proper ritual reasons.

Guard thou our genitals that life may only come of Love; and free us from all forms of falsehood into living light forevermore.

So Mote It Be. Amen.

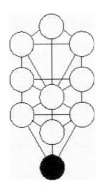

MALKUTH
Principle of the Life throughout the Kingdom

O thou Kingdom of all evident and obvious existence; thou art the special sphere in which we start our spiritual searchings.

Here as humanity we are thy cosmic children; formed by thy forces out of living flesh and blood.

Forgive us for our frequent failures; in recognizing our relationship with thy reality.

Tenth upon the Holy Tree of Life art thou; O Ruling One whose rightful name is Nature.

The entirety of evolution is thine empire; it extends all through our earth existence.

Blessed art thou as a blissful bride; bestowed on honored human husbands.

Resplendent is thy royal intelligence; exalted over everyone as the immortal way of wisdom.

Thou art the persuasive power of prayer; and by thy grace are we delivered from the gates of death.

Adonai ha Aretz art thou in the orginative world; O King of Kings and the unequalled master of our manifested universe.

May we always yield ourselves to thy Divine authority; displayed by thy bright yellow banner of obedience.

Archangel *Sandalphon* art thou in the creative world; thy feet are firmly on the floor of our far-flying cosmic chariot.

Steer straight our course throughout creation; O Close Companion cloaked with the sequential colors of the seasons.

O thou Angelic Order of the *Kerubim* in the formative world; thine is the fourfold force of mobile matter.

We recognize thy special signs of sable russet graced by golden points of power; may they be discerned through screens of smoke as dense as those of cretan dittany.

Thou art the elements of earth expressively; O physical phenomena within our working world.

We rely on thee for proofs of our reality as people; give us golden hints of higher meanings in the blackest of our basic matter.

O thou Mighty Daughter of Divinity and Lesser Mother of Our Lives; we value thy virginity as a most sacred secret which must be maintained inviolate.

Thou whose symbols are the altar cubes and cosmic Circle Cross, we seek to serve the spirit of thy cause.

Lead thou our faithful feet forever on the line of light; that lies between all human beings and their highest everlasting entity.

So Mote It Be. Amen.

iii. Invocations of the Paths

PATH 0-33
Connecting *Ain Soph Aur* with Sphere 1

O thou that Wilt or Wilt-not-be entirely as thou wilt. Be or unbe thy will with us.

Thou art our infinite impossibility. Of thee alone is inspiration to be anything we will within thee other than thine unidentity.

Thou art the void, yet breathest forth vitality and being as *Eheieh*.

Thou art uncreate, yet cause of all creation mediated through Archangel *Metatron*.

Thou art silence, yet the Holy Living Creatures sing in praise of thy perfection.

Thou art motionless, yet every moving nebula proclaims thy power made manifest through nature.

Blessed unto us be what thou wilt or wilt-not-be forevermore.

So Mote It Be. Amen.

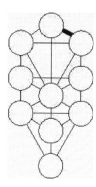

PATH 11 - B
Connecting Sphere 1 with Sphere 2

O Ruling Spirit of Summative Wisdom, grant in us that we may likewise know ourselves in thee.

May we become true pontiffs of thy power, and bridge with spiritual skill the distance that divides our state from thine.

Thou Breath of Life! Be in us what thou wilt.

Mediate our cause before the crown of our creation O thou *Metatron*, and proclaim our purpose to the Highest One, O *Ratziel*.

Thou living elements, sustain us through all cosmic cycles which we must complete.

As the nebulae, so may we come to life in light, and thence continue till the ending of the twelvefold Circle that contains our consciousness as separated entities within existence.

So Mote It Be. Amen.

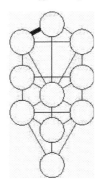

PATH 12-C
Connecting Sphere 1 with Sphere 3

O thou Crown of Understanding, let us comprehend what we shall be in thee above all else.

Let thy solitary single spirit be the only light in us that leads us into everlasting liberation.

Breathe thou forth from thee our souls that we may live.

Archangel *Metatron* uphold humanity unto the being that thou beholdest, and teach us truth, O *Tzaphkiel* when we are ready to receive it.

Thou Holy Living Creatures, set us most securely on our seats of sensibility.

From our first movement, may we gain sufficient gravity to proceed steadily like Saturn on our cosmic courses, holding thy most precious secrets safely in our souls till time reveals to all, thy total and most radiant golden truth.

So Mote It Be. Amen.

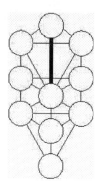

PATH 13-D
Connecting Sphere 1 with Sphere 6

O thou Supreme Crown and Beauty of all being, may we live forever in the state of thy perfection.

May every single star of Heaven be for us a sign of thy most holy spirit and a pointer of our ways upon the path of light.

Breathe thou in us that we may know thee in ourselves.

Be mindful of us, O thou Mighty *Metatron*, who dares to face Divinity directly, and do thou, O *Michael*, intercede on our behalf before the highest throne.

O Holy Creatures, be our active elements of life, and may the rightly ruling ones make straight our inner lines of light.

Like unto the nebulae may we bestir ourselves so that the sun of truth may surely come to light in us, and dissipate all doubts and darkness from us evermore.

So Mote It Be. Amen.

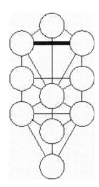

PATH 14 - F
Connecting Sphere 2 with Sphere 3

O thou Spirit of All Understanding Wisdom, be aware of us in thee who art the total truth of us in living light.

May thy judgment ever be the safeguard of our souls, arousing our abilities to comprehend our spiritual purpose and position in thy Cosmos.

Thou life of all! Be thou our will to live in light.

O Archangel *Ratziel* declare Divine intentions to us, and do thou Archangel *Tzaphkiel* help us to observe them.

Crush not our souls, O Circling Angels, but surround us with security upon our thrones of reasonable rulership.

Be thou not too seriously heavy in our human hearts, O *Saturn*. Let us sometimes leave the solemn side of life, and dance for sheer delight within the solar circle of our Cosmos.

So Mote It Be. Amen.

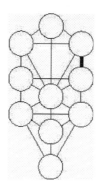

PATH 15 - G
Connecting Sphere 2 with Sphere 4

O thou Spirit of Beneficence and Wisdom, be magnanimous to us who may not live without thy mercy.

Be thou to us an emperor of gracious government, so that we may attempt to emulate thy ways of ruling on our earth.

Thou that wilt be what thou art, be Thou unique in us.

Proclaim this perfect power, O *Ratziel*, and do Thou Archangel *Tzadkiel*, preserve our rightful pathways leading us to light.

Encircle us with careful counsel thou *Auphanim*, and be kind to us, O *Chasmalim* with thy most welcome warmth within our souls.

May we indeed be jovial and generous throughout the twelvefold cycle of the solar seasons, so that we may ever claim compassion at the hands of earth or Heaven with a clear conscience.

So Mote It Be. Amen.

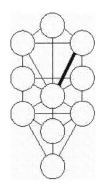

PATH 16 - H
Connecting Sphere 2 with Sphere 6

O thou Supremacy of Beautiful Omniscience, may we become aware of thee through wisdom and with wonder.

Teach us temperance with every way of life, that we may cross our chasms carefully, in firm control of every spiritual situation.

O thou that knowest what thou wilt, let us become enlightened in thee.

Reveal to us Archangel *Ratziel*, thy holy secrets, and deliver us O *Michael* from doubts and dangers.

Assist us, O thou Angels of the *Malakim*, to rule ourselves with reason in the living circles of the *Auphanim*.

May our secret sun behind the sun shine forth in glory through the signs of heaven, so that every soul may likewise live in light forevermore.

So Mote It Be. Amen.

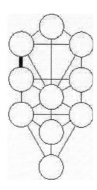

PATH 17 - J
Connecting Sphere 3 with Sphere 5

O thou Strictest Spirit of Controlled Severity, we pray that we may learn to understand thee.

Let thy decree of death deter us in no way from living, but encourage us to alter as we will within thee for the better.

O Mighty Life of Lives! Thou livest for us ever.

Archangel *Tzaphkiel*, observe what is unworthy in us, so that *Khamael* the burner may remove it, from us beneficially.

Support us steadfastly, O Thrones, so that the purifying seraphim may purge us of corruption.

Saturn, be thou our protective shield against all martial dangers of destruction, so that our surviving souls may live immortally in purest golden light forevermore.

So Mote It Be. Amen.

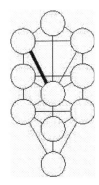

PATH 18-K
Connecting Sphere 3 with Sphere 6

O thou Most Beautiful of Beings, grant us sufficient understanding to become aware of thine existence.

In the sign of man suspended from the Tree of Life may we find our salvation and those secrets which our souls are ever seeking.

Thou art everyone! Thou knowest all we are.

Watch over us Archangel *Tzaphkiel* and *Michael* be thou our mediators as our souls are called to their account before Divine authority.

O thou Angelic Thrones and Rulers, guide and establish us with law and learning.

May our spiritual operation of the Sun and Saturn be successful in transmuting our base natures into souls of highest value to ourselves and the Eternal One in whom we live.

So Mote It Be. Amen.

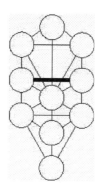

PATH 19-L
Connecting Sphere 4 with Sphere 5

O Most Compassionate Severity, may both extremes in us be balanced with the edge of thine exactitude.

Let us be delivered from afflictions and disasters by thy faultless justice, and the point of all we shall experience made plain to us.

Almighty One, thou livest by thy laws alone.

Archangel *Tzadkiel* stimulate our sense of rightness, and do thou *Khamael*, warn us from wrongdoing with thy fiery finger.

Angelic Flames of Fusion and of Fission, weld us firmly unto what is good, and separate our souls from evil.

May martial might and jovial mercy make us into finely balanced beings, completely compensated by whatever laws of life correct the errors of existence.

So Mote It Be. Amen.

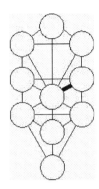

PATH 20-M
Connecting Sphere 4 with Sphere 6

O Most Merciful and Beautiful of Beings, thy powers alone are perfectly proportioned.

Thine is the strongest spirit in existence. All is accomplished by thine actions. Thine energy is inexhaustible.

Omniscient One, the whole of life is thine experience.

Archangel *Tzadkiel*, make thy right our might, and Michael, preserve our souls from peril by potency of thy protection.

O Warmhearted Angels, and our ruling guides to goodness, be thou kind and kingly unto us forever.

May the spiritual sun of our illumination shine eternally within us, and the magnanimity of *Jove* incline our feelings to be generous toward our fellow creatures of this Cosmos.

So Mote It Be. Amen.

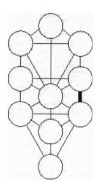

PATH 21 - N
Connecting Sphere 4 with Sphere 7

O thou Victorious One of all Achievements, may thy triumphant life be also ours to share with thee eternally.

Be thou like unto an empress, governing with grace, and let us similarly gain control of our emotions with a fair and firm benevolence.

Thou ruling one of everyone, may we reign with thee in ourselves. Archangel *Tzadkiel*, encourage us upon our way of right, and *Auriel* enlighten us, so that we may be led with loyalty and love toward our ultimate attainment.

Thou Shining and Celestial Spirits, help us to uphold the good opinions we should have for one another.

May our Lord and Lady, symbolized as Jove and Venus, signify to us true spiritual loving kindness, which alone will make our lives worth living in this world or any other evermore.

So Mote It Be. Amen.

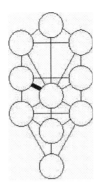

PATH 22 - P
Connecting Sphere 5 with Sphere 6

O Beautiful Severity, lay not the lash of thy most holy discipline too heavily upon us.

Break thou our selfish strongholds of stupidity as thou must surely blast the towers of those defying thy Divine authority.

Thou Mightiest of Mind, may we be strongly sensible.

Archangel *Khamael*, be thou our finest flame of spiritual freedom, and do thou, O *Michael*, become our leading liberator into light. thou Burning and controlling Angels, help us hold our tempers from becoming out of hand or overheated.

May the might of Mars be balanced by the poising power of solar strength, so that by equalizing energies peace will prevail throughout all actions on this path.

So Mote It Be. Amen.

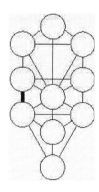

PATH 23-Q
Connecting Sphere 5 with Sphere 8

O Glorious Severity, try thou us not beyond our spiritual strength, nor send us sufferings we are ashamed to bear.

Thou tempting one, whose tests make us torment ourselves, we shall be delivered from thine influences by our inner sense of discipline and duty.

Mighty One of Multitudes, may all mankind mean most to thee.

Archangel *Khamael*, be thou the fire and *Raphael*, the sword which conquers whatsoever would corrupt our consciousness, or send our souls to senseless slavery.

O Flaming and Appearing Angels, help us to be forceful and apparent, utterly without ferocity, unkindness, or aggression.

By the help of Hermes, and the might of Mars, may all actions be averted which would lead to wicked wars. Let good counsel overcome the very worst of serious situations, so that peaceful power prevails with honor evermore.

So Mote It Be. Amen.

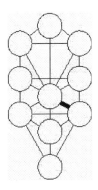

PATH 24-R
Connecting Sphere 6 with Sphere 7

O victorious Beauty, thou art winner of the cosmic contest. May we win this world of ours with thee.

Beloved unto everyone are lovers, and blessed be the bond between our living legions. Let us Love each other through our lives on every level.

Thou Experience of all, may thou be shared by every single soul. Archangel *Auriel*, enlighten us on earth, and lead us Michael, to our illumination in the living spirit of eternal Love. May we satisfy our spiritual sense with success.

O thou Governing and Guiding Angels, help us to achieve a genuine affection for each other's entities.

Thou Lord of Light and Lady of our Love appearing unto us as Sol and Venus, give us cause to conquer all conditions of confused antagonisms. May entire humanity, released from hates, rejoice within thy happy radiance forevermore.

So Mote It Be. Amen.

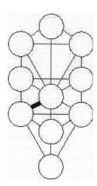

PATH 25 - S
Connecting Sphere 6 with Sphere 8

O Glorious Beauty, manifest thyself in all mankind. May our minds be made aware of thy magnificence.

Thou art the chariot that carries consciousness through cosmos. Take us with thee on thy travels so that we will also come to comprehend thy truth.

Thou knowest every issue of intelligence. Perfect thou our perception.

Archangel *Raphael*, instruct us rightly on our inner way, and *Michael*, point out for us the proper paths, which we must find and follow for attaining ultimate awareness.

O thou Controlling and Contriving Angels, help us to cleverly command ourselves with cheerful confidence.

Thou Solar and Hermetic Spirit of all hidden science, initiate our intellects into the holy inner secrets. May our searching souls be made full members of thy mysteries, and thus achieve admission to thine adytum therein forever.

So Mote It Be. Amen.

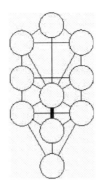

PATH 26 - T
Connecting Sphere 6 with Sphere 9

Thou Basic Beauty of all Being and firm foundation of our faith, let us never doubt thy true Divinity.

Thou art the centralizing Sun of Cosmos. Thy spirit is the light of every life. Let us exist through thee eternally, for thine illumination indicates our true identity.

All life is thine to know. Make known thyself through us.

Archangel *Michael*, send thou thy sacred staff for our support, and communicate to us, O, *Gabriel*, the contents of thy consecrated cup.

O thou Ruling and Reflective Angels, help us to believe that Deity knows what is best for us.

As Sun and Moon appear within the sky to man on earth, so may the souls of humankind be seen with their own light by the discerning spirit of Divinity in Heaven. May we be worthy of the will that works in us.

So Mote It Be. Amen.

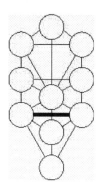

PATH 27 - V
Connecting Sphere 7 with Sphere 8

O Glorious Victory of Love and Learning, thou makest our mortality worthwhile. We pray and practice for thy sake.

Events fall as thou wilt, exactly as thy wheel of fate decrees our destinies. May we find favor from thy holy hand that casts our living lot into creation.

Thou art everything to everyone. Blessed be our share of thee in spirit. Archangel *Auriel*, assist us to make light of life, and *Raphael*, reveal some really suitable behavior to adopt in order to obtain the best of any situation.

O thou angelic Ones of Items and Ideas, tell us what we should think of things to make the most of them.

May hermetic wit and aphroditic winsomeness be with us when we will. Let us not be lost for lack of instinct or imagination, but be always ready with the right response in every chance or circumstance.

So Mote It Be. Amen.

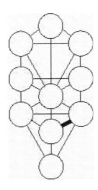

PATH 28-W
Connecting Sphere 7 with Sphere 9

O Victory of Life, thou art the spirit that inspires each soul to seek its individual existence. Let us become thy best-born beings.

Thou art like unto a pure priestess who prays for the perfection of all people. May we also mediate thy will in us which makes us more than merely mortals.

Our Overlord of Life are thou. May we truly recognize thy rulership. Archangel *Auriel*, shield thou our sentient souls, and Gabriel, arouse our finer feelings so that we are capable of contact with Divinity through our devotions.

O Representing and Reflecting Angels, make us meditate upon the inner meaning of initiation. May we be worthy members of the Holy Hidden Mysteries.

May the Moon and Venus bring before our minds that Virgin-Mother concept which connects a high identity with human incarnation. Let us also live to be illuminated in this mystic manner.

So Mote It Be. Amen.

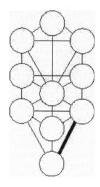

PATH 29 - X
Connecting Sphere 7 with Sphere 10

O Kingdom of Established Victory, in thee does man discover his essential meaning. May we preserve thy peace entirely.

Thou art our complete Cosmos, and the world wherein we work thy will within our words. May we always live according to the laws of light and Love.

Ruler of reality in everything art thou. Remember us eternally.

Archangel *Auriel*, enlighten us on earth, and do thou stand by us, O *Sandalphon*, when we strive to rise beyond its barriers toward a higher spiritual habitation.

O thou Angelic Ones of Living Likenesses, show us what we should be like, so that at least we shall attempt to live aspiringly.

May earth existence be made very comfortable when it is combined with ways of Venus. May all the arts of life become more lovely as mankind develops indications of Divinity, evincing true intentions of achieving immortality.

So Mote It Be. Amen.

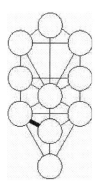

PATH 30 - Y
Connecting Sphere 8 with Sphere 9

O Ever Glorious Foundation, in thee begins belief by which we have our hopes of Heaven. May this be true for all humanity.

Thou art the Magician who makes man continue to seek more than mortal consciousness. Inspire us likewise with some spiritual interests in our lives.

Lord of Life art thou and its intentions. Live Thou thy will within us.

Archangel *Raphael*, remind us of the reasons we should stay alive, and *Gabriel*, supply us with the strength we shall require for our survival. Thou Angel Orders of Well-bred and Worthy Ones, help us honor our most holy heritage. May we deserve our destiny.

May mercurial resilience and lunar relaxation be a secret spring behind our lives. Let us never be despairing nor depressed beyond recovery, but restore ourselves to rights again with a recuperative will.

So Mote It Be. Amen.

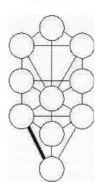

PATH 31 - Z
Connecting Sphere S with Sphere 10

O Glorious Kingdom, thou art the provider of that paradise on earth which we expect humanity to earn from Heaven.

Innocence alone art thou, and guiltless of all guile. May we also place a childlike confidence in thee, trusting in thine inner guidance for our everlasting good.

Monarch of thine endless multitudes art thou. Consider us thy children.

Archangel *Raphael*, reveal to us the meanings of the Holy Mysteries, and *Sandalphon*, support our search for the solution of their secrets.

O thou Angelic Families and Fourfold Forces, aid and assist our actions in our spiritual struggles. We welcome thee at work.

May hermetic help and earth experience evolve the souls of them that strive to live in light. Let every life that we endure within this world be worthy of the will that caused us to be creatures of this Cosmos.

So Mote It Be. Amen.

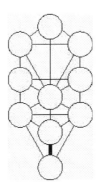

PATH 32-Th
Connecting Sphere 9 with Sphere 10

O thou Firm-Founded Kingdom, in thee is life established and expressed within the compass of our living consciousness.

Mankind is like the Moon, held back by earth while hoping for escape to final freedom. May our first steps in spiritual space be dedicated and directed to Divinity.

Lord of Life extended unto earth art thou. Be as thou wilt with us.

Archangel *Gabriel*, be Thou the heavenly mediator of that message meant for all humanity, and *Sandalphon*, make us see what lies before us by the highest light of life.

O Angelic Orders of the Friendly Flames and Forces, help us see and serve the cosmic cause. Aid thou our efforts to obtain enlightenment. Thou Light of Luna, representing upon earth reflections of humanity on higher holy subjects, shine thou so strongly in our souls, that we shall seek the spiritual side of everyone and everything forevermore.

So Mote It Be. Amen.

C. Notes—Prayers—Meditations

1. THE BLESSINGS OF THE *SEPHIROT*

0　**Blessed be the Light beyond all Being.**
　　Forever Blessed be the Living Spirit. *Amen.*

1　**Blessed be the Breathing of Origination.**
　　Forever Blessed be the Living Spirit. *Amen.*

2　**Blessed be Eternal Wisdom.**
　　Forever Blessed be the Living Spirit. *Amen.*

3　**Blessed be Omniscient Understanding.**
　　Forever Blessed be the Living Spirit. *Amen.*

4　**Blessed be Perpetual Compassion.**
　　Forever Blessed be the Living Spirit. *Amen.*

5　**Blessed be Almighty Justice.**
　　Forever Blessed be the Living Spirit. *Amen.*

6　**Blessed be Transcendent Beauty.**
　　Forever Blessed be the Living Spirit. *Amen.*

7　**Blessed be Unceasing Victory.**
　　Forever Blessed be the Living Spirit. *Amen.*

8　**Blessed be Surpassing Glory.**
　　Forever Blessed be the Living Spirit. *Amen.*

9　**Blessed be Infallible Foundation.**
　　Forever Blessed be the Living Spirit. *Amen.*

10　**Blessed be all Life throughout the Kingdom.**
　　Forever Blessed be the Living Spirit. *Amen.*

In the Name of the Wisdom,
⊕ And of the Love,
And of the Justice,
And the Infinite Mercy
Of the One Eternal Spirit. *Amen*

2. THE "I AM" FORMULA

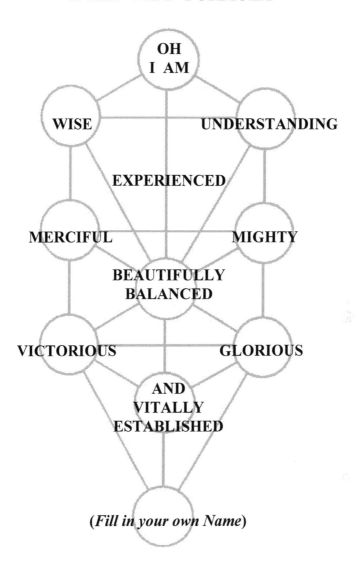

OH
I AM

WISE

UNDERSTANDING

EXPERIENCED

MERCIFUL

MIGHTY

BEAUTIFULLY
BALANCED

VICTORIOUS

GLORIOUS

AND
VITALLY
ESTABLISHED

(Fill in your own Name)

"MAY I IMPLANT THE HOLY TREE OF LIFE SO TRULY IN ME, THAT IT WILL ARISE AS EVIDENCE ON EARTH OF MINE IDENTITY ON INNER LIVING LEVELS."

3. THE QABALISTIC RULE

10	Man of Earth,
9	Faithfully Believe in Life.
8	Live Honourably;
7	Conquer Yourself;
6	Be Equable of Energy;
5	Self Disciplined;
4	Generously Merciful;
3	Understanding;
2	Wise;
1	Single of Spirit;
	and ultimately,
0 0 0	You will live in Light Divine,
0 0	Immortally beyond all limits,
0	in Perfect Peace Profound.

4. THE QABALISTIC CREED
i. Tree of Life up from Matter to Spirit

10	In Material Existence
9	I Believe,
8	with Reason
7	and Devotion,
6	in the Beauty
5	of Controlled
4	abounding Love,
3	whose Understanding
2	Wisdom is the
1	Only Light,
0 0 0	Illuminating
0 0	Boundless Being in the
0	Ultimate Unmanifest of
	Perfect Peace Profound.

ii. Tree of Life down from Spirit to Matter

0	**Of Perfect Peace Profound**
	out of the Ultimate Unmanifest,
0 0	**Boundless Being becomes**
0 0 0	**Illumination as the**
1	**One True Light of**
2	**Wisdom,**
3	**Understanding all with**
4	**Love outpoured**
5	**in full Control as**
6	**Beauty, whose**
7	**Achievement is a**
8	**Brilliance finding its**
9	**Foundation in**
10	**Material existence.**

5. QABALISTIC PRAYER

0	
0 0	**O Supreme Life Spirit,**
0 0 0	**You alone are**
1	**Cause and Crown of Cosmos**
2	**With Your Wisdom**
3	**and Your Understanding.**
	Grant us avoidance of the great Abyss in our
	Experience of Your Existence.
4	**Extend Your Mercy unto us**
5	**With all Your Might,**
6	**that we may realise the Blessed Beauty of Your**
	Being.
7	**Let us lovingly Achieve**
8	**the Glory**
9	**of Establishing ourselves immortally**
10	**in Your most holy Kingdom Evermore.**
	Amen

6. QABALISTIC THANKSGIVING

0

0 0   Gratitude to You, O Greatest

0 0 0

1   Sovereign Spirit

2   of Supernal Wisdom

3   and Omniscient Understanding,
since we are enlightened by
Experience of Your Existence.

4   Thanks be for Mercifully

5   tempered Might,

6   and blessed be the Beauty

7   of Achieving

8   Glory

9   by Establishing our Living Entities

10   within Your Everlasting Kingdom.
Amen

7. IMAGES AND THE TREE OF LIFE
i. Telesmic Images of the Ten *Sephirot*

0   NOTHING

1   HOLY HEAD

2   FAITHFUL FATHER

3   MATURE MOTHER

4   KINDLY KING

5   STERN SOLDIER

6   MAGNIFICENT MEDIATOR

7   LOVELY LADY

8   PERCEPTIVE PERSON

9   FERTILE FIGURE

10   MYSTERIOUS MATE

ii. Names and Qualities of the *Sephirot*

0   My name is NIL. I am the Origin of ALL prevailing past the point of personality in Perfect Peace Profound.

1   My name is LIFE. I am the Supreme Spirit of the Will. I am in everyone and everything existing everlastingly.

2   My name is FATHER. I am the willing Wise One who enlightens every soul sincerely asking for Illumination inwardly.

3   My name is MOTHER. I am the deeply Understanding One dispersing darkness from those seeking souls who call for Clarity.

4   My name is MAGNANIMITY. I am the Kindly Kingship and most noble nature of compassionate authority above all Cosmos.

5   My name is DISCIPLINE. I am the Control by will and word of every errant energy that calls for careful Compensation.

6   My name is HARMONY. I am the Poising Point of Cosmic Life, persuading Man to find the cause and meaning for its Laws.

7   My name is GRACE. I am the Loveliness of Life, so well worth winning by each single soul with hopes of Heaven.

8   My name is GAIN. I am the Incentive for each human intellect to rise above the rest by application of Intelligence.

9   My name is VITALITY. I am the Firm Foundation for a faith in Life by all that seek a spiritual sense in living.

10   **My name is NATURE. I am the ideal Mate for humankind to treat with trust and hold with honour in this mundane world.**

iii. Ideas Associated with the Sephirotic Images

KETER (The Crown)

1   Light from Darkness. Life from Light. Intention from Inanition. Divine Identity determining Itself. Self Cosmo-Consciousness commences. Being begins. All Awareness is One.

CHOCHMAH (Wisdom)

2   Paternal Power personified. Will with Wisdom. Supernal Sapience. Decisions of Divinity. Assertion of Authority. Maximal Masculinity. Impregnator of Ideas. Father of Force.

BINAH (Understanding)

3   Maternal Principle Personified. Universal Understanding. Acceptor of Awareness. Womb of Will. The Great Gestatrix. Full Femininity. Inherent Intuition. Mother of Form.

CHESED (Mercy)

4   Mercy manifest as Monarchy. The Concept of Compassion. Benevolence and Beneficence. The Grandeur of Generosity. Kindliness and Kingliness. Merciful Magnanimity. The All-Accelerator.

GEVURAH (Severity)

5   Duty and Discipline. Severe Strictness. Concept of Correction. Cleanser of Corruption. Efficient Economy. Stern Saviour. Divine Decreaser.

TIFERET (Beauty)

6   The Balance of Being in Beautiful Holy Harmony. Poising Point of Cosmic Creation. The Divine Drama as Innocent Incarnation, Sacred Sacrifice and Resurrective Redeemer.

The Mystery of *Melchizedek*. Man and Maker meet. Common union of Consciousness.

NETZACH (Victory)

7 The Triumph of Tenderness. Achievement of Aims by Affection. Enjoyment of Emotions. Cultured Consciousness. Artistic Ability. Victorious Vivacity. Graceful Gentleness. Sentience of Soul.

HOD (Glory)

8 The Splendour of Sagacity. Initiated Intelligence. Mind over Matter. Trained Thinking. Clever Consciousness. Scientific Skill. Humour and Honour. Adaptable Attitudes. Resilient Reasoning.

YESOD (Foundation)

9 The Founder of Families. Establishment of Evolution. Virility and Vigour. Sexual Stability. Best Biological Behaviour. Good Genetics. Respect for Reproduction. Love of Life. Fruitful Fertility.

MALCHUT (Kingdom)

10 The Nobility of Nature. The Perfect Partner for Material Man. The Mystical Marriage of Mankind with Matter. Human Hopes of Earning Emancipation from Earth. A Blessed Bride delivered by Divinity as Mate unto Mankind. The Kingdom that makes all Men kindred Souls in search of Spirit.

8. THE STATIONS OF THE TREE OF LIFE

To be able to work this ceremony, you need to have the previous installments of this series at hand. It is important to first read through the rite, then ensuring that you have the exact components prepared for you to do the invocations and visualizations smoothly and effectively, and finally to proceed with the ceremony itself.

It helps to prepare yourself beforehand, maybe by taking a bath and dressing in fresh clothing or wearing a robe, and then to prepare the room or Temple by lighting a candle and some pleasant incense. In this case the colour of the candle or the perfume of the incense is not really important. All that is needed is that you should feel prepared, relaxed, surrendered to your purpose of working the stations of the Tree of Life, without too much distraction. When this rite is worked in a group, the words are divided between a Preceptor (the person making the statements) and a Responsor (the person who answers or responds. This function may also be fulfilled by all present). Naturally all the lines are read by one person, if it is worked by a single practitioner.

An extremely important suggestion is to read or utter the words slowly. Try and get a "feeling appreciation" for the words, rather than a thinking one. Above all, do not go on "mental trips," trying to reason out the meanings of the words. Feel them out as it were. By saying the words slowly, you pause on each words just long enough to "feel the word out" without losing the overall sense of the sentences. If you "feel the words" out in this manner, you will find you naturally begin to "feel the meaning" and invoke an "inner response" inside you. In this way you will practice a very intense form of meditation, while at the same time practising the "art of invocation" or calling up responses inside yourself.— Jacobus G. Swart

i. Opening
(*Form the Cosmic Cross*)

In the Name of the Wisdom,
And of the Love,
And of the Justice,
And the Infinite Mercy
Of the One Eternal Spirit. *Amen*

Preceptor: **Blessed be to us the Holy Tree of Life that symbolises our belief in Supreme Spiritual Being, and formulates our faith in the Divine Design thereof.**

Responsor: **Sacred be to us the Stations on the Tree that point our purpose in its plan, and lead us step by step along our paths to Perfect Light in Peace Profound.**

Preceptor:	**Welcome be our Way of Light around the Course of Cosmos centred on the unique Total Truth uniting all our Universe.**
Responsor:	**So mote it be, *AMEN*.**

ii. Signalling the Sphere

Preceptor:

1. *The Sefirah is signalled by knocks or the lighting of a candle or lamp of an appropriate colour.*

2. *An associated Blessing and response is selected from the "Blessings of the Sefirot."*

3. *An associated Invocation is uttered from the "Names and Qualities of the Sefirotic Images."*

iii. Personification of the Sphere

Preceptor: **By what Image is this Principle to be personified?**

Responsor: **That our Inner contacts with it may be made more closely.**

(Here the associated Image-Concept selected from the "Sephirotic Telesmic Images of the Tree of Life" is given)

Preceptor: **We acknowledge our associations with this special Sphere.**

Responsor: **Let us live to learn what comes in consequence.**

Preceptor:

1. *The Signal of the next Sphere and Blessing is given.*

2. *A verse of the "Hymn of the Angels" or another appropriate linkage may be sung or recited while moving from one station to the next.*

3. *When all the stations, or those selected,*

have been worked, the Preceptor utters the
"Thanksgiving Prayer," followed by:

Thanks also be that we have worked our Way with Will around the Points of Power upon the Holy Tree of Life. May this pilgrimage of purpose we commenced by faith conclude in fellowship with those belonging through belief within this Spiritual Family whose Sacred Principles we have proclaimed.

(Form the Cosmic Cross in the same manner as before.)

In the Name of the Wisdom,
And of the Love,
And of the Justice,
And the Infinite Mercy
Of the One Eternal Spirit. *Amen*

iv. Holding Formula

(If the Rite is worked in stages, or if there are interruptions, the following holding formula applies)

(Appropriate knocks or a cymbal clash is given)

Preceptor: **Here shall we hold our conscious situation, until we come to its continuation with Words of Will.**

(Form the Cosmic Cross)

In the Name of the Wisdom,
And of the Love,
And of the Justice,
And the Infinite Mercy
Of the One Eternal Spirit. *Amen*

v. Continuation

(Reopen at a different time with the Cosmic Cross formed as before)

Preceptor: **In the Name of the Wisdom,**
⊕ **And of the Love,**
And of the Justice,
And the Infinite Mercy
Of the One Eternal Spirit. *Amen*

With those words will we continue on our Course of Consciousness thereto connected.

Responsor: **So mote it be.** *Amen*

9. THE QABALISTIC ROSARY

The Qabalistic Rosary is similar to the Christian rosary. The pattern in this case is quite simple, comprising ten large beads each divided from the other by single small beads. The symbol of the Tree of Life is used instead of the crucifix. The large beads are for meditation on the Spheres and Life-Elements, while the small ones are for the Paths between them. In working the "Qabalistic Rosary" in its entirety, one is required to move between a large bead, representing a Sphere, and the succeeding smaller one, representing a Path, until all the related "Paths" have been "activated" as it were, before moving onto the following large bead representing the next Sphere, etc.—Jacobus G. Swart.

i. Plan Prayer

O Supreme Life-Spirit, Thou alone art Cause and Crown of Cosmos with Thy Wisdom and Thine Understanding.
Grant us avoidance of the Great Abyss in our Experience of Thine Existence.
Extend Thy Mercy unto us with all Thy Might, that we may realise the Blessed Beauty of thy Being.

Let us Lovingly Achieve the Glory of Establishing ourselves immortally in Thy most Holy Kingdom evermore. *Amen.*

ii. Beads
Sphere—Principles

Statement: **Blessed unto us upon the Holy Tree of Life be Thou, the Principle and Power of ....**

Response: **Permit and prosper Thou we pray, our present purpose with the Perfect Plan.**

iii. Paths

Statement: **Blessed be the Path of .... upon the Holy Tree of Life that links the principles of .... and ....**

Response: **May this, and every way within the Perfect Pattern lead us truthfully toward Enlightenment in Living evermore.**

iv. Thanksgiving

Gratitude to Thee O Greatest Sovereign Spirit of Supernal Wisdom and Omniscient Understanding since we are enlightened by Experience of Thine Existence. Thanks be for Mercifully Tempered Might, and blessed be the Beauty of Achieving Glory by Establishing our Living Entities within Thine everlasting Kingdom. *Amen.*

Chapter 6
LANGUAGE OF THE GODS

A. The Power of Names

Assuming that higher forms of life and intelligence than human beings exist independently of our physical universe, how might we communicate with them? What terms of consciousness (if any) should we use, and how could these be translated into expressions our normal awareness would understand? In other words if there are Gods can humans talk to them or more importantly, talk *with* them?

Esoteric adventurers of all kinds have sought such secret spiritual speech from one century to another. Ever since language began, there have been stories concerning "Magic Words of Power," both sonic and written, which were supposed to link man and God together for some purpose indicated by the Word-Symbol itself. There was a belief that Man could say something which would persuade the God to do something. This developed to a point of arrogance when Man became convinced he could actually compel Divinities to co-operate with his whims. All sorts of ideas abounded, but their fundamental basis was that specially trained humans could indeed make intelligent contact with higher orders of being which lived invisibly and intangibly behind or apart from our ordinary world of matter.

Far from fading out in modern times, this communication-concept has condensed into scientific studies of consciousness which it is hoped will enable experts to computerize codes of pure energy impulses recognizable by intelligent beings beyond our earth, when a two-way channel of communication can be set up and operated for the mutual advantage of both parties. As yet there is no indication how far such experiments are progressing or what results may or may not have been achieved. The only certainty is that no information would be likely to reach a literate public which might deny or disturb its acceptance of authorities dictating the courses of civilized conduct throughout our socio-economic structures.

As it happens, the bulk of our past scriptures and other writings purporting to be "God inspired" consist of either admonitions calculated to encourage alterations of human attitudes, or projective ideas of what life might be like if we were better people living in different worlds. There is very little in any sacred literature or oral tradition to suggest satisfaction with the world we have made for ourselves on this earth. One might almost suppose that scriptures on the whole were communicated to and by dedicated revolutionaries against current states of stasis. Their single constant and consistent message is: Alter awareness. Change consciousness. We are frequently told what such changes ought to be, yet never told precisely how to accomplish this apart from praying and hoping for eventual enlightenment. If the Gods did or do communicate with us through recognized religious teachings, we are surely entitled to wonder how close their human translators came to the original meaning of their messages.

How would humans communicate with Gods anyway? By direct telepathy? Listening to voices in their minds? By means of oracles, through mediums, or some other kind of divination? All these and many more methods have been employed including simple prayer, but in the end the problem is one of how to bridge between the deepest and most recondite normal consciousness as intelligent human beings. It is not that we cannot communicate to some degree or another with the Life-Spirit which vivifies our Cosmos. As individual items of that Life ourselves, we must automatically be in some sort of contact with it whether we are conscious of this or not. The question is, can we translate this fundamental contact-sense into terms understandable by our average waking minds, if so, how and for what reason?

An important point is that only a very minimal fraction of humanity are interested in establishing communication between such opposite levels of their lives. The overwhelming majority are quite content to focus attention on the details of finite living in this world and occupy themselves with those to the exclusion of everything else. There is therefore a very limited field of human experience to call from when investigating the topic of conscious relationships connecting the human mind with its inmost sources of supply. Furthermore we are all too familiar with the many instances of unbalanced minds claiming direct contact with God and promulgating every kind of insane or dangerous doctrine. Obviously there has to be a "quality control" standard applied somehow, so that we may have at least reasonable confidence in any communication we receive from other than ordinary sources. There is no point whatever in trying to deal with "Deep Awareness" in ourselves unless this can be channelled through to our normal minds without harmful effects to all concerned. It is probably an instinctive appreciation of this fact which makes the majority of humans let the sleeping dogs of Divinity lie undisturbed in their own depths.

Perhaps it might help us to probe the problem a little deeper if we went back somewhat closer to its origins nearer the dawn of human history on this earth. So far as we know, men were much more familiar with the "Voice of God" then than they are nowadays. They heard it speak with every sound of nature. It uttered warnings, encouragements, soothings, stirrings, and every variety of sonic stimuli causing men to react with their environment and change consciousness to cope with each emergency arising. They learned by listening, and their lives depended on how they interpreted what they heard. Sight and scent augmented their ultimate decisions very greatly, but it was mainly hearing which alerted early man into action. What he could not see clearly or smell strongly was mostly likely too distant for immediate concern. Man has always depended chiefly on hearing to provide basics for his life-decisions. It is the first sense we develop in the womb and the last to leave our dying bodies. Without speech in aural, and its words in written form, we could not have developed our civilization.

Early man established sonic communication among his own species by imitating the noises of nature. Those would be further enhanced by visual motions of limbs and features possibly again with mimetic meanings. We can understand in our own times how the almost universal "SSSSS" warning sound came from imitation of a snake. The intention was to cause immediate stillness and silence, since it had been learned that sudden movements cause snakes to strike. Eventually the ejaculation has come to cover all situations demanding silence or alertness. Piece by piece over the centuries, humans built up their vocabularies by combinations of sounds they learned from natural life all around them. If a religious person can believe that the Voice of God can indeed be heard in nature, then it might accurately be said that the same God taught man to talk in the first place. In which case there really is a common language common to both levels of life.

Our most primitive speech was undoubtedly very close to that of animals, being a collection of their characteristic sounds mixed with elemental imitations and combined Sonics indicative of intention of condition. Man's basic need is to communicate his state of being, and then his intention arising from that state. He first says in effect: "I am this" and secondly: "I want - that." Something like: "Hungry - food. Tired - sleep. Frightened - shelter" and so on. By those simple sounds he hopes to arouse recognitive responses from other humans who might help him gain his objectives. From the first, our prayers were mostly a monotonous repetition of: "Gimme, gimme, gimme."

Chances are that early humans spoke very seldom until urged by sheer necessity. Speech meant effort of mind over muscle, and man's control of consciousness was still in its experimental stages. His instinctive reactions might have been rapid, but his creative thinking could be a very slow and frequently painful process. A man might live as long as he could on earth yet never achieve a larger vocabulary than was needed to cover essential necessities. He simply had no inclination to learn further. That is still true in our modern world. Conversely there were many individuals intensely interested in gaining sonic skills and inventing combinations of sound which attracted attention from fascinated human hearers. They soon learned the value of such an art in terms of reaction from their audience. Admiration and bribes were often forthcoming from hearers who enjoyed the experience. Perhaps needless to say, the descendants of such types are with us yet as entertainers, preachers, and politicians. Once they discovered that their vocabularies brought them actual power over people by persuasion or coercion, there was no holding their word-making back.

It was undoubtedly some of these sharper-witted folk who noted that specific words seem to automatically arouse set reaction-patterns from an audience. Those were words evoking energies arising from the well-springs of human existence itself. Survival words arousing fears, greeds, ego-enhancements, and other basic motivations behind human earth-life. It must have been very early in the history of Magic that its practitioners were discovering "Words of Power" which gave them advantages over other humans when used skilfully. From then on it was a case of straightforward progression to the "closed shop" for professional word-smiths. They soon had "Secret Names" for Gods and demi-Gods, leading to all the rigmarole bringing us to our present day state of jargoneering and computerization of consciousness.

Perhaps it is difficult for us now to understand the impact of names in really ancient times. Especially personal names. There was a magic in them connected with the identity of an individual which affected him to the very depths of his being. The name literally *was* that particular person, and whatever happened to the name also happened to him/her. No wonder it became a custom to take secret names which no other human must know except perhaps most trustworthy intimates such as blood kindred. To be identified in public by an authority figure and then hear its intentions towards the individual spoken of is still a profoundly impactive experience. Even today a legal arrest or sentence formula always employs the full name of anyone. Anciently it was often enough for the authority to point directly at the condemned man and say solemnly: "So and so, son of so and so, you will die!" Fear-inspired vagal inhibition sometimes caused the death of the subject on the spot, probably helped by the knowledge that he would be hacked painfully to pieces if words failed to accomplish what stones certainly would. Children still sing the: "Sticks and stones may break my bones but words will never hurt me" chant of defiance. We still consider it wrong to point fingers at people. Our ancestral memories are a lot longer than we think.

Naturally the most feared and respected names were those which might identify the Mighty Gods who controlled the environment allowing humans to live on this earth. To identify a God by name was to invite its attention at once, which could be a very risky thing to do. Possibly this is why humans frequently preferred to think of their Deity as a Mother-Figure. Experience had taught them that mothers treated their offspring better than fathers on the whole. Mothers fed them, and usually protected them from dangers. They might scream and slap but they seldom inflicted serious injuries intentionally. Moreover, they were available most of the time. Fathers were not only more remote, but liable to hit with heavy and sometimes fatal swipes. They could be more generous with gifts but were also dangerous to deal with. A Mother-Goddess was a much more approachable Divinity, and it was a long time before a Father-God became supreme in human concepts of their Heaven-home.

Even then he was not to be named with impunity, and most human God references were euphemisms such as: "Him, It-up-there, That, The Oldest, The Governor," and so on. Only important priests dared to claim they were on first-name terms with Divinity, and a particular horror of blasphemy or careless use of God-titles was common to most of mankind. To this day we do not really have a name for our Deity. The word "God" only means "that which is worshipped as source of good," while Jesus Christ means no more than "anointed Saviour." These are not personal names at all, and neither is Holy Spirit." Our Gods are still anonymous.

Man' s greatest breakthrough in language came when we began to pictorialise our words and so record thoughts for the benefit of posterity or a wide range of other minds able to interpret the marks made on stone, baked clay, or other convenient surfaces. At first, writing conveyed ideas by illustrating them. If a hunter meant to record: "I have killed three deer," he would sketch three deer lying dead with spears or arrows sticking in their bodies. It was only a question of time before a whole series of symbols contracted and conventionalized like shorthand until ideographs grew into a complicated collection of symbols expressing states of mind, emotions, and abstract speculations. Our written language evolved from the purely mundane towards the metaphysical.

The enormous improvement on ideographology came with the invention of alphabets or classification of human speech into a standard set of basic sonics each with its special Symbol. For the first time words could be represented as they were spoken and the readers could translate the symbols into audible speech within their own minds, thus clarifying consciousness very considerably and coming much closer to the writers original meaning. Of course this left less freedom for the reader to interpret the symbols according to his imagination, but it did guide his mind along channels leading in definite directions for specific purposes, so making him focus attention on points he might otherwise have missed or mistaken. Writing became a mixed blessing. On one hand it opened up awareness to information which might otherwise have been unobtainable, yet on the other, it often discouraged original thinking since it enabled people to stock their minds entirely with the ideas of other humans instead of creating their own concepts. This was one of the main reasons why later "Teachers" of spiritual systems, particularly the Druids, forbade the writing or reading of sacred subjects, preferring the old oral methods of passing them from one generation to another.

The major use of early writing was for commercial and other practical transactions between humans involving calculations and bargaining processes between interested parties. Deals could be done at a distance, and more importantly the terms could not be argued with or denied after conclusion. The writing was the word, just as the name was the individual. Moreover the use of an alphabet code enacted figures to be represented by letters instead of the older method of making separate strokes or ticks for each unit. It was much simpler to write *FH* instead of putting ninety-five strokes one after the other. As our consciousness evolves we tend to condense increasing amounts of it into less and less physical space. We also speed up the process of communication. Ideas which once took weeks to explain can now be imparted in moments. Extrapolation of this process indicates an almost incredible expansion of our consciousness within the foreseeable future. This all began with joining ideas one to another in slow succession so as to make sense between humans. It is ending with split-second linkage of multi-impulse energies to convey whole masses of consciousness between human minds and other orders of intelligence. The days of our baby-talk with the Gods are coming to a close and we are beginning to reach a higher and more adult level of communication with Divinity.

In primitive times and conditions the early training of a Shaman or God-mediator compelled him to wander around natural surroundings alone, listening intently to the slightest sounds from elements and wild creatures while reacting intelligently with all, and trying to interpret them in terms of his deepest instinctive understanding. He listened with ears pressed to earth, against trunks of trees, standing stones, under water. He strained to hear silence itself in the desert, and under every conceivable condition of environments unspoiled by man. With no other human to talk with, he was forced to attempt communication with the pervasive Life-Spirit expressing Itself through sheer Existence. Only when he had grasped something of the meaning and purpose of Life per se, was he considered fit to rejoin human company and help guide their destiny by his conduct and spiritual service to the community. It is rather a pity that this ancient practice is not more insisted on today. There is so much to be gained from it even in the difficult circumstances imposed on us by human encroachment into almost every inch of our environment.

Nearly every initiatory spiritual system advocated some form of this natural communication of consciousness between human and higher intelligence. Some worked out detailed programs of approach which almost amounted to an alphabet of instructions, and others left it entirely to the trainee how to manage his do-it-yourself letter-learning in company with the Gods talking to him through every voice of nature. Training by this method lasted for varying periods according to different schools of practice. Jesus on his desert sequestration and Buddha under his Bo-Tree are examples. Individual isolation like that was usually undergone by more advanced types of initiate. It became a more general custom to train in small groups so as to form collective foci of consciousness. Today the Zen system in the East, and the Quaker methods of the West are cultivated survivals of mediative meditational interpretation of Inner Intelligence. Both work by disciplined application of awareness beyond bodily boundaries aimed at higher than human sources of consciousness. Many other systems operate equivalent schemes built up by experience over the centuries, but in the end each individual must emerge for themselves and make their own unique relationships with Divinity as best they can.

Despite the discovery of writing, some spiritual systems still preferred transmitting their teachings by direct sonic means for one very good reason. The written word only reaches a reader's mind visually by means of an inanimate medium - the surface bearing the letters. In the case of oral instruction the message is mediated from one human being directly to another, and apart from any sonics it is also being "beamed" from teacher to pupil by immediate exchanges of psychic energy. That means the message is being imparted by straight contact between soul and soul on inner levels. Written teachings can but impart intellectual information from mind to mind, which is not the same thing at all. True spiritual teaching is only possible along direct lines that lie far above the limits of human words.

This brings us up against an inevitable realization that God or "the Gods" do not communicate with us in human speech or writing of any kind. That is not *their* language but ours. The most we can do is try and translate their consciousness into terms of our own as closely as we may, which process is necessarily governed by our skill and experience of the art. If we are to be honest, we shall have to admit that our efforts are always limited by the extent of our best knowledge, beliefs, and ability. Everything depends on our capabilities of mediatorship and natural gifts of communicative expression. No earthly "Teacher" of spiritual subjects could claim more than: "This is what came to me as I have interpreted it into our tongue. May it encourage you to seek likewise for yourself."

Many initiatory and other spiritual systems which see this point quite clearly because of long experience, believe that the best type of "Teaching" reaches human consciousness without written or spoken words being used. They have found however, that some kind of focal collecting agency is definitely needed to receive and concentrate the consciousness concerned. Mostly this will be a human being, though some suppose it possible for an invisible presence to locate itself focally through an inanimate medium and radiate its awareness towards humans within range. The Catholic Church has been practising this idea for centuries with the concept of a "Sacred Host" bread-wine medium acting as a concentrator for the consciousness of Christ. A literal host of other agencies have been employed by every sort of human seeking contact with Inner Awareness however described. From early stone monuments right down to plastic charms, men and women have made use of talismans intended to connect them with supra and infra human orders of intelligence. They certainly appear to achieve some measure of linkage between their objective and subjective levels of consciousness by such means.

So for quite a number of people looking for systematic

means of relationship between themselves and Divine Intelligence, it is sufficient for them to "sit in the Presence" of whatever agency they find brings them into best contact with their own highest abilities of Awareness. Some believe they absorb "Inner teachings" straight from the aura of their human mediator, and it is only necessary for them to stay awhile within its ambience in order to communicate with a common consciousness of Deity. The "Teacher" need not utter a single word, or conversely he may chatter away incessantly about the most trivial topics while his pupil are busily taking in truths from the spiritual silence behind his flow of words. His sonic speech is acting as an hypnotic which engages the lower part of his hearers awareness and prevents this interfering with direct communication along higher lines.

Methods of this vary enormously. Some chant repetitive rhythms for prolonged periods during which they try to raise the reach of their inner awareness and make contact with the consciousness they are aiming at. The Zen method of "sitting *zazen*" is particularly interesting. During this practice the instructor or Roshi gives a ritually positioned group their "*Koan*" or code-question, which should be just beyond logical reasoning and normal intellectual grasp. While they are struggling inwardly to reach some sort of conclusion with this, the Roshi moves quietly among the group sensing the currents of consciousness circulating amongst them. When he notes (usually by slight changes of posture) that the attention of anyone is wandering or losing force, he corrects this immediately by striking that particular student smartly on his spine with a short flat staff. The Roshi knows precisely which place to hit with exactly the right impact. Nerve stimulus should restore the student's concentration in the proper intensity for his exercise. The whole performance is highly disciplined and conducted with virtually military precision, its object being to aim at and hit a target far beyond range of ordinary human thinking so that an "explosion" of awareness at that point becomes possible. Maybe this is but a momentary realisation on our levels, yet a single instant of such Eternal Awakening in earth time is worth maybe a multiplicity of incarnations needed to gain it otherwise. The Zen school call this transcendency "*Satori*." This amounts to realising ones own immortal identity while yet inhabiting the body of a superior animal, which is the common aim of most spiritual systems.

Apart from advocating private prayers and meditations, the Christian Church on the whole believes in "preaching power" to stimulate conditions of God-communion. Some set phrase from scripture is usually taken by the priest-mediator-minister which is then supposed to arouse the faculties for mediating messages from Divinity directed at his congregation. The ensuing flood of words (mostly from the mind of the minister), are hoped to be inspired or modulated by the Divine Spirit of Life trying to make contact with its humans who are willingly awaiting Its word within themselves. Their scriptures tell them that this Spirit *is* a Word, or Expression of consciousness in and as Itself. If humans could actually hear that Word they would certainly be saved by achieving immortal entity in the consciousness of their Creator. Therefore they listen with bodily ears limited to a very small range of sonics while their preacher pours forth a spate of speech which is only too frequently nothing but noise that his hearers have not learned how to override and reach superior realms of awareness along inner lines. Masonic mythology also carries the legend of the "Lost Word" said to be originally given by God to Man which contained all secrets of the Universe. It became lost due to human perversity, and its rediscovery should be the aim of all right thinking "workers of the will." Once found and understood again, our troubles in this world would be over. Both Word and Will would be One.

Many Christian-oriented sects and groups have experimented with the so-called "Gift of Tongues" for a long time. This is actually one of mankind's earliest practices dating back to very primitive people. It meant that a human medium must induce a state of semitrance in themselves wherein control of the larynx would be transferred from focal to subjective levels of awareness. An almost involuntary tremor would then be induced to activate the vocal cords into glossal sonics which then developed and turned into articulations resembling speech, though seldom intelligible or recognisable as any conventional language. In the old days most of this was done by female pythonessa, whose male associated priest claimed to translate her vocalisations into ordinary human speech. This is nowadays practiced by Spiritualist mediums and Pentecostalists who usually leave it to hearers for finding whatever interpretation they can. If a careful enough connection is made with the coherent part of the subconscious mind, some very interesting and informative results may be produced with this method, though in every case these need to be assessed with extreme caution and critical judgement.

However much dedicated mystics of every system realised that genuine spiritual teachings simply cannot be put into human words, they had to admit eventually that both spoken and written words might be useful as symbolic indicators which at least pointed in the direction of Divinity. Words were the media of intellect, and this was a developing faculty of humanity likely to become the commonest method of expression among humans of the future. Therefore, providing the limitations of verbalism were recognised and understood, it could be usefully employed for the furtherance of Humano-Divine relationships. So symbols and scriptures began to make their mark upon Mankind. An advantage was that these enabled the intellectual content of Inner teachings and traditions to reach a much wider range of consciousness among literate people. A disadvantage was that literature tended to constrict consciousness within the limits of its definable and debatable circles. These might seem very wide to uninstructed humans, but in fact were very finite in comparison to the far-reaching sweeps of consciousness possible to those extending awareness beyond the confines of verbalism.

However much dedicated mystics of every system realised that genuine spiritual teachings simply cannot be put into human words, they had to admit eventually that both spoken and written words might be useful as symbolic indicators which at least pointed in the direction of Divinity. Words were the media of intellect, and this was a developing faculty of humanity likely to become the commonest method of expression among humans of the future. Therefore, providing the limitations of verbalism were recognised and understood, it could be usefully employed for the furtherance of Humano-Divine relationships. So symbols and scriptures began to make their mark upon Mankind. An advantage was that these enabled the intellectual content of Inner teachings and traditions to reach a much wider range of consciousness among literate people. A disadvantage was that literature tended to constrict consciousness within the limits of its definable and debatable circles. These might seem very wide to uninstructed humans, but in fact were very finite in comparison to the far-reaching sweeps of consciousness possible to those extending awareness beyond the confines of verbalism.

So in general throughout the Holy Mysteries, literature served to awaken interest, classify consciousness, and record routines of procedure or other intellectual indications of inner actualities. For the expression of greater conceptions pure symbology was employed to convey meanings above verbal limits. This was where mathematics came into the picture as a system for thinking in terms of abstract value-relationships. Originally it was a sacred science with an objective of enabling a human to comprehend something of Divine consciousness. Pythagoras observed his famous dictum: "God geometrises," and specialised in teaching his followers the use of pure values applied to formulating concepts leading towards higher than human states of awareness. To this day it is mainly mathematics which lead to scientific discoveries which ultimately must push us past humanity altogether into vastly greater areas of Life. It should be realised however that like other fields, mathematics are a strictly limited means of gaining spiritual magnitude and they alone will never achieve our ultimate liberation from bodily boundaries.

Throughout initiated circles it became recognised that written symbolism based on human language alone could only supply the early needs of awakening souls. Nevertheless, there seemed no reason why this should not be brought to as fine an art as possible. Through the centuries of our civilisation we have been working in this direction with varying degrees of success and considerable amounts of failure. There are perennial complaints that esoteric literature tends to be vague and incomprehensible, full of metaphors, hints, allusions and uncertain topics. From one point of view this is quite true. Authors with a limited vocabulary themselves have been trying to verbalise states of consciousness beyond words altogether. Some make a better job than others, but all are bound by their abilities of expression and the coverage of consciousness by any human language. We may suppose ourselves extremely erudite, but even the maximum extent of human erudition falls far short of requirements for reaching clear understandings of Inner intelligence. The most we can achieve verbally are approximations and reductions to our scale of thinking.

Comparatively few authors are capable of reaching very high up the scale. Poets have done their best, but mathematicians, musicians, and artists outreach them every time.

In modern times especially, most humans have fallen into the trap of deliberately confining consciousness within strict word-definition. If something will not fit into our narrow network of words we almost automatically refuse to recognise it. Anything outside our purely intellectual boundaries becomes an unwelcome disturber of our status quo, and is therefore to be avoided. It is true that we need to exercise particular care in introducing fresh varieties of consciousness within our working range, but it is also true that we may be losing the art of using words so as to liberate our awareness from their limits into wider worlds of Inner experience. Instead, we are trying to widen our vocabularies in hopes of covering all the consciousness around us clamouring for our objective attention. Sometimes this may partially succeed, but often it causes more confusion and misunderstanding than enlightenment. Sadly to say, such misdirection is often quite deliberately engineered by those with greed-gain motivations among both human and anti-human intelligences.

This literalisation of letters can constrain consciousness repressively. The old text: "The letter kills, but the Spirit gives Life" is entirely accurate. Letters only provide a body for meaning to live in, and if we keep mistaking body for soul we are losing something worth living for. We can see this plainly enough in those who take scripture at no more than word-value alone, often mistranslated and wrongly applied to circumstances of purely modern derivation. The misery they make for themselves and others is surely enough evidence of their inner conflictions. Self righteous souls are seldom very happy. On the other hand, unless we can rely on some common, or at least average meaning within our words, they will cause nothing but bewilderment and confusion. Ideally our language on several levels of comprehension, each built on a basis of the one closest beneath it. In that way, our consciousness can travel back and forth between the extremities of our understanding. To some extent this is possible already, though how many people make full use of the facility could be anyones guess. An accurate answer would certainly be a small minority figure.

Everything depends on how we want to use words. If they are only intended to communicate commonplaces with other humans, then restriction to that field should be legitimately accepted. If we mean them to indicate more recondite spheres of consciousness, we shall need some kind of mutual agreement amongst ourselves to determine their values in those terms. Words are the currency of our consciousness, acceptable according to prevailing rates of exchange on all the different levels of Life. Words which may purchase a great deal in this world might buy nothing at all elsewhere, and words we think worthless could well be of enormous value in higher venues. Like money, words are worth no more than their exchange acceptance, which has as many alteration factors as material finance, if not more. What we have to learn is the art of arranging transactions between different lifestates with interchangeable values of consciousness negotiable in all.

From the beginning of recorded history we hear of attempts by men to communicate intellibly with Gods or other categories of non-human beings, including demons or anti-human types of consciousness. Passages of scripture frequently commence with: "And the Lord spoke to Moses (or whoever it was), and said....." Evidently the Mosaic method of communication was via a "still small voice" or audio telepathy received probably while in a contemplative state of silence. In the light of modern science, we cannot entirely rule out the idea of micro-energy transmissions beamed at his brain by extraterrestrials intending to influence an entire people through the thoughts of their prophet. Such an alarming possibility comes closer to actuality in our times. How can we possibly guarantee that energies of such a nature emanate only from sources intending the welfare of humanity? If a human mind or brain can be sensitised enough to receive transmissions of intentionalised energy from other than our native states of Cosmos, then who knows from whence or whom they originate?

Old timers were well aware that by no means all Inner contacts brought benefits to our species of Life. They roughly classified such distinctions into "Guidance of God" and "Temptations of the Devil," depending on whether the impact of these influences impelled humans towards better or worse courses of conduct. At the same time they realised that neither type of influence was entirely irresistible by an average human being, and we had some latitude of decision which stream of suggestion we followed. This degree of determination was then known as our "Free will." It depended entirely on ourselves whether we were led "upward" along an Inner Line of Light towards eventual Identity in Cosmos, or were dragged "downwards" towards total extinction in Chaos. Most of the mystical and magical systems were concerned with learning how to evaluate such Inner impulses, make ourselves independent of either and evolve into a superior state of being beyond human fate altogether.

There are many legends traceable to early periods of our past concerning the "Secret speech of Angels" which very advanced humans might learn in order to gain information or make conscious contact with higher orders of Life who were helpfully inclined in our direction. Most of these stories have implications that indicate Angels did not use our language, but we might eventually come to understand theirs. This places "Angelic" communication above sonic range altogether. In instances where these beings were said to have employed plain human speech, they are supposed to have assumed a humanoid appearance at the same time. Whether this was a "materialisation" in the Spiritualist sense, or an associative mentalisation made by the mind of the hearer, or a mediated message through an actual human person, is seldom clear. For all we know, it might have been some kind of projected image from a transmitter in another state of Time-Space. The fundamental factor is that a communication of consciousness truly takes place between human and non-human species of life.

Be this as it may, it has been the centuries-old dream of most mystics and magicians to discover a common code of consciousness whereby Gods, Angels, and Men could communicate with each other in acceptable terms of their normal intelligence. Since humans have recently succeeded in making their ancient moon-dreams come true, there seems every likelihood that some day a "hot line to God" may become a practical possibility. Whether humans would really welcome observations on themselves from other angles of Existence is another matter. They may yet wish they had left well alone, and not insisted on attracted articulate attention from classes of Cosmic Life beyond their present means of living up to.

Meanwhile it is proposed to examine a particular system of

spiritual communication which was evolved several centuries back, and is yet in its experimental stages. This is the so-called Qabalistic Tree of Life scheme with its alphabetical attributions. We shall first look at its origins and ideology briefly, and then turn attention to practical applications. Though the basic ideas behind it are quite old, it seems to have enormous possibilities for future expansions of awareness. If its methodology can be modernised and put into practicable working order, we might make some significant changes of consciousness affecting the courses of our life-careers during this Earth-existence. All changes are most likely to be for the better, because the Tree-scheme by its very nature will not translate impulses of Inner intelligence into any evil meanings, whatever their origins may be. Which is more than can be said for many systems purporting to put human minds in touch with the Creative Consciousness that imagined them into existence in the first place.

B. The Talking Tree of Life

The Qabalistic Tree of Life and its attributes have been so thoroughly written up in other publications that there is no real point covering the same ground here apart from references and comments. So far as can be traced however, no one seems to have dealt with its alphabet coding by making mental links with modern languages, which is the topic of this study. Therefore we shall be breaking a fair amount of new ground. First let us have a few thoughts on its early developments and the general ideology behind it.

The basic scheme behind the Tree of Life is believed to have been conceived by philosophers seeking a single formula which would express our entire Universe in a way that human consciousness could grasp and handle so as to improve and increase our intelligent dealings with Divinity and Its intentions towards us. Many of the scholars involved were Hebrew, but they were associated with others who belonged to different official faiths, though most of them were emancipated from formal religions of any kind. They were all looking for fresh relationships with a common Life-Spirit through an intellectual and co-operative interest in the workings of Life Itself operating through every field of existence. Hence they tried to find some approach to the problem which might co-ordinate their combined conclusions. The "Tree of Life" as we meet it now is the result of several centuries effort among its designers.

Fundamentally the idea is a straightforward one. Take ten concepts intended to cover every category of Creation from God to Man. Connect these together so as to explain themselves in a logical and reasonable fashion. At the same time they should suggest openings leading toward Inner experience or expansive consciousness on higher than human living-levels. In other words the Mind of God and the minds of man might be provided with a useful meeting point. One might say the Tree growers were seeking a translation scheme so that God and Man could converse sensibly in a common tongue.

Why should the Tree of Life be ten-based? Probably because that was the oldest way of bargaining known by men making transactions without knowing a word of each other's language. All humans except freaks or mutilates had eight fingers and two thumbs. By means of gestures with these an entire code of wordless communication was possible, though mostly limited to commercial conversation. For example, to point at the sun and hold up two fingers obviously meant two days, whereas the moon would mean two months, and so on. Eventually this finger-talk elaborated into quite a language of its own, and experts could reach a fair speed of exchange. Early hunters used it because it was silent. Modern tic-tac men on race courses use it for convenience and codification of meaning. Previous Qabalists thought the principles behind finger-talking might be a good basis for learning how to talk with a God who seemed to speak without human words, and best in conditions of silence and stillness. Besides, they were hoping to strike some kind of a bargain with Him.

Nobody knows how long it took to arrive at agreement concerning the ten Concepts needed to cover our Universe from four angles, while allowing a Zero-idea to connect inconceivables with a human consciousness which could not yet imagine them. Eventually the Concepts arranged themselves into a natural geometric relationship, and since there were twenty-two direct lines of contact between them, the obvious thing to do was to identify these by characters of the Hebrew alphabet which was consonantal.

A curious point arising which most commentators seem to avoid, is this. Since the Hebrew alphabet was also their numeral system, why did they not start numbering the ten Spheres of the Tree by letters? Moreover, it was the Arabs who produced the cypher to identify a Zero-concept, and our modern numerals are derived from the Arabic system of mathematics.

Ancient Egyptians used special symbols for figures, and so of course did Romans and some other Mediterranean cultures. It seems clear that the Tree-engineers intended to identify the Spheres as pure values beyond speech limitations, yet capable of combination with each other to make units of definable intelligence. That is to say the Spheres of Life themselves might best be sensed or appreciated with our spiritual abilities, while harmonics between them could be grasped by our minds and rational processes of thought. The text of the "Book of Formation" (*Sepherr Yetzirah*) tells us that God created his Universe by "Numbers, Letters and Limits." That is by values, distinctions of awareness, and confinements within Time-Space. Perhaps it might be more correct to say that it is Man's consciousness of the Universe which is determined by those specifications. They are the intelligent appreciations through which we look at Life. Therefore it makes good sense to build up the Tree of Life glyph from a formula consisting of those basics.

Alphabets were originally composed from symbols representing the initial sonics of words in general use. *Alef* - the Ox, *Bet* - the house, *Gimel* - the camel, and so on. All quite common items of mainly agricultural or bodily significance except the last one, *Tav*, meaning a signature mark in the form of a cross. We used to teach our alphabet in a similar fashion saying: "A for Apple, B for Bed, C for Cat," etc., and the telephonic alphabet of initials is still with us. This is to say in order to clarify consciousness of letters forming a word, we associate a complete concept with each unit of that word. The whole word is thus made into a collection of concepts which may have no direct connection with its total meaning, yet help explain that meaning because they have helped our overall consciousness put it together piece by piece for analysis by our intelligent awareness.

The Tree of Life will do just this for us in a somewhat different way. By conjoining two distinct spiritual concepts, it produces a single intellectual issue. If we treat this like the letter of an alphabet and start combining it with others similarly produced, we shall begin making "words" in a language of its own which speaks from mind to mind. Not so much from one human mind to another, but between a human mind and an altogether higher form of mentality to which the very finest of our conceptions are but primitive and minor abilities of its awareness. In learning the language of the Tree, we come closer to understanding that of the Gods themselves.

In the case of a human language we first learn our words whole by imitating other humans and copying the way they speak. That is not very difficult as a rule. Plenty of people with quite a workable vocabulary never learn to write, read, or spell, so we call them illiterate. With the Tree of Life it is rather a reversal of this picture. We first grasp the ideas then the letters, then the words, and after that how to put the words together. It is like learning writing and grammar except that is a lot more difficult. To some extent it may be compared with solving crosswords, because a number of associated concepts have to be held in the mind at the same time in order to produce a related conclusion. Widely divergent items of consciousness have to be connected through devious and difficult lines before they all coalesce into a completed concept. That in its turn may be taken on higher levels as a unit among others of its kind forming part of a wider consciousness altogether. Metaphorically, we are but fractions of letters which "Gods" connect together to make words in their language. It would be as difficult to read their writing on its own scale as trying to understand banner headlines of a newspaper by studying it under a microscope. Yet if that headline were projected through reducing lenses it would become a microdot picture clearly readable to human sight focussed through a microscope tube.

As humans, we have a specific rate of awareness within a limited scale of consciousness. Even the greatest genius alive cannot penetrate beyond certain points. The Three Rings of our Time-Space-Event Cosmos confine our consciousness within their magic circles of Life. True, we are constantly though slowly extending those limits, but we cannot progress faster than our natural safety-factor allows without running considerable risks to the coherency of our consciousness which constitutes what we call our "sanity." Like all energies operating mechanisms, consciousness can really "burn out" minds unable to use it effectively through their working. "Blown minds" is a fairly good description of this in modern times. History shows what happened to medieval minds which tried to make closer contacts with Gods then they could cope with. Religious wars, persecutions, and other associated horrors and insanities are matters of relatively recent human memory. We have our own equivalents in terms of our times which are just as terrifying if not more so. Unless we are able to keep our conscious contacts with Inner intelligence controlled by boundaries of reason, they may do us more harm than good.

That is why the Tree of Life system proves so reliable. It may seem very slow compared with others, yet it builds solidly on a spiritual scale enduring a lot longer than a lifetime, and a great deal more safely than a drug-induced flash of insight without relevancy or cohesion of consciousness. It works by steadily expanding awareness through linking humanity's highest concepts of Creation with quite ordinary levels of existence, adapting our awareness on each level so that one flows into the other naturally enough along lines of communication resulting in rational and satisfactory progress for minds and souls committed to its pathways.

To use the Tree of Life as a consciousness-converter, we have to learn how to THINK THROUGH IT. It has to be set up at the back of our minds as it were, so that all our thinking filters through it both ways. The Tree covers every type of thinking a human mind can tackle, and has the unique effect of aligning our consciousness with the purpose of the Life-Spirit living through us. Once it comes into practical operation as a sort of console controlling the consciousness of a human being, it will have the apparent power of changing evil thoughts into good ones, neutralising harmful currents, stabilising thought processes, and generally organising our inner awareness so that we come to realise the meaning behind our lives and our relationships with the Invisible Universe.

Few humans have any form of central control over their thinking at all. They would not dream of buying a car without an instrument panel, a typewriter without a keyboard, a television with no control knobs, or similarly useless productions. Yet they will think their thoughts along reaction-patterns conditioned and suggested by factors outside themselves with repetitive monotony and unenquiring lack of interest in life below its most superficial surface. They drift from one current to another as the stress of circumstances carries them from point to point between birth and death. Such control as they sometimes try and exert amounts to pressing random buttons in hopes of something happening. They may occasionally be very lucky on lower levels of life, but until they learn how to take over control and guide their living from a higher vantage point in their "Chariots of Consciousness," they will gain little from life except another experience of incarnation to boil down for the sake of its Golden Drop, if there is one worth finding.

Some humans do try and set up some method of centrally controlling their conscious relationships with Life, but use very short term materialistic values as push buttons. Providing these are correctly patterned they will work, but only within their very limited capabilities. They cannot carry consciousness outside the areas they serve, so they are not much use beyond those boundaries. Conversely we find so-called "spiritual" people whose guidelines are so vague and undefined they lack any effective coordination or directive drive. It may sound all very well floating along from one life to another on the strength of "Gods Goodness," but Divinity projects Itself with strength and precision through the Cosmos of Its Creation. We have to learn how to live according to at least a semblance of such a system, and that is exactly what the Tree of Life was designed to represent.

So the first thing we do is think of and about the Tree of Life with an objective of discovering how to think *with it.* Thinking *of* it supplies information, but thinking *with* it brings actual intelligence. The channels between the Spheres on the Tree were called the Paths of Intelligence for that reason. Spheres were for soul-sensing and feeling with, while Paths were for mind-working and thought processes. In that way, it was the deep feeling of Divinity acting on life which determined the thinking of whoever was using the Tree-Paths for focussing the forces of their minds. Thus "converse" could be held between humans and the Creative Consciousness behind their beings. Because we are now "word thinkers" concentrating our awareness of Life into alphabet-associated chains of thought, the linkage of Paths with letters of our language allows translation in our terms of intelligent thinking. Originally the language had to be Hebrew but now that the English alphabet has been arranged to cover the Paths of the Tree, we should be able to use our native tongue quite normally.

For those of us who learned to speak and write the ordinary way, the Tree of Life scheme means that we shall have to re-learn our language in alignment with its system. This implies a great deal of hard work and patient application. To memorise an alphabet code may not take a great deal of time by itself, but to attach enough meaning to each unit so that this effectively evokes consciousness from our deepest levels of Life when used, can be a very prolonged process. Each Sphere and every letter has to be worked with again and again until an automatic system of thinking begins to build up and show some results in our realms of normal awareness.

Anyone supposing this might bring amazing supernatural knowledge, revealing secrets of the Universe or advantageous information about the stock market or racing results, had better be disillusioned at once. It will not necessarily do any such thing. The object of the exercise is to put our ordinary everyday awareness in this world into closer conscious contact with the Life-directing Intelligence of Divinity behind our beings. That it will indeed do. A Jungian psychologist might say it was a system for making direct links between our objective and subjective minds meeting in the Universal Unconsciousness. An occultist or mystic could consider it a matter of Higher Self governing lower self by revelations of intentions. A religious individual might believe he was listening to God speaking within his soul. A magician would perhaps suppose he had discovered the secret speech of Angels which brought "Knowledge of, and conversation with, ones Holy Guardian Angel." However it is thought about, the Life-Tree letter-system amounts to the same thing. A communication code with ones own normally dormant sense of Divinity. Something of little or no interest to materially minded people solely concerned with affairs of this world, and their socio-economic successes therein. Alternatively of the utmost importance to someone looking for Life beyond boundaries of physical bodies, and having an intelligent interest in other types of existence than those confined to expression on this earth alone. The final decision whether or not to devote time and trouble for following this particular system must rest entirely with individual investigators.

The obvious starting point on all this work is learning the Tree of Life itself from top to bottom and inside out. Doing this by rote is something most people of average intelligence can accomplish fairly well. Learning what to do with it afterwards is entirely another problem. A dull child can learn the alphabet, but it takes a brighter child to build a vocabulary with it, and a brighter child still to become a fluent and interesting speaker or writer. Shakespears are few and centuries apart in our world, and neither does an ability for counting to ten produce many Einsteins, though even his brain had to begin that way.

Books may and do supply intellectual information about the Tree, but even the best of them can only go so far in laying out its plan, ideology, and authors' opinions or experience in connection therewith. All very helpful and interesting no doubt, yet necessarily limited in coverage and presentation. If every book about the Tree were read and grasped from cover to cover, that would no more produce a practitioner of its principles than reading descriptive textbooks alone could produce a qualified surgeon or any other professional person. The Principles of the Tree have to be lived in practice, before they will teach us the least thing about the Language of Life they speak from one level of spirit to another. What is the use of suggesting that an "S" sonic in English expresses the harmonic between the Principles of Beauty and Honour to someone without any real concepts of, or beliefs in either? As well play the finest music to a tone-deaf and disinterested hearer? To him it will only be noise.

Therefore before the Tree will start speaking its unique language to anyone, they must first have found each Sphere within themselves and formed clear concepts of relationships between these according to the Tree-plan. It is utterly insufficient to think about Mercy qua Mercy and "place it on the Tree" in theory. The Principle has to be identified in oneself and recognised as an individual relationship with a Divinity having the same quality albeit in different degrees and applications. The Ten Principles or Spheres of the Tree are all qualities which humans should have in common with their Gods, thus forming a mutual bond of the best kind between them. Relationships based on such an agreement can only be beneficial, and any conversation or conscious connection coming along such lines is bound to be both enlightening or encouraging, however much it may have to deal with the worst experiences encountered in Life at all levels.

So it is definitely not enough to sit contemplating pleasant pictures of the Tree while thinking nice thoughts about it. That is a necessary exercise during initial stages of introduction to it, but where do we go from there once our minds have grasped its rudimentary mechanics and lay-out? Ritualisation of its arrangements will help considerably if only part way along the paths of its projection into Life. Nevertheless we should not overlook the possibilities of psychodramatic art for coalescing the concepts of the Tree into formalised forces of consciousness. Anything that assists our inner awareness to come forward and manifest its meaning through our human living is well worth trying, and ritualism is as old as humanity. Its potentials are not yet exhausted because they have never been fully developed, so there is plenty of interesting material to discover and use in the light of contemporary consciousness.

Ritual is basically the practice of co-ordinating and concentrating our consciousness between Inner and Outer living by means of rhythmic and repeatable energy-patterns linking both levels. Our purely physical senses are intentionally associated with their equivalents on higher and hidden areas of expression, so that what happens at one end of this combination will tend to reflect itself at the other in its particular terms of reference. In our times we can think of this as an electronic circuitry connecting our bodies, minds and souls with the Spirit of Life for the sake of a communicative experience. Ritual is always a kinetic expression of living as contrasted with contemplative states of storing up spiritual energy in potential form. Therefore meditation is a natural approach to ritual, and it is always a good idea to begin every type of rite with a meditation, however brief.

Designing rituals is exactly like designing any other construction of consciousness. There has to be an objective in view and appropriate ideology arranged systematically so as to lead the awareness of participants thereto by the most practical and preferably the most direct means. We have to remember that in this case we are dealing with Western People who are seldom prepared to spend a single second longer than strictly necessary on formalised spiritual activity. They also expect an element of entertainment in their rituals in the sense of being dramatically impressive and intellectually impactive. Strictly speaking, it is best for Westerners of variant Life-attitudes to design their own rites, since they are so unlikely to accept others without critical and conflicting opinions. Conflicts of consciousness are part and parcel of Western struggles for independence of spirit. Early non-conformists used to speak of "wrestling with the Spirit," meaning their inner psychological struggles between instincts and imposed idealism. The original Western way of accepting very generalised procedures for communal practice, and highly specialised ones for individual or small group working is a very useful method of tackling this problem. Nevertheless since ritual arranging is somewhat of a skilled art, it seems most practical for non-adepts to start with some ready-made system until they develop their abilities enough to commence ritualising on their own initiative. With this in mind, let us see what we can do about using modern methods of ritual to help us understand the Language of the Gods behind the Talking Tree of Life.

C. Thotols: Keywording the Tree of Life

All ritualising of the Tree of Life has to start with its basic pattern. It becomes a matter of using every practical means we can think of for sinking this pattern deeply enough into the awareness with which we relate ourselves to Life along its main levels. We can dance the Tree, sing it, hear it, see it, taste it, smell it, or invent any scheme we will for making the Tree "come true" as a realisation of our inmost relationships with Cosmos and Its different degrees of consciousness. What we have to remember all the time is that the Tree does not show the actual truth behind our beings, but is a workable Symbol for that truth which we can grasp and handle so that it will lead us in the right direction. That is as good as we expect to find in this world, and we are unlikely to find better for a long time to come.

Everything really depends upon what type of ritualism is favoured. The essential factor is to associate each one of the Ten Spheres or Principles with specific classifications of consciousness which connect with our spiritual structures projected into existence on this earth. We can take the old Hebrew ideology if we like and translate this into modern terms, or compromise with it and approximate its meaning into more familiar language. There is one point to be very careful about if we insist on updating all the old terminology. In making the mechanics clearer, we must never lose complete touch with the element of "Magic" behind them. That is the indefinable "soul" which brings everything to life and Inner importance. A long time ago it was said "Change not the barbarous Names of Power by a single syllable." There was a certain amount of good sense in this, because those were sonics linking right back to our very early times, and they could clear human consciousness back to its beginnings on earth when we were struggling with our Gods as best we might. Maybe the sounds we made then did not stimulate our purely intellectual perceptions, but they awoke or intensified instincts which brought us a lot closer to contacts with Creation Itself. So we should not make the mistake of banishing all the "Magic" connected with the Tree just because it seems clever to make everything sound modern. We could quite easily lose more than we gained by converting vital concepts to commonplaces or important allusions to mere trivia.

The old classification of consciousness on the Tree was fourfold. Originative, Creative, Formative, and Expressive. That is to say apart from our spiritual end of existence, Life-consciousness condensed as it were, and focussed down into limits of the finite human mind. As St John put it, "The Word became flesh." So for the flesh to "Know the Word" this process has to be circulated onwards along the return route. Put another way, we have to alter the condition of our ordinary awareness from its normal focus and broaden out the beam of consciousness enough to encounter the Creative stream of Life behind our beings. Otherwise God and Man meeting each other half way along the communicative channels of consciousness between them. There is no reason why we should not use the old descriptions of these arbitrary divisions rather than say "State A,B,C, etc." On the other hand there is everything to be said for single-headed call symbols intended to evoke awareness of enormous areas of ideation into our focalised forces of mind.

This coverage is important, because it employs only one unit of awareness to represent and release powers involving far greater and more effective energies usually lying dormant or in reserve at our deepest Life-levels. That is why invocations of "God Names" can work. They really amount to quick call-ups of conscious forces we normally have no great need for in dealing with routine daily affairs. Under pressures of emergency a "God Name" was once a vital Key-release of Inner consciousness, desperately essential to assist escape or at least for ameliorating some threatening situation. It might summon enough intelligence to help someone cope with things on his own, or it could communicate enough with others to attract their assistance, and, if sufficiently strong, might even launch some psychic stress factor into a predicament, which could alter it. Failing everything else, it would help adjust the utterant's awareness to the actualities of what was happening. So only good could result even by negative effect. It was scarcely surprising old-time people had a horror of blasphemy which would automatically weaken, and eventually wipe out the power of such "God Names" to summon help from the Divine depths of human consciousness with speed and efficiency. It is a pity we seem to have no equivalent sonics in our times. Copulation and excreta are very sad substitutes, even though psychological grounds might be argued for their usage as biologically expressive expletives.

Therefore in keywording the Tree of Life, we can either use concepts saved explicitly for that purpose, or we could use convenient sonic symbolism with some attached prefix which indicates its application to the Tree for such an instance only. Whatever it is, it must direct attention to the Tree and nothing else. There should be no tracking our minds aside to remind us of advertising gimmicks or TV programmes and the like distractions. Our consciousness has to be coded so that it will lead us to the Tree by the quickest and most direct line. A century or so ago this was relatively simple, but today our crowded minds have to be dealt with in rather different ways. Even the Principles of the Tree are connected with sheer commercialism. To mention Beauty may link minds with cosmetics, Foundation with corsets, or Victory with bonds. We have to identify our ideas with a clarity beyond suspicion of confusion.

Grammatically we can do this by tacking on "of the Tree of Life" to whatever Concept or Principle we are thinking of, but this is a very cumbersome and clumsy device indeed. Most of our modern "Magic words" are acronyms, or words made up from the initials of some complete descriptive phrase. Radar and Laser are examples. So why should we not do the same here and specify Tree-meanings by means of a conditioning acronym? Let us try and choose a really satisfying one while we are about it. Supposing we settle for the slightly unusual title **THOTOL**. This derives from **T**he **H**oly **T**ree **O**f **L**ife, and pronounces not unlike "total." There is thus an immediate suggestion of completeness and thought, almost like "Total Thought," or "All Awareness." Surely a good word to invent.

With this simple device of objective consciousness we have secured the Tree-speech and Concepts from contamination by unwanted interference or other intrusions as far as we can. To stipulate that our thinking must be "Thotol," means that it had to follow the system and pattern of the Life-Tree plan. We could go a bit further and specify that our Inner speech is translating into "Thotolese," or that we were "Thotolosing," instead of thinking about and with the Holy Tree of Life. The more we get used to the word and give it significance by employment, the better. That is providing we use the word in no other sense except dealing in some way with the Tree. To try and make it mean anything else would spoil it entirely. So long as the word has no other meaning apart from the Tree it will remain potent. It is fairly easy to adapt with grammar and fits naturally enough into normal phraseology as an acronym.

Armed with our new word, we may head-up the Tree Concepts with power and precision. To merely speak of "Concept 1" by itself does not concentrate consciousness nearly enough. What sort of Concept? We could say in full, "The first Concept of the Tree of Life" and so on, but how clumsy compared with "Thotol One" which carries every thought concerned with *Keter* the Crown-Summit in that single specific heading, once consciousness is properly compressed into it. That can only be done with a lot of work and effort just like learning shorthand, but once accomplished its advantages are enormous. Not that we always want to think in shorthand, and spelling out words by syllables is not only needed for babies. Adults can sometimes make useful points thereby. Nevertheless a gift for "speed-reading" does enable humans to cover an enormous amount of conscious ground which extends awareness a long way past the limits of average intelligence. Therefore "Thotol" will be a vitally descriptive word for us, if we do not abuse it. At first we shall probably have to employ it quite a lot in order to get accustomed to it, but as it gathers significance, an occasional usage will be adequate to serve its best purposes, and though it may never supplant the full phrase of "The Holy Tree Of Life," it is about the most practical adjunct of this sublime Design to arrive on the scene recently.

The aim for first-stage grasp of our Thotol alphabet is a state of practical familiarity with every Sphere, and recognition of their relationships with each other and the entire Plan, so that consciousness can be classified and concentrated in an instant to cover all workings up to current condition. That is really a formidable task which has to be tackled the hard way at first. Whether the Tree is learned by any special system or simply by gradual acquaintance and investigation, the upshot has to be complete familiarity with its format and ideology to a steadily increasing degree of awareness. Everything also depends upon individual interest and determination to discover its deeper meanings. As yet there would seem no limits reached in those possibilities. There is always something new to be discovered on the Tree somewhere. Who knows what the limits to human consciousness may be? To say nothing of consciousness experienced and used by higher types of Life co-existing with us in conditions of Cosmos almost beyond our believing. Beings existing in energy-states independently of what we call "matter," of whose existence we have no "evidence" at all except intuitively and inferentially, somewhat supported by such communications of consciousness we have been able to translate into our own terms. So far as we are concerned, they are our "Gods" whose language we are attempting to learn through our Thotalised streams of thinking. It might help a bit if we briefly recapitulate some principal headings of the Ten Concept-Principles, trying to find perhaps an angle or two which has not been written into the ground already. The pre-first Concept is of course:

Thotol 0

The Eternal Negative Existence. All we have not yet become that we intend to BE, and all that we have no intention of ever becoming. The Unexplored Universe. Apparent Emptiness. The word "Nothing" in Hebrew derives from two small interjections — "*Eh na*" signifying "What (or where) now?" In modern colloquial speech, "And so?" That makes all the difference in the world as to how the Tree-Zero Concept should be approached. It is the Eternal Enigma of Life which we will never solve on this earth, yet without it our lives are indeed as Nothing. Take it away from us and we have nothing really worth living for. Change the letters *AIN* (Nothing) to *ANI*, and this means "I, me-who-is." The becoming Self. In Arabic the word *Ain* also means a well-spring. The Fount of Life. The NIL which produces All. In the West, we make the mistake of equating our word "Nothing" with unimportance and insignificance, whereas in reality it is the supreme meaning behind all possibilities of being anything. "Nothing is greater than God" means exactly what it says. Infinity behind Divinity. A Law larger than Life. We cannot think *of* Nothing, but only *with* it. The most we can do is search for symbology which might inspire us to become living Question Marks aiming ourselves at an infinitely receding reality from the Voice of the Void. In arriving Nowhere, we shall encounter everything else on the way. However we connect ourselves to this Preconcept of the Holy Tree, the entire chain of consciousness has to be focussed in mind through use of the magic formula: Thotol Zero. A specification and numeral selected for the sole purpose of collecting our consciousness concerned with Infinity.

Thotol 1

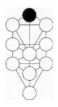

Here we have a concept dealing with Ultimate Being at the very Summit of Life or Crown of Consciousness. It is the absolute end of our evolutionary experiences, and the Single Spirit which contains all Awareness in Existence, so that its incalculable individual lives amount to only ONE. At the end of everything, there is only One of us all. This is It. Thotol One. Every idea of Uniquity, our slightest suspicions of a controlling Cosmic Consciousness, beliefs in the possibility of a Supreme Being. The mere suggestion of a purpose within our Life-stream which is steadily leading us towards some inscrutable state of perfection. These are all intimations pointing in the single direction of Thotol One. Whether we will ever arrive at this pinnacle with awakened awareness in communion with Its Life, and participating in Its powers, or alternatively be broken up for fuel to supply Its energy-expenditures, It will have to employ us one way or another because we are essential to Its ecology. The Tree teaches us that we do have a choice in deciding our ultimate fate, if we really intend to individuate through our incarnationary experiences, and evolve beyond animal body types of human housing. It further indicates that such is the very reason our Gods are ready to talk with us, if we are capable of listening intelligently. They, like us, are linked to the Single Life Spirit evoked in our ordinary awareness by the Tree-Concept Thotol One. They have specific functions and obligations to fulfil within the Great Life analogously to those of our Microcosmic organisms in our lives. It is all part of the Serial Story they are trying to tell us for the sake of our eventual education and possible inclusion in the "intelligence network," which amounts to a "nervous system" distributed throughout the Cosmic Corpus. Like them, the complete cycle of our existence begins and ends with Thotol One. That must be the "magic word" initiating every train of thought leading us along any lines connecting with this Concept.

Thotol 2

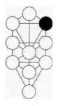

Now we come to a special category of consciousness sometimes considered "male" because of its analytical characteristics as contrasted with its complementary stream of intuitive or "feminine" awareness. It is really one side of a polarised power which cannot exist without the other. This "duo-division" of Life is the primary pattern of its initial activity. Life cells multiply and commence making themselves into complex constructions by the simple process of splitting (mitosis) and subsequently recombining in another fashion. The Tree does exactly the same, and did so long before biology became an exact science. The root "bios" (the two), indicates the male-female nature of all living creatures even when both occupy the same body. Here we have the essence of masculinity per se, its old title being Wisdom. This puzzles a few people who associate that word with femininity in the Scriptures due to the bi-valency of gender. It could be used either way like the Greek Sophos or Sophia. Wisdom as a principle is common to both sexes, but either may use it as their polarity determines. In this case we are considering the male half of humanity, and its equivalent cycle of energy in Creative Consciousness. An ideal human being may be a perfectly balanced combination of both sexes in one individual, but we have not yet evolved to that point on this planet, and therefore we should think about taking the facts of life as we come to them. We must never forget the Tree of Life is a Perfection Pattern, and we have to see its Spheres and system only in the light of whatever helps humanity develop and grow towards a condition of "Divinity" relatively to our present position on the scale of Existence. So in using Thotol Two types of consciousness, we should be specifically directing ourselves into good relationships with Deity as a polarised power from the "masculine" angle of approach.

Thotol 3

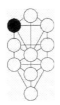

Thotol Three is the equal and opposite complementary of Two, and neither could exist without the other, like halves of the same body. We usually think of it as "feminine" because its awareness is of the intuitive type. One might say the gestative sort which creatively develops and brings forth what Thotol Two implants embryonically. If Two is the seed then Three is the soil and its nutriment. Two may be the inspiration of an idea, but Three is the soil and its nutriment. Again, two may be the inspiration of an idea, but Three is its germination until it is ready to emerge as an independent unit of intelligence. Theologically, if Thotol One were the Holy Spirit, and Two were God the Father, the Three would be God the Mother. God the Child does not appear until Six, the apex of another trinity. The sequence is logically One, Two, Three, Four, but with the Tree design Spheres Four and Five are essential Life-adaptive factors assuring the mutual relationship of Six with Two and Three. Considered for itself, Three is the matrix of our consciousness carrying it into constructive continuity and keeping it going from one generation to another until the end of Time. Birth and death alike are equal events here. This is the Mother from whose womb we emerge and whose mouth eats us up at the end of an incarnation. We cycle our living through Her. She is Nature on a very high level of Life indeed, and we are only One species of her Cosmic children inhabiting this temporary home. Our happier habitat is the depth of Her subconscious mind where we may dream securely in Her womb, awaiting projection into whatever objective world She sends us. When we have worn out our welcome there, She will run us through a regenerative process and think us out again, so long as our little lives contribute something of value to the Whole Idea behind everything. Summoning all contacts with this kind of thinking by the single concentration point of Thotol Three, might seem an unlikely proposition, yet it can be done!

Thotol 4

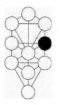

Thotol Four could be thought of as the ne plus ultra of "Live and let live." Mercy on a scale almost akin to madness, except that method saves it from exploding itself to extinction. Here we have the analogy of the human male orgasm which pours millions of sperms out with apparent abandon. "Let them all have an equal chance" cries their cheery Creator at the starting line placing sporting bets on likely winners. We might well imagine a genial Father God holding a human race-meeting for his entertainment. Some old wit thought God invented Man with a shout of laughter. May we hope not to be disinvented some day with a sigh of regret. Laughter is actually a very high form of worship, and here is its origin in the release of rightness as a flood of fulfilment. Providence with a capital P. All the resources of Cosmos assured to anyone willing to accept them regardless of responsibility or price of payment for them, all the benefits of Jupiter with their cunningly built-in banes. Every expansive (and expensive) idea of improvement and enhancement of Life. Blessings, benefices, and wonders worked on our behalf through alignment with this class of consciousness. Virtually no end to the liberality and compassion of a Creative Consciousness anxious to build Its human play-people into the best specimens they are capable of becoming. Put in childlike terms, the better we make ourselves, the happier God would be for His own sake. Though commonsense should be curtailing our notions of euphoria, it is still pleasant to think we can have contact with Thotol Four on tap by concentrating its meanings through that single phrase.

Thotol 5

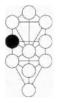

Thotol Five brings us up with a salutary pause. This is the law of strict selection for the sake of survival. One sperm out of millions is saved. One individual out of many will reach puberty. Few out of those will make old bones. Spiritual survival works on the same principle. Unless this control factor limited the largesse of Four, our lives on this earth, and probably elsewhere, would have become impossible long ago. Both Four and Five are indispensible to each other for the economy of Existence. We may be reminded of the Good Fairy godmother who wished the pampered princess a little trouble, to counterbalance the idiotic plethora of gifts the other immortals had presented, but she knew very well what she was doing. It is often true that Thotol Five seems to over-control our lives, but while we swing them around so widely and wildly in this world, it has little other option. The Cosmic laws of compensation are exact in the end, even if they take many of our little lifetimes to operate. There is no question whatever of "Divine punishment" in the sense of an offended God retaliating like an upset child on misbehaving humans. There never was. It is simply that Cosmos can only keep functioning correctly by balancing Its condition continually. We have to do the same in our small states of being. If our bodies cannot correct their unbalances adequately—they die. Literally we have to wipe out millions of viral and microscopic lives every day in order to go on living. So does God - with us! To save what we need, we must eliminate whatever threatens its integrity. Insofar as we ourselves are involved with the Lifestream of Cosmic Consciousness, the Law by which It lives compels It to take equivalent measures with us. If we become incompatible with that Consciousness, It must ultimately and automatically either neutralise us, or convert us into absorbable energies. Nothing more complicated that that. There are very wide issues involved here with Thotal Five, and they will all come under that heading once we can work it as a call-sign.

Thotol 6

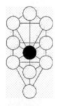

Thotol Six is the point of Balance and Harmony in the entire Tree-Plan. The general picture so far is that consciousness originates at One, separates at Two, gestates at Three, expands at Four, contracts at Five, and now settles into its regular Life-rate at Six. All Life-systems have natural rhythms which are regulated by some special center, and this is it on the Tree, which is why it corresponds to the heart of a human body, or the Sun in our planetary scheme. Every idea linking concepts of centralisation, harmonious relationships among groups, beautiful arrangements of associated units, and similar connections has a Thotol Six connotation. In fact without it, Life as we know it could not continue here at all. Four and Five would cancel each other out at their level and short-circuit back to their origins. That is what happens with a still-born child. Birth and death cancel one another. Focussed from Thotol Six, the Life-force can continue projecting closer to our world by its normal procedure of going from one extremity to the other and then coming to a compromise between both. That is the way Life works, which is why Thotol Six is connected with the "Redeeming Principle" of mankind and associated with a Messiah or Christ-Concept. If we can once get past Five and reach Six we have a chance of continuity in consciousness, and so long as we keep contact with Six somehow, we are unlikely to be eliminated from existence down the Abyss of the Abandoned. So all thinking along such lines from any direction may be linked together by Thotol Six.

Thotol 7

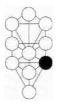

Thotol Seven is a Life-quality which amounts to the triumph of our best emotions over our worst feelings. Here are all the ego-expanding experiences which develop us into sensitive appreciative souls, realising the loveliness there can be in Life for those able to live it with even a fraction of Divinity conditioning their consciousness. Here the rhythms of Six are translated into dancing and music, movement and singing. This is the consciousness enabling us to constantly improve our artistic and aesthetic standards of living, making us want finer and fuller lives along such lines for every other human being. It governs the civilised side of our natures from every angle of emotional and empathic approach. This is what gives real depth to sex-relationships between people, and makes them of spiritual importance and significance. Consciousness through this Sphere is one of our most wonderful achievements in this world. Without it we should lead very dreary and colourless lives with no vivid and heartening experiences to bring us confidence, that there is more to Life than mere survival from one body to another. Thotol Seven is where we gain some incentive to look above the lowest levels of mortality, and see something joyous and gladsome behind the surface of everyday existence. It may be that relatively few human beings experience Thotol Seven to very intense degrees many times per incarnation. In fact it can be unbearable to a killing point for those unable to mediate its energies properly. Nevertheless, even an average assurance of its inner reality from time to time will help most people through otherwise desperate periods. Thotol Seven holds more than welcome lifelines to otherwise hopeless humans struggling with waves of depression and worse in this frustrating world. It is a remarkable feat achieving ability to summon its state at will, by means of the Keywords linking all contacts with its happy conditions of consciousness.

Thotol 8

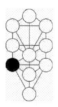

Thotol Eight is the complement of Seven along purely intellectual lines. This is where mankind develops its technology and science from, together with literature and skills connected with inventive applications of awareness. As Seven was concerned with music, so Eight is concerned with mathematics. Our modern electronics and other techniques for dealing with the finer forces of nature, derive from our Thotol Eight type of consciousness. It has led us along a line of intelligent enquiries into the workings of our universe, while we mastered one secret after another sufficiently to have produced our present civilisation, and it is now pointing us a long way past this planet. Small wonder it was called the Glory of our Life-Tree. Admittedly its uncompensated energies could quite well destroy us, and we need to learn how such curbs can sensibly be applied to regulate a flow of consciousness beyond our power to handle properly. Undiluted intellect is too raw a spirit for humans to stomach comfortably. Thotol Eight is needed to control the overabundance of Seven just as Five works with Four, but, likewise its constraints and specifications should act as conditioners, which channel consciousness along living lines aimed at the perfection of our species as a whole. Intellect is useful for rationalising emotion compatibly with our advancing spiritual status, but unless it is tempered with the warmth and kindness of human feelings, it can shrivel our souls to a frightening extent. Once the best blend of consciousness is made at Thotol Eight, the result will be ready for flowing into Thotol Nine.

Thotol 9

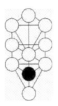

This is a "collecting in" of consciousness in order to make a basis, or foundation, out of which to construct lives which have some coherency and continuity of meaning. We could call it a pool of thought or reservoir of basic beliefs. It is full of dreams, ideals, and ancestral memories, together with all the seperate items of inner awareness we need, for making ourselves into whatever we aim to become in each incarnation. Thotol Nine holds our immediate source of supply behind the workings of our everyday consciousness. Perhaps we might think of it as a wholesale warehouse from which we stock the retail shop, where we transact business with other humans like ourselves. We could also see it in reverse as a collecting point, where we hand in quantities of consciousness we have processed by our own living and thinking, so that this may be sent back to source along lines of Life linking with our particular origins. Here we have a consciousness which speaks with us in symbols, representations, and impressions. Because of its reflective characteristics, Thotol Nine was connected with the Moon by earlier Qabalistic students. It actually forms an adaptive filter allowing humans to deal safely with modified intensities of consciousness, which might otherwise drive them insane. This is something like the way our atmosphere protects us from Solar and other radiations, which would kill us in their pure state. One way or another, we need Thotol Nine all our lives to protect us from potencies we could not cope with unshielded. In one odd sense, we have to rely on our dreams to save us from our realities, until we make those dreams come true enough to handle harmlessly. Once we appreciate the function and value of Thotol Nine, we might have more respect for the so-called illusions of Life, and realise why it is often wrapped up in so many protective layers which we rip off wantonly at our peril. How many of us can remember the shock of our births as we were suddenly stripped defenceless, and shot naked, wet, and wailing into this alarming world? Thotol Nine has an analogous function to the placenta while we are yet spiritually enwombed, awaiting our awakening on higher Life-levels. It does that for us, and a lot more besides which we can discover by enquiry.

Thotol 10

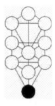

We should all know quite a lot about Thotol Ten, since it is this very world around us and the consciousness we normally employ for living in it as best we can. In particular, it is the consciousness concerned with the constant improvement and development of humanity as a species of life on this planet, and our prospects of living away from it in better conditions still, whether in physical form or otherwise. That is to say it is really the consciousness of the Gods working through us. Humans with no wider views on Life than those confined to single-incarnation limitations, are not likely to appreciate this aspect of Thotol Ten awareness, however much they may be influenced by its subtle action on themselves. Why anyone should suppose all their thinking and intelligence originates only in their own minds, encouraged by what other humans have been thinking, is quite a minor mystery. In old days people believed their Gods talked to them through Nature. Nowadays some might suppose telepathic communications reached them from some other dimensions of Life, or more simply via Space from Life-forms outside our Solar system. Whatever happens, the end-effect is that the reach of human consciousness is undoubtedly extending in range and qualities over the centuries, and we have witnessed a great leap forward during the last space of a single incarnation. Thotol Ten has made its most impressive movement for many millennia.

So there they are, the two fundamental types of consciousness which have the God-like powers of lifting humans from purely animal levels of living, and evolving us into altogether higher and finer specimens of sentient beings. It should be particularly understood that Thotol terms deal exclusively with consciousness of this perfecting kind. If we choose to disregard its promptings in ourselves, and deliberately follow counter-currents for one incarnation after another, there will be none to blame but ourselves for eventual reduction to non-entity. This awareness of immortality does not speak through the Tree of Life alone of course. It contacts us in every way capable of reaching the human heart and soul. The Thotol system is but one way devised by humans and their Gods between them for communicating with each other to some degree of mutual recognition. Like other systems it is limited by individual ability of humans to align their 'Inner sensoria' with agreed arrangement of integrals, and their willingness to work at this until able to apply the art to their actual living and thinking.

The first completed stage of this ability is gaining such familiarity with the Ten Concepts, that they can easily be called to focal consciousness by a single call-up. For normal minds this demands a lot of concentrating and meditating every day, until it is possible to hold the Concepts as states of actual Inner experience for more than a few moments. This means to say that if we are working on Thotol Five for instance, we have to create it as a state of mind and soul in ourselves by imaginative artistry, and stay in that state long enough to recognise our relationships with it and realise its significance in our lives. In other words it has to be as real for our minds and souls as a physical contact would be for our bodies. There is no denying this takes a lot of effort to achieve.

To "take the Concepts in from outside" as it were, we have to absorb them as any lesson is learned, particularly through ritualised psychodramatic methods. In these days with the aid of tapes, files, projectors, coloured lights, musical effects, and all kinds of similar equipment now within range of even modest incomes, there should be some quite powerful and interesting arrangements contrived. Imagine, say, a small modern Temple set up to mediate a Thotol Four experience. Lighting of the correct blue flashing at fourfold intervals, or in groups of four, would be one method of starting. So would a full-detail Tree of Life plan with Thotol Four spot-lighted. A lot of lighting effects are possible. Cedar, or some Jupiterian scent could fill the air. Music would be to match, maybe "Jupiter" from "The Planets" by Gustav Holst. There would be velvet or similar rich fabric to feel, nor should taste be forgotten. A sweetshop is the obvious place to look for something with a Thotol Four flavour, or for real enthusiasts, an entire meal could be concocted to suit each Concept. Additionally, a projector might show changing scenes, symbols, or even whole moving episodes entirely connected with Thotol Four topics. Anything whatever is in order providing it links directly with Thotol Four through a human sensorium. For those with means and ability, it could be a delightful pastime to plan and perform a whole set of Thotol experiences from one end of the Tree to the other.

Perhaps needless to say, yet advisable to remember, no amount of elaborate procedure and expensive equipment is of the slightest use, unless conscious attention within such framework is held and exercised strictly according to the spirit of the Concept being worked. The mind especially must not be allowed to wander from the fundamental frequency of the Concept while it is under consideration. Nor is that enough. The soul too has to coincide in its feelings with what the mind is thinking. Everything has to be a whole experience, integrated by the individual or group conducting it. In point of fact, there is really no need for any of the costly and decorative ritual gear at all. It is a great help for those who cannot keep their minds focussed easily, and probably a benefit during the first experimental runs through this system, but sooner or later the early cumbersome exercises have to be superseded by neater, faster, and increasingly improving techniques. People should not normally continue communicating with picture books for the whole of their adult lives.

The very simplest equipment will serve perfectly well. A

hand-made and detailed chart of the Tree is an essential to start
with. If a copy of: "The Office of the Holy Tree of Life" can be
obtained, this could be a help also. It is a collection of statement-
invokations dealing with the traditional characteristics of each
Concept, plus one for each Path conjoining two Concepts. It is
these especially we are concerned with here, since we are
considering the alphabetic basis of our God-language. Reading the
Office at the rate of a Path a day, is a very practical way of
commencing work with the Tree alphabet, but there is no use
progressing to this until each Concept can be called to
consciousness, banished, and replaced by another in the matter of
a moment. Nor is this a casual flicking them over with no depth of
contact. Everything depends on the depth of awareness used rather
than its duration. At first we have to work slowly, in order to
achieve penetration of perception. As we progress, we should reach
the required depth with increasing rapidity, then move from
Concept to Concept so that these spell out the pattern, syllables,
words, and sentences of our God-talk. In that way we shall soon
begin to build up an Inner vocabulary of spiritual speech.

What we are in fact doing is learn to talk all over again, but
this time in terms of "God-language." We are deliberately
associating items of consciousness together, which are specifically
connected with the Divine Perfection Plan behind our lives and the
Cosmos we live in. Each collection of items is being taken as a
single sonic. Combinations of double sonics become letters, in this
case consonants only. Our five vowels associate with the Elements
of Life, symbolised by Air, Fire, Water, Earth, and Spirit or Truth.
The consonants are taken as the bodies of words, while the vowels
are the enlivening Spirit without which words by themselves are
dead. Thus each word is really a concentration of consciousness
from a vast source of supply, concerned with our survival and
status as individual integers of the One Great Life comprising our
whole Cosmos. In other words, we shall be learning how to speak
intelligibly with our own Immortal Identities, and recognise the
reality of our spiritual selves with our ordinary waking
consciousness.

How long it takes to get a basic grip on the Ten Concepts
of the Tree and their interrelationships, is a matter for all to
discover by their own efforts. Parrot-learning and superficial

skimming is nowhere near enough to expect any noticeable results from. The only sensible thing to do, is continue working away until the Tree begins "talking back" by entering the mind of its own accord, and relating itself with specific Life-situations. For example, something might have happened, which necessitated a swift and stringent countermeasure of disciplined action. If this automatically suggests a Thotol Five situation, then the Tree is indeed relating itself to Life through the consciousness of the individual concerned. In other words, it is "coming alive" or making itself felt from inside someone in connection with ordinary experiences. When we start measuring the conduct of our lives in this waking world by the scale and standards of the Holy Tree, then we shall be ready to make more elaborate use of its other facilities.

There are endless opportunities for practice, and inventing exercises is an interesting experience by itself. For instance, we could look for Thotol Concepts wherever we encounter numbers in ordinary ways. Try looking at the number of a book-page and seeing it simply as that, then think: "This is Thotol numbers such and such." Make a flash-contact with them at the same time. Then switch off and see it as only a page-number again. Try this with car numbers, telephone numbers, any kind of numbers, until they start suggesting the Concepts by themselves, yet always keep control of the decision whether to see ordinary numbers or their Thotol linkages. Develop and practice the knack of seeing figures from either viewpoint at will. Look at a watch-dial and think: "It is half past Harmony" or whatever. At eleven the Abyss might be thought of, and at twelve, Zero, so the whole Tree-scheme could be considered over the course of a day. For those who like prayer beads, the "Qabalistic Rosary" is rather a lovely procedure. It is similar to the Christian rosary in decats of ten with dividing single beads, and a Tree of Life instead of a crucifix. The large beads are for meditation on the Spheres and Life-Elements, while the small ones are the Paths between them.

It could be a good plan to include Life-Element work with that done on the Sphere-Concepts before Pathworkings are seriously began. What this amounts to, is a comprehension of Life under four main headings, grouped around a central Concept, and poised between the extremities of God and Man. This Cosmic Cross arrangement has been exhaustively dealt with elsewhere, and here we are principally concerned with its communicative function via its associated vowels. This is sufficiently important to think of in some detail, since it outlines the principles involved when tackling the consonants of our "God-Language."

D. Vowels and Life Elements

The old familiar Magical Elements of Air, Fire, Water and Earth were supposed to be the four Principles from which living Creation was constructed. Philosophers eventually added a mysterious Fifth Element of "Aether" or Spirit which was the inherent Truth of Life. It was carefully explained to Initiates that the perceptible phenomena known to mankind as air, fire, water, and earth, were actually symbols illustrative of unknown energies responsible for maintaining Life throughout Cosmos.

Living creatures breathe or need atmospheric air in some way to stay alive on this planet. They also need body-warmth, fluids, and solids for the same purpose. Even if all those were present, there would still have to be the vital principle of "Spirit" to animate an otherwise dead body. So the Four Elements of Life are really prerequisites which make this world possible for the Fifth Element to manifest here. We might call them the rock-bottom basics enabling us to become human beings. These Life-Elements would have some kind of equivalent in any world we lived in, physical or otherwise. Whatever we call them, they constitute an environmental condition compatible with our species of creature, so to think of them as Elements is quite a valid description. Every art, science, or construction of consciousness has its "elements," and Life is certainly all of these and infinitely more.

The elements of speech and consequently alphabets are the vowel sonics, without which no consonants could be combined to make any sense. Those can be lined up with the Life-Elements simply enough like this:

A (pronounced "ay") as Earth, the solid sound of a thump
E (pronounced "ee") as Air, the light sound of a whistle.
I (pronounced "ah-ee") as Fire, the crackling sound of a flame.

O (pronounced "oh") as Water, the flowing sound of a river.

U (pronounced "oo") as Life-Truth, the acknowledgement of actuality.

The last sonic, *OO*, *HU*, or *IEU* is one of our very oldest God-names. Most of the "Secret Names" of the Gods were vowel combinations alluding to the fundamental forces behind Life from one angle or another. The "unpronounceable Name—*IHVH*," mostly transliterated *Yahweh* or *Jehovah*, was the vowel combination *IAOUE*. Not pronounced, but breathed. That is uttered without closing the mouth. Its Latinised form of course is *IAO—YO-WEH*, or *Jove*.

Associative exercises linking vowels and Life-Elements together are straightforward enough. It all depends how far anyone is prepared to go in pursuit of this practice. The objective is to make each vowel represent an actual experience of living rather than a merely intellectual mention of It. In old times, magical initiates were literally pushed into contrived situations which positively forced them to focus attention with utmost intensity on the meaning of whatever was being driven into the depths of their consciousness. They were not just told things, shown them, or advised to read about them. Their magical lessons were imparted as symbolic living experiences which altered awareness on causal levels of consciousness. They had to work attentively at them or they might die from a single careless move. In our times troops are trained to cross country with live ammunition aimed above their heads. They learn to lie low very quickly. We might bring some of the old magical lessons up to date without applying quite such drastic stimuli as the ancient idealistic methods of naked exposure to howling winds on hilltops, burial to the neck in earth, swimming in dangerous waters, and submitting to branding with hot irons. Yet it cannot be denied that such ordeals endured for the sake of accepted ideas were certainly conscious-changers of a very definite kind. Nowadays we should call them stress-techniques.

Short of such methods we shall have to substitute more regular ritual procedures, and hammer home little by little the points which would otherwise have been driven home forcibly and unforgettably. It is now more a matter of arranging illustrative and impactive psychodramas, for the association of vowels with the basics of Life. If we set up the sense-sonics for each in turn, we might arrive at something like this:

A ("AY") EARTH

Touch:	Anything giving impressions of weight and solidity. Earth itself, stones, heavy cloak, etc. Roughness, heaviness, coolness, dryness, slow.
Hearing:	Slow dragging and thudding sounds, cavernous echoes, deep drumbeats, very low notes, stones being struck with stones.
Sight:	Darkness or very dim light. Caves or vaults. Earth-colours. Symbols suggestive of Earth. Lights should be screened so that no source is visible. The scene can be night if required, but no stars.
Smell:	Fresh earth if possible. Otherwise thick heavy incense such as dittany or poppy.
Taste:	Raw mushroom, or whatever stimulates Earth-Ideas. Roots of some kind maybe.
Action:	Slow regular-rhythm dancing, low and deep chanting, invocation of Earth-Mother or Earth Archetypes such as Archangel Auriel. Prostrations, considerable accentuation of *EH* or *AY* sonics, periods of silent seated meditation. Mimetics of digging, striking a staff on the ground. Lying listening with ear to earth.

E ("EE") AIR

Touch:	Anything very light and insubstantial. Loose free clothing, feathery ornamentation. Breeze blowing with varying intensity.
Hearing:	Wind in trees sound, whistling, wind instruments suitably orchestrated. Birdsong.
Sight:	Sky blue colours, cloud effects, symbols of Air. Dawn-morning light for preference. Sunrise.
Smell:	Any fresh, natural breeze-born scent or incense suggestive of some Pine forests, heath, light flower

perfumes.

Taste: Effervescent and "fresh" flavours. Aerated drinks. Soda water.

Action: Graceful "flying" dance motions imitative of birds. Invokation of Air Archetypes such as Archangel Raphael. Whistling in a high key with accent on *EE* sonic, Invokations of Air Archetypes such as Archangel Raphael. Sword whirling exercises or fanning activities. Imitations of birdcalls.

I ("AH-EE") FIRE

Touch: Warm-feeling yet light garments. Place must be well heated, dry, and sweating encouraged. Air can circulate but it should be warm. Nudity permissible if high temperatures employed.

Hearing: Crackling flames. Any "fire" music, especially orchestrated for strings.

Sight: Bright lighting wavering for fire effect. Symbols of Fire. Full noon illumination. Colours to match.

Smell: Woodsmoke. Pleasant cooking or roasting smells. Frankincense.

Taste: Hot spices. Ginger wine or warming drinks. Peppermint.

Action: Swaying semi-static dancing varying from "brisk flame" to "glowing ember" movements. Invokation of Fire Archetypes such as Archangel Michael in firm ringing tones. Accentuation of the *AH* sonic. Great care must be taken to emphasise the beneficent aspect of Fire at all times. Lamps or candles may be lit. Incense offered.

O ("OH") WATER

Touch: Theoretically should be water but practical difficulties impose problems. Could compromise with a basin of water in which hands are dipped and face laved. Enthusiasts might swim in a pool or dance in the rain. Anything to convey wetness.

Hearing: Recordings of water sounds and suitable orchestrations. Rain pattering, tinklings. Sistrum shaking.

Sight: Green-blue lighting, wave effects. Symbols of water. Evening illuminations. Sea-sunset.

Smell: Seaside, seaweed and ozone. Lily perfume or similar scent.

Taste: Plain water, preferably from a spring.

Action: Swimming movements, including floating. Invokation of Water Archetypes such as Archangel Gabriel. Accentuation of *O* sonic. Lustration in a ritual bath. Meditation while rocking gently as if moved by waves. Handwashing.

U ("OO") TRUTH-SPIRIT

Touch: Normal sensation of comfortable vesture at a pleasant temperature. Nothing constrictive or awkward. Everything smooth and easy.

Hearing: Natural background of wind, sea, shingle, and beach fire, or suitable orchestral pieces. Organ music. Chanting.

Sight: Daylight colours of all kinds. Symbols of all elements. Iridescent effects. Time and season changes of lighting.

Smell: Varied scents of stimulating kinds.

Taste: Changes from bland through sharp, hot, bitter, sweet, etc. Complete with something leaving a sense of satisfaction.

Action: Comprehensive. Walk, run, dance, hop, jump, stand, sit. Move as inspired. Invoke Universal Truth of Life under whatever Archetype recognised. Accentuation of the *OO* sonic. Invoke its action on and in own individual life. Sing or recite code of belief and standards followed in pursuit of Truth learned through living.

This is the briefest outline of Elementary ritualism. The idea is to tune each agency of awareness in keeping with whichever Element is being worked. An entire experience is dramatically contrived to condition the overall consciousness into maximum harmony with the central theme being mediated. As a rule, there is no need to practice such a performance more than a very few times before the ideology becomes deeply enough rooted in a mind and soul to operate of its own accord with maybe an occasional prod to keep it going along the right lines. Very elaborate rituals are principally for conditioning commencements of conscious courses. Later they should shorten and condense till virtually imperceptible to a casual observer, yet remaining fully effective from Inner angles of Time-Space which have no noticeable intrusions into our normal Life-dimensions. It is as if we took a whole section of our Time-Space-Event consciousness and turned it end-on at right angles inside ourselves. That is to say a series of events over a normal hour long can be polarised so that their whole content would be retraversed in the slight fraction of a second with barely a flicker of muscle-tension anywhere. Yet the total intrinsic value of such compressed consciousness remains constant. Our whole lives are everything we have ever been, said, thought, done, or intended, all concentrated into the split instant of our NOW. It and our Eternity are identical in principle, though constituting the Alpha and Omega of Time in our Life-dimensions.

If the vowel associations can be made to the necessary depths of awareness without all the sensory conditioning, then whatever is superfluous may be dispensed with. It might be possible to achieve associative identification by less complicated means via simple audio-visual stimuli only. For example, gazing at the vowels painted in appropriate colours and forms while listening to or reciting short mnemonic versicles. A set of cards can be made with the vowels, verses, and maybe the magical symbols of the Quarters on them. A brief workout with these at odd opportunities would eventually drive them a little deeper each time toward the causal levels of consciousness underlying our commonplace waking state of awareness.

By these and any other available means we have to recognise and realise the Life-Elements in ourselves and our Universe. For instance with *I* (ah-ee) we resonate the heat of our bodies, force of our minds and fervency of our souls. With *A* (ay) the solid structures of our bodies, the stable dependable thoughts of our minds, and the enduring qualities of our souls. With *E* (ee) the breath of our bodies, freedom of our minds, and aspirations of our souls. With *O* (oh) the fluids of our bodies, fluency of mind, and fluidity of soul. With *U* (oo) the Truth of ourselves relatively to Life through all its Elements. Everything amounts to condensing and concentrating consciousness from wide fields into very fine force-foci. That is the essence of the exercises we shall be engaged on in this work. Once upon a time there was a mystical belief that everything in Existence could be summed up into a single Word, and that Word was the "Ineffable Name" of God. If nowadays we could conceive every energy as reducible back to One Prime Power, we might get a more modern understanding of the Universe.

The question is one of relationship between two totally different Life-states. How are Gods and humans to talk with each other unless they both agree on some mutually acceptable scheme of awareness? If our millennia are but moments of "God-Life," what sort of time-twist would be needed to adapt their thinking with ours? They would have to use some kind of "reduction-gear" which relates our consciousness with theirs, and we would correspondingly have to accelerate our consciousness until the two altered streams of awareness came within recognisable range of each other.

Let us put it this way. What amounts to a single word of "God-talk" might cover an extent of our consciousness which would take millions of words to tell in ordinary human language. So if we could represent that same extent of consciousness by a single symbol or short combination of symbols, we might come a lot closer to learning the Language of the Gods. Similarly, if they "conversed" with us by combinations of basic Life-consciousness reduced to terms we are capable of appreciating, they would come closer to perfecting the part we were designed to play in their Cosmic ecology. All this is exactly what we are trying to do through this "Tree-talk" system. By making each letter of our alphabet sum up and symbolise collections of consciousness which have taken us centuries of study and application to acquire, we are developing a code calculated to communicate with those whose consciousness contains ours like a mind holds all its individual thoughts.

By getting used to vowel-association first, we are preparing the way of dealing with the consonants, which are somewhat more complicated since they are resultives of double-concept combinations. There is no real point in trying to rush ahead with consonants until the vowels are properly absorbed. That will be known when they start "talking back" of their own accord. When elemental associations put letters into the mind, they are reaching basic levels. Perhaps garden digging suggests *A* (ay) sonics, wind in the trees whistle *E* (ee), lighting the gas or fire snaps *I* (ah-ee) at us, and washing up murmers *O* (oh). Not continuously of course, but enough to sound as if the source came from outside our ordinary consciousness like thoughts arriving unexpectedly which claim attention.

Keen Tarotists will naturally see the Elements as the four suits of cards, and there is no reason why they should not if this will help them classify the Life-Elements through one Thotol Concept after another from top to bottom of the Tree. The original designers of these remarkable cards considered that Life as we know it on this earth was divisible into four parts, viz. —

Gladness
CUPS
WATER

Learning		**Earning**
RODS		COINS
FIRE		**EARTH**

Sadness
SWORDS
AIR

Or the Good (Cups), the Bad (Swords), Obligations (Coins), and Opportunities (Rods). Other comparisons can be made under any suitable quarternal headings. By marking a scale from one to ten, an attempt was made to cover every contingency of Life from top to bottom of its Ladder. That is why the cards line up with the Tree and parallel its Pathways. Any decimal view of Life from four angles must do the same. People were classified by the Court cards also into four kinds of dominant characteristics. Tolerant (Cups), Exacting (Swords), Industrious (Coins) and Sociable (Rods). They were further divided into males and females of mature or immature natures. Mature males are Kings, and immature Knights or Princes.

Mature females are Queens, and immature ones Pages or Princesses. Any individual human is bound to be covered by one of these categories unless insane or otherwise excludable from average human company. The Tarots seemingly were not intended to deal with the detritus of Life, but only its redeemable or perfectible properties, human or not.

So according to the Tarots we react with Life gladly or sadly while we learn and earn our way through Cosmos with it. Quite a reasonable way of looking at things from a human viewpoint. Combined together they form the four strands of the Truth-Cord which connects the incidents of Existence with each other as a continuum of consciousness. To see how this quarternal thread joins up all the Thotol Concepts in a Tarotically presented Tree, we might begin looking along these lines.

Thotol 1

Cups	Gladness in Life	Heavenly hopes	Pleasure
Coins	Effort in Life	Willing Work	Profit
Rods	Interest in Life	Alert attention	Purpose
Swords	Sadness in Life	Constraining care	Pain

Thotol 2

Cups	Glad Wisdom	Enjoyable experience	Happy choice
Coins	Earned Wisdom	Rewarding experience	Careful choice
Rods	Learned Wisdom	Grasp of intelligence	Determined decision
Swords	Sad Wisdom	Sadder but wiser	Difficult decision

Thotol 3

Cups	Glad Understanding	Cheerful concord	Pleasing encounter
Coins	Earned Understanding	Deserved discovery	Dedicated design
Rods	Learned Understanding	Acquired knowledge	Widening outlook
Swords	Sad Understanding	Bitter experience	Unhappy affliction

Thotol 4

Cups	Glad Mercy	Welcome beneficence	Kindly ideas
Coins	Earned Mercy	Rightful rewards	Appreciated affluence
Rods	Learned Mercy	Thankful thoughts	Festive feelings
Swords	Sad Mercy	Suffering spared	Peace after pain

Thotol 5

Cups	Glad Severity	Sacrificed happiness	Lost illusions
Coins	Earned Severity	Distressing deprival	Poor prospects
Rods	Learned Severity	Salutary lesson	Taught through trouble
Swords	Sad Severity	Defeated schemes	Abandoned struggle

Thotol 6

Cups	Glad Harmony	Blessed beauty	Sweet sympathy
Coins	Earned Harmony	Deserved delight	Patience repaid
Rods	Learned Harmony	Cultivated control	Dignity displayed
Swords	Sad Harmony	Tranquility in trouble	Protection in peril

Thotol 7

Cups	Glad Victory	Alluring ambitions	Seeming success
Coins	Earned Victory	Patient progress	Worthwhile work
Rods	Learned Victory	Situationary skill	Opposition overcome
Swords	Sad Victory	Empty triumph	Dangers delayed

Thotol 8

Cups	Glad Honour	Search for satisfaction	Quest for glory
Coins	Earned Honour	Honest achievement	Admirable activity
Rods	Learned Honour	Attaining aim	Laudable attempt
Swords	Sad Honour	Bounden duty	Precarious position

Thotol 9

Cups	Glad Basis	Hearts desire	Wish won
Coins	Earned Basis	Social success	Pleasure provided
Rods	Learned Basis	Lesson learned	Warning and worry
Swords	Sad Basis	Fear of failure	Rueful regret

Thotol 10

Cups	Glad World	Benign brightness	Happiness ahead
Coins	Earned World	Advantageous affairs	Prosperous proceedings
Rods	Learned World	Information gathered	Facts found
Swords	Sad World	Bloody betrayal	Ruin and wreckage

So there we are. The Tarots are a set of symbols covering about every possibility of ordinary life which humans are likely to encounter in this kind of world. Reading them is a question of interpretations in the light of modern meanings and focussing the fundamentals down to fine points of projection. They can certainly help very considerably in thinking out concepts and ideas connected with the Life-Elements as traced through the Tree. A single Element could be taken and followed right up and down the Tree from Concept to Concept. Then again, one card might be selected and pushed along its line of significance from one angle of meaning to the next. It is a useful scheme to keep a "Tarot book" with loose-leaf pages, so that the meanings of each card can be extended by meditation and thinking, as fresh ideas about them arrive. Possibly the Court cards might be compared with real people known to the recorder, or public figures which relate. The

Trumps could be linked with actual incidents connected with ones own life or other people's experiences which seem apposite. In that way the cards could interpret living in terms familiar to the enquirer, which is really what they were designed to do rather than tell fortunes.

The meaning of each card does not lie in its design, but in whatever its fundamental formula evokes from the consciousness of an interpreter. To some extent the cards are like Rorsach blots which suggest all kinds of things to different people, yet have specific limits of rational interpretation with each. For instance, if an intelligent person were asked to classify the gladness of Life into ten stages of importance with an example of each, we should have that person's concept of the Tarot suit of Cups. The same could be done with the other suits and the Trumps identified by twenty-two Key ideas concerning Life, Death, and the Universe. In other words, every thinking individual has a Tarot already in them. The packs we use are no more than artist's conceptions of common ideology, relating humans with their shared state of existence from a Western viewpoint.

Theoretically a Tarot pack need be no more than seventy-eight cards with nothing but names on each for identification. "2R" should be enough to invoke every idea about the Two of Rods in a skilled Tarotists mind. The cards are only headings for long chapters of consciousness in the Book of Life. Nevertheless, various designers over the centuries have somewhat standardised their visual presentation, and we have more or less come to accept many of their features on face-value. At the same time there is no doubt that specific packs suit individual interpreters better than others, and it becomes a question of discovering which pack is best for any particular person. The solution lies in finding the pack which evokes the widest and deepest reaction from anyone's subconsciousness. This is only possible if several are studied, and careful notes made of results, to decide the issue. Possibly the most evocative of modern packs is the Waite-Coleman Smith issue (Rider-Waite pack), on account of its intricate detail and involved symbology, but mention should also be made of the Regardie-Wang pack based on Golden Dawn ideas. This series is clinically clear with no superfluous sidetracking, and links in with most of the advanced studies covering human psychology. In the end however, the choice of pack depends on whichever has the closest visual affinity with someone's subconscious mind.

Once all the Life-Elements and Thotol Concepts have been connected with the vowels with the help of Tarot symbology, we can start concentrating on the Path-consonant arrangements. Providing that the necessary preliminary work has been done faithfully, this last stage should not be too difficult because the early techniques learned are the same which apply here. Should many serious snags be encountered, that would mean the early work was not accomplished adequately, and revision must be carried out until consciousness is sufficiently conditioned. This will be known by the ease with which combined Concepts are identified in the mind by their call-up codes, and the impressions they convey of linking the mind concerned with them to superior sources of intelligence. Let us next try a tentative run-through of the consonantal Path-plan of the Tree and see what happens.

E. The Tree Alphabet, Tarot Trumps and Pathworking

Each consonant of the Tree alphabet is formed by the confluence of two Concepts. To utter them consciously we have to focus awareness on both Concepts simultaneously. At first maybe we must think of them sequentially, but step by step this has to be advanced until the two extremeties blend into a single mid-resultant symbolised by the alphabetical sonic. This is really no more than the Tree-principle of "Right-Left-Centre," or "Plus-Minus-Neutral" extended in practice. It is a basic Law of Life. Always follow the centre path between extremities. Between Black and White, follow the thin Gold line. Buddha called it the "Norm" and made it the central point of his Life-philosophy. Our Life-Tree is arranged on the Three Pillars of Life, and we are always being told how important it is to regard the Middle Pillar as the ideal Way of Life, even though so few humans can actually follow it. Here we are trying to do exactly the same thing between the Concepts of the Tree, by treating each pair as outer Pillars, and making a Middle Pillar of Path stand for the relationship significant to both.

This is not easy, it demands an ability to hold two enormous pools of consciousness in focus under a single symbol-heading each, then merge these into reactive relationships with each other so that an energy eddy is set up between them which takes on an identity of its own, symbolised by an alphabetic consonant. Since each Concept already has vowels attached via its Elemental associations, there is always a good supply of these for connecting consonants into pronounceable words.

The old way of thinking about Paths on the Tree was by numbers. The Concepts went from 1 to 10, then the first Path from Concept 1 to 2 become Path 11 and so on. Strictly speaking this was a misnomer, since a Path is not a Concept but a connection between two of them. It may be difficult to change already accepted ideology, but it would be more correct to think: "Thotol 1 and 2 - B" instead of "Path Eleven." In the first place we are identifying the Concepts in question linked with a representative symbol. In the second instance we would be using an inaccurate enumeration for conjoining Concepts, since One and Two cannot possibly make eleven by any stretch of the imagination. If we were laying out the Tree by a point system starting from Zero, we might fairly say the first Path was the Eleventh point of the Tree and carry on from there. But we are not doing this. The Tradition is most forcible and persistant in saying "Ten and not Nine, Ten and not Eleven." There is no Eleventh Sphere and never was. We only use an "Eleven" idea with the Tree by making it "Ten plus One," and so forth. Therefore the Path identification by ordinary figures was a convenience which served a useful purpose but was scarcely in keeping with the fundamentals behind the Tree design.

If we are going to employ conventional figures to symbolise the Sphere Concepts of the Tree, it seems but reasonable to keep the figures for that specific purpose and adopt Letter symbols for identifying the dual-Concept Paths. This in fact seems to have happened with the old Hebrew-letter attributions. Here they were evidently meant to be thought of sonically rather than numerically. Using our modern English alphabetical linkage with the Paths, we should have but little difficulty in thinking "Paths B and C," rather than "Paths Eleven and Twelve" (or more correctly Paths One and Two). It is probably asking a very great deal from people accustomed to thinking in terms of previous Path enumerations to alter their approach angles, but in fact it is rather a matter of improving these than abandoning them. Instead of thinking "Path Thirteen" (or Path Three), we have only to think "Thotol D" and mean: "The Path on the Holy Tree of Life which connects the First and Sixth Concepts." Plus of course all the implications of both Concepts combined to form an harmonious stream of consciousness acting on its own frequency.

Putting two concepts of anything together for production of one is a commonplace of human consciousness though mainly on smaller scales. We do it every time we blend two colours or strike chords. We do it whenever two humans combine to engender a third. Here we are creating a "child of consciousness" by mating two Tree-Concepts. We cannot do this unless the concepts themselves have been created in our minds first and matured there or "grown to puberty" enough to ensure their fertility. An immature idea cannot propagate its species any more than a non-adult human is able to perpetuate our race. That is why it is so important to mature our Concept-ideas properly before we can fairly expect to begin breeding from them. Consciousness is a living force, and consequently subject to the laws of Life like other vital energies.

Combining Concepts through human sensory media is mostly an audio-visual process. The simplest method is going over and over a coloured chart of the Tree with the Paths identified by consonants, while audibly repeating some standard formula for impressing the combinations into retentive levels of awareness. This is also the cheapest way of course. Alternative methods of experience may be much more impressive and elaborate to start with as a basis, but in the end they have to be condensed to momentary processes of perception too small in duration to be measured except theoretically. In other words we shall be doing much what happens with a computer. Literally millions of factors are all taken into account in less than a second, though each had to be programmed into the scheme separately. At this stage we shall be setting up the integers of a computer deep in our consciousness which is calculated to "print out" in some form of "Godspeech."

It should need little imagination to work out interesting ways of combining Tree-Concepts in our consciousness. An "Electric Tree" could be constructed with coloured lights illuminating each Sphere connected to a keyboard, so that single, combined, or any collection of Concepts might be selected at will.

This might be elaborated by the Paths being identified by illuminated letters being shown up by colours blending from both Spheres. On the audio side, each Concept could be allotted a specific note, while the Paths were harmonies, or a tape made for each Path as in my "*Office of the Holy Tree of Life.*" Again the tape recording might comprise the briefest recital of Concepts and Paths from top to bottom of the Tree, and then listened to over again until the outline begins to stick in the memory. Something like this:

> Thotol A (ay) is Living Earth,
> Thotol B is One and Two,
> Thotol C is One and Three,
> Thotol D is One and Six,
> Thotol E (ee) is Living Air,
> Thotol F is Two and Three,

and so on to the end of the Alphabet. Alternatively the letter may be emphasised at the end of a line so:

> Thotol Earth of Life makes A (ay)
> Thotol One and Two makes B
> Thotol One and Three makes C
> Thotol One and Six makes D
> Thotol Air of Life makes E (ee)
> Thotol Two and Three makes F

and so on to the end of the alphabet. When chanting or reciting alphabets, the vowels should be included for the sake of continuity. About the shortest and fastest list would go:

> Earth is A (ay),
> One Two B
> One Three C
> One Six D
> Air is E (ee),
> Two Three F, and so on to the end of the alphabet.

Any of these formulae will serve or others can easily be made up to suit individual requirements. Providing the connections between

236 / *A Beginners Guide to Living Kabbalah*

Concepts and Path codes are clearly and precisely indicated, that is what really matters.

The practice of "Pathworking" is quite an old Thotol exercise, favoured a lot by the Golden Dawn and derived schools of thought. In many instances it consisted of a meditational session, during which awareness was supposed to be confined entirely to a single Path between two Spheres. If attention wandered, efforts had to be made in recalling and directing it along the lines chosen. This gave good practice in attuning consciousness to specific frequencies and holding it on course at will. It also assisted at "loading the Paths" with units of consciousness for forming the stockpile, out of which meanings might be drawn by future use of Key-codes. There was another important angle seldom mentioned by practitioners. This was the communication of mind by means of this system via the "Common consciousness" shared by those who thought in its terms of reference.

What this amounts to is that minds habitually using a symbolic code of consciousness in common, eventually communicate with each other along those lines through what Jung called "The Collective Unconscious" or maybe better "The Universal Mind." Whatever this may be in actuality, it is certainly something we all have access to on particular levels. It would seem to be stratified, or maybe "frequency responsive" might be a better term, in such a way that specific types of mentality have their own especial areas of action. That is to say our common consciousness is not a conglomerated mass of disconnected impressions from every sort of human, but an ordered arrangement of awareness classifiable into all kinds of categories, just as in the case of an individual mind. We are not collectively insane, much as cynics may be tempted to query such a statement. Granted, humans vary enormously in ability to tap and use this amazing reservoir of consciousness behind our embodied beings. Everyone has some limited degree of ability, though probably very few ever extend themselves anywhere near those limits. Not a lot of people realise they are just ticking along on minimal consciousness-consumption like an idling engine, and this rate could be considerably raised by making a few necessary efforts. One of these efforts is the Pathworking exercise.

The keys for making contact with our common

consciousness are held in Symbol-systems applied at surface levels, where they penetrate to much deeper sources of supply and release long chains of connected intelligence. That is why they were called "Keys." A key is an implement pushed into a mechanism and operated so that a barrier is opened and access obtained to some desired area. That is exactly what a Key-symbol is supposed to do, and that is why the entire Tree of Life consists of an enormous collection of them, affording entry to otherwise hidden Inner chambers of consciousness. Let us consider this comparison. An ordinary alphabet is a series of Key-symbols offering its users a share in all the accessible printed or written awareness, accumulated by the whole of humanity since literacy began in this world. The ordinary mind boggles at attempts to grasp or appreciate the incredible importance of this fact, which is taken for granted so casually by millions of unthinking humans. When we think of what we owe to just one short set of symbols, it is small wonder alphabets were treated as sacred in long-ago times. More recently the late Aleister Crowley complained contemptuously about being solemnly entrusted with the Hebrew alphabet as a Grade secret during an early initiation. Had he sought the symbology of the act, instead of being offended by what looked like an insult to his intelligence, he might have learned a lot more. It never pays to leap at hasty conclusions during occult operations.

With the Thotol alphabet we are using our ordinary symbols of literacy, but specialising these so that they convey rather more recondite shades of meaning than when used in the normal way. An alphabet can be employed to spell any phonetic language in the world, yet the words would only be understood by those able to think in that language. In effect we shall be using our alphabet to "think Thotolese" with, and since each letter is linked to specifically spiritual values, it could be said that we are tyring to learn the "Language of the Gods." It should also put us in touch telepathically with other humans and orders of Inner Life, who share the same speech-system in the depths of our common consciousness.

Many occult writers have made longish lists of "attributions" to the Paths consisting of different colours, perfumes, and other esoteric items they felt were appropriate. Few are of much help, except maybe the Tarot Trumps providing the right pattern is applied. So far, the lay-out shown in "*The Talking Tree*" has neither been seriously challenged or superseded. (*This very large and detailed work on Tarot attributions to the Paths of the Kabbalistic Tree of Life has been out of print for several years, and it would appear that its size and attraction for only the most serious student of this subject, would cause it to stay out of print. See the illustration below for William Gray's attributions of the Tarot Trumps to the Paths. - Jacobus G. Swart*).

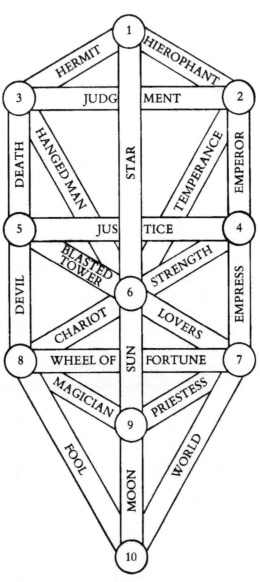

In the end, there is only one way to reach the Paths. Go to each in turn personally and experience them. Note and record the experiences as they come, then sum up each one looking for dominant characteristics. This in every case will be whatever factor of that Path has made a maximum mark on the consciousness of individual mediators. That, or its symbol, will be what they need to put them in touch with the Path rapidly and reliably. The ultimate aim of course is to achieve this contact by means of the Letter-symbol, thus taking a further step in search of a common language shared by an Inner intelligentsia.

Arranging psychodramatic experiences for Pathworking is not always an easy project. The *"Office of the Holy Tree of Life"* was compiled for that purpose, but it restricts the practice to a religious rite. The basic requirements are good audio-visual symbols indicating the Path being worked in connection with its code-letter. Other senses are very tricky to handle. Touch can be usefully brought in by means of a solid alphabet much as those used to teach small children. If the Path letter is felt and fingered during the exercise this often helps to buttress the impression being built in the mind. Providing perfumes could be chosen for each Path unmistakably, they would be valuable. Possibly the most practical would be blends of both the Sphere scents, just like the colours. Taste combinations could be a fascinating subject for experiment. As a general rule, some all-purpose incense, not too powerfully present, is quite a fair background for most Pathworking purposes. The really important factor of the whole proceedings is confining consciousness entirely within the limits of whichever Path is being worked. Any symbols being employed should only be present to act as constant reminders to this effect.

We can only be conscious of a Path because we are constantly aware of which Concepts it lies between. This means that during the whole of the exercise, both concepts must measure the limits of consciousness between them. We can start by thinking of one and then the other, but in the end they have to form the right and left hand Pillars of our progress. That could be ritualised by literally placing a representation of each Concept on Physical Temple Pillars and locating the Path-letter between them. With this, or some similar arrangement, a good beginning exercise can be worked something like this:

First call up mentally a condition of the leading Concept and hold it momentarily. Project it out to the left round the room, and as it reaches the mid-mark opposite, feel it changing condition when it returns by the right as the concluding Concept. Synchronise breathing, and inhale during one concept then exhale equally with the other. Be conscious of the code-consonant illuminated somewhere above the centre. If possible imagine the Telesmic Figure of the Path stationed opposite and governing the changeover. Keep this going at an increasing speed till it reaches a maximum, yet be very careful not to hyperventilate. While keeping breathing steady, imagine each breath covering more and more cycles. At first one cycle per breath, then two, then four, and so on. Eventually conceive the cycles so rapid, they cannot be counted by any normal consciousness, but realise they are producing a "power platform" which provides the energy for animating the Inner experiences peculiar to this Path. At the end of the exercise steadily reverse the procedure so that the circle is slowed down till the Concepts come to rest again. If the Telesmic Image is used, always make some courteous acknowledgement to it as if it were activated by a real Inner entity, which it probably will be eventually.

Variations of this exercise can be made quite interesting. The old mirror-image practice is also fun. It is best to make a set of letter-cards for this. They need not be larger than ordinary playing cards. Each one figures the consonant shown centrally, and the Concepts indicated by numbers in the simplest and most effective ways. Also needed will be a set of twenty-two discs or cards coloured on each side as one Concept of the Paths with appropriate symbols. Any writing or figuring on these will have to be in mirror-image script. The mirror itself should reflect head and shoulders at two or three feet away, or a closer and neater image can be obtained by using a convex driving mirror.

To start the exercise, set up the mirror with lights at the side so that a good image is obtained. This illumination may be coloured to suit the end-Concepts concerned. The letter-card is displayed just above the mirror centrally against a colour back-screen in keeping with the Path-significance. As an ultra refinement, a simple headband can be worn with an adjustable plain circular mirror on the forehead. This is fixed so that it reflects the letter-card to be readable in the mirror-image where of course it will appear the right way round. Select the Concept-card of the Path to be worked and hold it about breast level edge on to the mirror. When everything is ready and the operator in a correct frame of mind, begin with the assumption that the person seen in the mirror is an actuality confronting the Godlike Path-propounder who will speak and direct all action. In other words the "you-in-the-mirror" is the Earth-personality of the operator, and the "you-that-speaks" is his or her "Higher Self," Holy Guardian Angel, or whatever anyone likes to term his or her inner identity. "Personifying a God" is a very old mystical practice, calculated to put people in touch with their immortal principles. When this disposition of consciousness has been duly achieved, start speaking and thinking something along these lines:

"Listen, so-and-so, I am going to show you the such-and-such Path of the Holy Tree. I will now begin by sending one of its Spheres to you. I want you to catch this, absorb it, change it into the other one and send it back to me. I shall bounce it back to you again, and so the game goes on for a while. Then, whichever you send to me I will change and return to you. Catch this, think, and then alter it into the other. This is called the (Path-Letter) practice whereon you will learn one single letter of God-language, so keep that in mind as we go. Now get ready because I am going to begin."

After that proceed to act exactly as outlined. With each "throw," turn the disc appropriately so that the mirror-image responds to instructions. Later on the roles may be reversed and the operator in *propria persona* will respond to whichever the "God-Image" in the mirror displays. The important point is to feel the Sphere-state as fully as possible, then work the changeover proper for the Path and experience of the other Sphere to the same degree. This should be rhythmically done, and a metronome or music-beat can be very useful to guide the action which increases in speed as expertise is gained.

All sorts of variations can be played on this theme. Yet another set of cards may be prepared, this time with only a Path-letter and only one Concept-colour on each. These are to be shuffled and drawn at random. As each appears, the complementary colour is strongly imagined. This is actually an important exercise, because it moves the focus of awareness around the Tree in ways it would have to follow if words were being spelt out. Small sets of these cards may be made for the pocket to occupy odd-moment occasions. The aim is to attain a conditioned response with each consonant, so that it automatically causes a Sphere-stimulus in the mind triggered by whichever produces the Path between them. Since we only want this reaction to occur when dealing with the Tree of Life alphabet, and certainly not when reading daily papers or usual literature, the Keyword "Thotol" must be thought of at least on commencing the exercise.

Hypnotists have long been familiar with the principles of this technique which some call "post-hypnotic release." The idea is to lock an instructed or other item of awareness into a "compartment" of the subconscious mind, where it will stay inactive but potent, until released by an audible or visual signal acceptable to the hypnotised subject. For that reason the release-key has to be something most unlikely to be met with, except under circumstances or conditions needing its immediate employment. Here we are using the word "Thotol" in a similar way to change our awareness of an ordinary alphabet into consciousness of it, as a means of communication with higher than human beings who have their equivalent of it in their normal states of existence. That is how a "Magic word" works. It does not alter anything in itself. What it alters is the consciousness dealing with it. When a hypnotist hands a subject a pencil and tells him it is a heavy hammer, that pencil symbolises sensory impressions of a heavy hammer in the subjects mind which he accepts in preference to what his fingers, eyes, and common-sense are telling him. Those tell his brain quite clearly: "This is nothing but an ordinary pencil," but his mind rejects this and overrides the brain in favour of a hammer which is what he wants to believe in, so that is what his consciousness becomes concerned with.

Something similar is happening here through what might be described as auto-hypnosis. Our brains are visually or aurally stimulated to recognise familiar letters of an alphabet we consider commonplace. Because of all the conditioning our minds have been voluntarily undergoing in relation to those same letters, once our attention has been triggered by the word "Thotol," we see them as symbols representing the basic units of spiritual speech. Thotol is a "turn-on" word. Now we will also need a "turn-off" word, which will send Thotolese back to our subconscious until we need it again. That will allow us to use the language of literate humans for everyday purposes. For this, we will have to coin some other unusual word, and one practical suggestion is just to reverse Thotol, into "LOTOHT," pronounced something like "Low-toht." Vaguely reminiscent of "Lot-out," or "Everything away." Not a bad banishing Keyword.

It is advisable to start using the On/Off formula fairly early in the exercises at the beginning and end of every Thotol session. This is because we need to keep the Thotolised consciousness as a clear stream unconfused with normal awareness. People who mix up "Inner messages" with ordinary thinking, are liable to become mentally imbalanced if one set of values are mistaken for another. Our verbal on/off switch does not wipe out a single impression on subconscious levels. The Thotol system will be working safely away there all the while, communicating inwardly with those speaking its language and awaiting its linkage with focal consciousness via its Word-Keys. In one sense this is not unlike setting up an electronic phone answering device or a "voice-controlled" tape recorder. Once the system is operating effectively all "messages received" will be automatically recorded for future play-back. Interpreting them correctly however, is not quite so simple.

So the thing to do at this stage of study is work away at the alphabet until familiarity and usage allow rapid identification and loading of each letter-symbol. Here the solid letters can be a considerable help. Mix them in a bag or box, and pick out one at a time without looking. In the dark, under a desk, or in the pocket will do. Identify each by touch alone, and mentally call up the Concepts, colours, symbols, or anything at all associated with that Path. These must not simply be seen or heard mentally, but summoned as an actual soul-experience for the briefest split-second. This is highly important. These inner letters are not just for looking at, but for *living with*. They are, after all, letters from the Tree of Life, and until they are vivified by the will and awareness of whoever is creating them, they will speak nothing but a dead language. Everyone has to bring their own Thotol alphabets to life through creative consciousness. Letters by themselves are dead, but the Spirit speaking through them is essentially *alive*. That does make all the difference.

Suppose, for instance, we are tackling the Path symbolised by its letter **L**. Here we should be treating that letter only as indicating an actual spiritual state of balance between the Principles of Mercy and Severity. A sense of Justice is absolutely essential for following this Path, hence the appositeness of the Tarot symbol. Unless a condition of consciousness in keeping with this and all other significance can be conjured up and considered a fact of Inner Life, the letter is not being "brought alive" properly. Therefore it cannot be expected to speak much sense in the soul of its user.

Although everyone should experience each Path for themselves, and keep some kind of a record concerning whatever they encounter on it, there may be some value in making rough estimates of what anyone might expect in connection with the different Paths. It should be obvious enough that if a sternly fierce warrior appeared on the Thotol **M** Path, something would be wrong, and the exercise must be re-examined in search of the fault. It is always well to built a framework of estimation in which to work. This does not mean that anything which will not fit that framework must necessarily be wrong. The framework itself could be inadequate and need adjustment. Whatever looks like a misfit should be examined to find out why, and if possible directed to the Path where it should have been. This was the meaning of "Magical banishment," which did not signify mere dismissal, but more importantly relocating items of consciousness to their proper places. The fierce warrior should probably have belonged with the **P** Path, but could have appeared on the **Q**, or much less likely on the **X** or **Th** Paths depending on context. A lot would depend who or what he was supposed to be fighting for or against. Therefore we might as well run quickly through the Paths getting general ideas of what they should convey to our consciousness. This is no more than checking a map before making a journey into foreign territory. The map supplies information about routes, geographical features and so forth, but it cannot tell what the weather will be like and what will befall the traveller. These will have to be discovered by experience, yet knowledge of the map must contribute to the success of the excursion.

F. Questing for Definite Objectives

When rapid recognition by means of Path-letters on the Tree is achieved, Pathworking becomes a lot more practical. A good test is with the loose solid letters. Select these randomly from a box, bag, or the pocket without looking. By feel alone they should evoke all the major attributes of their Paths. Colour, God-names of Spheres, and every salient point of both concepts should come quite clearly to mind. When this happens consistently it will mean that the Paths are indeed establishing themselves properly in the subconsciousness. Tarotists may find the first image behind the letter is the Trump of that Path, which is entirely a valid symbol providing the Spheres and their details also appear distinctly.

In Pathworking the Path itself is first invoked by any or all means considered previously. Other methods are also to be encouraged if they produce equivalent results. Once the Path is clearly in the mind there are several procedures possible. The Sphere-Concepts may be allowed to drift towards the right and left edges of Inner Space where they are held semi-subjective, to control the free forces of consciousness between them which the operator is dealing with. Here they may be visualised as forming a sort of huge ring around the perimeter of awareness, while attention is focussed on the empty enclosure within. For instance, with Path **L** a blue half circle on the right would be matched by a red half circle on the left, making a purple background against which mental images could be received or projected. This background might be faded into suitable scenery for the Path, out of which happenings should begin to build up and commence action.

Alternatively a journey could be imaginatively made from one Sphere to the other along a connecting Path. First a decision would have to be made as to which Sphere to start from. Create that Sphere-condition consciously around oneself, experience it, then be aware of a call from the other Sphere a Path-distance away. Travel towards it mentally, seeking adventures en route. These should change character as progress is made, first in keeping with the starting-Sphere, then being symbolic of both in the middle where the sound of the Path-consonant is clearest, finally altering in character with the destination-Sphere as this is reached, and the consonant fades to a distant murmur. The Spheres could be considered as two different countries with the Path as a frontier-road between them and a post, demanding passports and identity checks, or some similar procedure for admission. If this is carried out ritualistically, the sonic and visual or other stimuli would have to make the change also. Many interesting musical effects could be contrived to ensure this is a fascinating exercise.

Then there is the Quest-idea. A definite objective should be thought of which is likely to be found on some particular Path. Then the Path is entered imaginatively and the Quest-aim sought for. It need not necessarily be found, because the questing adventures themselves are the real purpose of this exercise, since consciousness is intentionally projected through Inner Space in pursuit of a purpose. Following this idea through, a useful old practice was the close questioning of every unexpected figure arising on the Path, something like antique initiation rituals. Whatever appeared as if entering the field of awareness on its own without being intentionally summoned, had to be stopped, challenged, and compelled to give some explanation of itself. It was asked who or what it was, why it was there, where it was going, and other pertinent points. In particular it was asked its connection and function with that particular path. If replies were unsatisfactory, then the figure had to be banished in the magical sense by dismissing it to wherever the Pathworker felt it properly belonged. In this way a valuable association was made, and more importantly consciousness was being brought under the increasing control of the practitioner.

Some workers found a reasonably quick way of entering a Path was just by imagining a door in front of them with the Path name and a few details painted on it. Its posts, lintel and threshold had the colours or characteristics of the two Spheres concerned. The right knocks for the Spheres and Path had to be made on the door, which would then open. To help impress this action into the mind, an actual door would be marked in some easily removed manner and ritually entered maybe only once for every Path on the Tree. After that, the idea of entering each path by its proper portal should be deeply enough driven into the subconsciousness, to make memory-recall practical for all future usage. Workers with a fondness for arcane procedures made up passwords and countersigns for each Path, something similar to entering a lodge. To some extent this helped establish a recognition route.

Once a suitable technique has been adopted for entering a Path, it is well to have some advance ideas what to expect thereon. There is not a great deal of benefit to be obtained in looking up lists of what former workers have encountered in the way of plants, animals, stones, signs of Zodiac and so forth, because this is no more than the way their individual awareness interpreted the influences they felt upon that path in their time. The decisive factor in determining Path-phenomena is its motivational relationship with the prevailing spiritual purpose of the Path itself. This means is it appropriate for the nature of a particular Path or not? If yes then it belongs, if not then it must be sent elsewhere. That is the essence of the whole exercise. So let us get some ideas of what the twenty-two Paths might probably present in general terms.

The first four Paths of the Tree, **B C D F**, connect with the Supernal Concepts above the Abyss. They are concerned with pure consciousness in three distinct streams. If we consider consciousness as a spectrum of energy, **B** would be the top end, **C** the bottom, **D** the center, and **F** as a link between top and bottom. They are sometimes colour-coded by **B** being silver for the white Pillar side of the Tree, **C** being bronze for the black Pillar, and **D** being gold for the middle Pillar. **F** is half silver, half-bronze. The Spheres themselves are shown as 1 being brilliant white, 2 light grey, and 3 very dark grey. It is a mistake to show 3 as black. Black only occurs at the very bottom of the Tree as the winter-tint in 10, where it balances the brilliancy of 1 very well indeed. The real colours of the Tree commence beneath the Abyss, where silver becomes blue, bronze red, and gold yellow.

It is a good plan if possible to try and make Concepts above the Abyss relatively outside limitations of human history. That is to say costumes, accessories, and scenic effects should be as timeless and "otherwordly" as can be imagined. The lower down the Tree we get, the more contemporary we can become. The Cosmic circles of Time, Space, and Events start with the Supernals, and link with the Divine Principles of Omnipresence, Omniscience, and Omnipotence. Though these must naturally apply to all Paths of the Tree, they are generally taken as being symbolised by Cosmo-Omniscience-Space associating with the White Pillar Side of the Tree, Cosmo-Omnipresent-Time belonging to the Black Pillar side, and Cosmo-Omnipotent-Events being linked with the Middle Pillar. The sense-phenomena of the Paths can quite reasonably be classified under the headings of People, Places, and Things. Nor should the Pathworker forget his own adaption to the Path in the way of appearance and behaviour. These have to conform with the happenings of the Path too. So bearing all these points in mind, let us have a first look at:

Thotol B

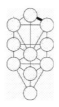

This is the primal move from Spirit towards Matter by the way of Wisdom. Not wisdom as the result of experience and learning, but the ability of Wisdom as a potential Life-power inherent in individual souls. It is Wisdom already within us awaiting attainment through evolution. For us humans, it is our inherited Wisdom from the male side of our genetics, which naturally varies from one incarnation to another. Few humans come anywhere near fulfilling their quota of Wisdom, which came with them at birth into this world. The parable of the unused talents certainly applies here. True Wisdom is gained, not learned, and its essence is something we bear through the gates of birth and death alike. This is the Path whereon we must come to terms with the Inner Wisdom we were born with, and must enrich by our experiences of each incarnation. So our imaginary audio-visual impressions are most likely to be:

People: Father-figures and Archetypes of the All-Wise kind. Seniors and superiors of a very high order. No mere instructors, but actual *imparters* of Wisdom by contact of consciousness alone. Some of these Beings would not necessarily appear ancient so much as ageless, having an absolute authority beyond question. They can only be approached with respect and reverence in the true sense of the term. Their united purpose would be to awaken and encourage the ability of Wisdom in the Path traveller, so that he is inspired to seek Perfection at the summit of the Life-Tree.

Places: Very probably magnificent vistas on grand scales as if from mountain tops, well lit and quite clear. The phallic symbol of a mountain peak may be realised. There could be a Temple with nine pillars, since this 10 -1 on the descending Tree. Or two upright monoliths with a lintel across them might be seen, because this is the 1 + 2 Path. There is always a sense of altitude here. Another impression is sometimes a mountain monastery or retreat of "Masters in the Mysteries," where the Ancient Wisdom is safeguarded from worldly desecration, and passed on from one generation of initiates to another. The topmost battlements of the Grail Castle would be appropriate here. An odd feature of this Path is that the traveller never seems to be alone, yet seldom sees his immediate companion whom he senses as being slightly behind or above him.

Things: It is seldom wise to overburden the Supernal Paths in particular with a plethora of attributed articles. It is better to let these make their own appearance, and then query their appositeness. Scrolls of Wisdom would certainly be appropriate here, a common sort being the Scroll of the Law presented as a single roll for the sake of phallic symbolism. The Grail-Hallow of the Lance is also valid for the same reason. So is the Torch of Wisdom illuminating doubtful passages of Life. There is a possibility that the Pathworker may have the sensation of being seated as a Hierophant charged with mediating the Wisdom of God toward the minds of men, or this idea might be visualised in some other way. Many symbols associated with pure Spirit and the Principle of Wisdom are likely here.

Thotol C

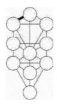

This is the path linking the Superself with the way to Life through the Principle of Understanding. Here we have an inheritance from the female side of our genetics enabling us to comprehend what Life is about, not so much by learning anything, but by being able to appreciate the ineherent meaning of things because of an automatic responce from our Inner depths corresponding to this level of the Tree. Consequently the influence here is maternal. At Thotol B we had God-the-Father, and here we have God-the-Mother to match. From Her we inherit all our intuitive-instinctive abilities which are so vital to Life on all levels. We understand things mainly because their basics are already in us from experience gained in former incarnations, plus what our ancestors have given to our genes. Understanding is something we have to dig from the matrix of our own natures. To classify some expected encounters on this Path.

People: Mother-Figures of all kinds. Sympathetic and understanding seniors, more likely to be female than male. The Sophia-ideal. Athena and her owl. People on this Path might seem somewhat serious, and there is not much likelihood of loud laughter here. Quiet smiles might be the most. There could be a sombre note here and there as warnings are given or admonitions made, yet never any oppressive sadness or grief. Only thoughtful and "pregnant" silence.

Places: Often nocturnal or shaded backgrounds. Soft lighting, quiet and dignified surroundings. Could be a seashore with very calm sea, or simply the ocean alone. Womb-conditions symbolised. A comfortable chamber with very soft cushiony chairs and thick deep carpet. Nothing rushed or hurried, all very orderly and controlled. Environments suggestive of timelessness. A hermitage in sheltered conditions is not uncommon. Sometimes dark pools of water reflecting a spot of light will appear, or deep wells with a star reflected therein. Flat polished stones, usually deep grey. Occasionally a cavern-Temple. The night-vigil of the Grail chapel.

Things: Womb symbols of every sort. The Grail Hallow of the Cup. The Cauldron of inspiration. Sanctuary lamps. The female breast and emblems thereof. An ark as a chest to contain the phallic Scroll of the law from Thotol B. An ibis or crane is sometimes seen standing in water here, because it suggests contemplation while patiently waiting to catch a fish. This symbolises finding food from the ocean of thought. Hence a Fisherman image could belong with this Path. No Path is exclusively male or female, it is simply a question of proportional relationship between the sexes. Here the female predominates. The Hermit-symbol for instance could be either sex. There is often a sensation on this Path of being wrapped in a heavy hooded cloak such as hermits are reputed to wear. This of course is a womb-suggestion.

Thotol D

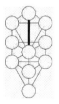

This is the Golden mean Path of Life which plunges past the Supernal state of pure consciousness across the Abyss and emerges into a condition of Expressive Energy symbolised as Solar power manifesting in our universe. The Superself links up with the Innermost nuclei around which we construct our microcosmic beings. Spirit speaks the Word we recognise as our Solar Logos.

Here, with God-the-Child, we ourselves become the Children of Creation, relating ourselves directly with our Primal Parents as sons (Suns) of the Gods in the truest meaning of the term. This Path crosses the Abyss by the Gate of Eternal Life, and here we have to recognise that every soul is indeed a Star, and every event we experience in Life should help us bring our Immortal Identities closer to consciousness. Here we would expect to encounter:

People: Radiantly beautiful Beings abounding with energy and Life. They are much too bright for us to identify, but somehow we know they are Avatar-Figures passing in and out of incarnation for the sake of human salvation. We may find humans of transcendent appearance radiating a type of harmonious happiness unknown on earth, and so intense it can be quite unbearable to ordinary materialistic mortals. Here people appear as they are in their highest spiritual form closest to absorption in the Absolute. We may be aware of a strange bitter-sweet sadness because of comparison between their state and our own.

Places: There are really no earthly standards of comparison to describe situations on this Path. They might be likened to the most wonderful environments imaginable to the Pathworker and then extrapolated from those. Every human idea of "Heaven" applies. There is a brilliance and intensity here which can only be termed a condition of pristine perfection. If anything were more perfect it could not exist at all. A sort of *ne plus ultra* for humanity just short of entering Divinity.

Things: Almost anything associated with entirely harmonious and perfectly poised wellbeing. Musical instruments capable of the most sublime and magnificent sonics imaginable. Solar symbols connecting with a Cosmos of Stars. We have to remember the Apollo connection here and his association with medicine and music. Since no disease can cross the Abyss all healing processes must be kept to the Solar end of the Path. From a purely modern viewpoint spaceships could be considered here, because this is where our Solar system ends and reaches out towards the galaxies in search of Life on other planets. Here we hope to make conscious contact not only with others of our kind elsewhere in Space, but also reach the awareness of far more advanced species of Life than ours who will help us evolve towards Infinite Identity.

Thotol F

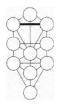

This Path connects the Concepts of Wisdom and Understanding together on Supernal levels of Life, so it is concerned with a stream of pure consciousness we call Judgement. This faculty of accurately assessing, estimating and adjusting with any circumstance of condition of Cosmos is almost our highest ability, and our lives are constantly depending on it. Without it we should not survive very long on this side of the Abyss. Here is blended the rational and intuitive side of our natures, so that together they will guide us through every Pathway on the Tree of Life. Neither Wisdom from the paternal, nor Understanding from the maternal side of our natures would be sufficient alone for this tremendous task. Combined and concentrated into a single conscious ability of Judgement, those who walk its Inner way can travel from one end of Creation to the other. This is the Path where we have to acquire that faculty, and whereon we are likely to meet:

People: Mixed male and female figures of great ability, acumen and gifted with exceptional accuracy for summing up situations on all Life levels. They are capable of directing consciousness so that everything is evaluated correctly according to its proper place in Cosmos, and therefore treated exactly as it should be relatively to the rest of its connections with Creation. These beings are far above any possibility of bias or error. They deal with each decision entirely on the intrinsic merits of all involved factors. This is where we have to make those deep decisions which once made will alter our entire lives, and these are the "Inners" who will help us reach them rightly.

Places: Halls of Judgement. Any scene where calm deliberation is possible, and maybe discussion to decide outcomes of vital issues. Courts presided over by wise and understanding judges. Conference rooms. Consulting chambers. Grail Castle Council Chapter. Outdoors in any favourable environment for furthering the purpose of this Path. Possibly a pleasant garden, or impressive vistas with view of sea and mountains.

Things: Anything calculated to aid faculties of judgement. Usually combinations of male-female symbols. For instance the phallic pen and the feminine ink-well. The masculine seal being impressed on virgin parchment. The Judgement scales with level pans holding either man and woman or other sex-symbols. Everything here has to suggest combinations of consciousness between the sexes resulting in correct courses of action and procedures. Spiritual sex-equality is an essential keynote of this Path.

Thotol G

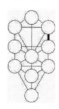

This Path is an Abyss-crosser by the Gate of Birth. Here we enter extended existence between Wisdom and Mercy via the birth-process. It is interesting to note that Wisdom must govern Mercy to prevent this quality from becoming mere supine permissiveness. We have to learn here that Mercy and Wisdom should be used conjointly. Unless love and compassion is controlled by Wisdom it can have fatal results, as so many humans discover to their costs. On the other hand, Wisdom without Mercy can impose a terrible threat to Life. Theoretically we should come into incarnate living because we have attained enough Wisdom to recognise the value of real Love. Wise souls on the Supernal side of the Abyss should be attracted to loving souls on this side, and so come into birth by conjugal means. We know this may very seldom do so in fact, but we are still seeking the Paths of Perfection, and this is one whereon we must learn how to combine Wisdom and Love in order to make closer identification with the Divine Intention which animates us. On this Path we might meet:

People: Good governors and rightful rulers. That is what the Tarot Emperor means here. Such figures are symbols showing us what we ourselves ought to be on the Paths. Self-rule is vital before we attempt any involvement in other peoples lives. Here we must learn how to govern our "invisible Empires" and control our consciousness just as a ruler might to run his State for the benefit of all living in it. Here too, we should find out what Royal Responsibility means, and now to behave regally within our realms of living. Those we meet on this Path are supposed to help us discover the Rules of ruling.

Places: Throne rooms. The Round Table scene with the King-Figure centrally and his court in a circle around him. The Good King Wenceslaus story. Almost any setting for a Kindly King being wisely generous to his people. There could well be a lot of laughter and happiness on this Path. Outdoor events might be the announcement of an amnesty, or proclamation of a public benefit. Crowds and heralds will fit in here. Courtyards and balconies of the Grail Castle.

Things: Symbols of Wisdom and Mercy. Sheathed swords. Rule books for procedures of good government. Royal regalia such as sceptres and orbs, but not crowns since those associate with Thotol 1. A ruler here would wear a Cap of maintenance and circlet only. Cradles might be seen on this Path too, and anything linked with either Royal birth, or incarnation between loving parents.

Thotol H

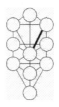

This is another Abyss-crosser by the Gate of Grace. Here we have to consider the Wisdom of living in beautiful Harmony and balance with Cosmos. This is where we must come to the conclusion that health, happiness, and everything else worthwhile in Life depends on a condition of balanced poise between every extremity of existence. Avoidance of extremes and keeping close to midway courses through them is the main message of this Path. That is why the Tarot trump of Temperance fits so well here. Temperance should never be understood in any kill-joy sense whatever. It does not mean abstention, but the enjoyment of everything up to the limits where an excess would endanger the well-being of those entitled to its usage. So this is the Path whereon we should acquire the elements of common-sense which will allow us a maximum of freedom in Life within a minimum of peril to it. Here we learn how to handle potencies by balancing them against each other with advantage to ourselves. This is where we are taught the value of moderation in all things. Therefore we could expect to encounter:

People: "Guardian Angel" types, counselling restraint against rash or hasty actions. The "faithful friend" who always seems available in times of trouble or difficulty to give sensible advice and assistance. Dependable and reliable companions who can be trusted completely. Wisely benevolent and beautiful beings.

Places: Could be any scene suitable for thinking thins out or talking them over. Possibly a library or cloisters. A pleasant country place with cheerful sunshine. A favourite walk with close friends away from crowds. This is an intimate Path to share with valued company only. There is always a bright and hopeful atmosphere.

Things: Symbols of moderation and tolerance. A calming hand over a clenched fist, or to prevent a weapon being drawn. Water in wine. Storms abating. Temperate winds. Hot iron being tempered. Masonic trowel levelling rough plaster. Anything creased or uneven being smoothed out. Equalising weights or heights. Symbols suggesting patience in solving problems. Shaken poise restored. Rocking Pillars replaced firmly. Ragged rhythm regulated.

Thotol J

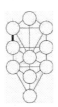

This Path crosses the Abyss from Understanding to Severity by the Gate of Death. Here we must discover the necessity for death as a complementary to birth. Death is not an opposite to Life, but an essential Part of it along our progress to Perfection. It lies between Understanding and Severity as a function of the "Economics of Existence." Without death, we could never become any more than mere mortals bound to animal bodies until extinction. We need death in order to find higher forms of Life elsewhere than on this earth. This is the Path on which we have to come to terms with ideas of parting from our physical bodies so that we may make better progress along higher lines of living. In other words we must see death as our great Cosmic chance of improving our identities. Either we grasp and use it properly, or lose it and have to be recycled back to birth without much real advance in our spiritual situations. Death is a fact of Life as a bodily phenomena, but here we have to see it in the light of its spiritual significance. Its horrors remain below the Abyss, while its hopes arise eternally above that Chasm dividing our consciousness from that of Divinity. On this peculiar Path we might meet:

People: Possibly an "Angel of Death" figure in some very kindly guise such as a Dark Mother who hushes us to sleep on her breast. She might wear a deep grey cloak lined with warm red. Here too we could encounter heros of wars and disasters who gave their lives for others. Those who understand death, and having experienced it maybe many times themselves, try and help other souls through its dreaded gateway. Here we meet those Inner guardians, and if we are sensible, listen carefully to what they tell us. We might also come across some other types of being that supervise the process of purification by directing rubbish down the Abyss for disintegrative reconstitution, while the worthwhile remainder is sent on to the Supernals for incorporation into Divine Identity. The cleanliness of Cosmos depends very much on its "Sanitation Department," and this is one Path where workers are always fully employed.

Places: The dangerous Bridge before the Grail Castle. Avenues of tall cypresses. The edge of the Abyss. Elysian fields. A dark ocean imperceptibly meeting a sky of the same hue. Everything to suggest serious thought and facing change or a journey into the Unknown. A waiting room for a very important life-altering interview. On the lower part of the Path, battlefields, deathbeds, or scenes associated with necessitous severity for the sake of restoring a state of ruin.

Things: All symbols of Death and Change. Hourglasses and Scythes, etc., but symbols of resurrections such as a trumpet should be there as well. Christians might see an Easter Tomb here, or an empty Cross, yet never a crucifix with a Christ-corpse on it. That symbol belongs to the central Concept of the Sacred-King. There could be some battle-accoutrements, but on the lowest part of the Path only, and they should be seen as if in retrospect or as being abandoned in preference for peace. It might be useful to remember this is a Saturn-Mars Path, so both steel and lead artifacts would connect through the symbolism of swords and plumb-lines.

Thotol K

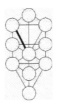

This is the last Abyss-crossing Path by the Way of Obligation. Here come those who are yet bound to incarnation mostly because of some duty they have either assumed or been obliged to accept in order to further the Cosmic cause of evolution towards Ultimate Perfection. That might be on account of uncompleted work commenced in previous lives which they are asking time and opportunity to finish. Between Understanding and Harmony comes our final payment of Karmic debts and freedom from the last bonds binding us to continued material existence. Sometimes there may be only a single loose end to tie off before we are free to seek heaven in its true sense. This is where we have to recognise our Life-responsibilities balanced between higher and lower Life, and reconcile them with our principal purpose for living. This is also a Sun-Saturn Path, so alchemical associations would be appropriate with transformation symbology to match. In particular this is the Path of perceptive poise, and on it we are likely to meet:

People: Those alternating between serious and sunny outlooks. We might remember the Hanged man of the Tarot and his significance. Here we have souls with serious motives of mission who are cheerfully confident of success before them. They are all deeply convinced of a major purpose behind their lives, having a very strong sense of duty to their religions, countries, families, or wherever their loyalties lie.

Places: Wherever any particular cause is being upheld for the advancement of humanity towards Divinity. Possibly a Temple. An amphitheatre for presentation of dramas encouraging people to seek the highest ideals of living. Could be a laboratory dedicated to research of humanitarian benefit. Might even be a hospital on the lower part of the Path, but of course no suggestion of sickness is to be allowed above the Abyss. Perhaps a vessel cruising through days and nights on a questing voyage. Many places are possible on this Path providing they do not counter-suggest its purpose.

Things: Solar-Saturnian symbolism. Gold cased in lead, valuables in dull protective packages. Portia's lead casket? Dark cloaks with gold linings. Most alchemical symbology and items suggesting transmutation of basic human nature into pure spiritual gold. On the other hand remember the screening effect of lead on radiations harmful to Life as we know it. Note also the Masonic symbolism of a plumb-line (Hanged Man), for ensuring uprightness and therefore stability and endurance.

Thotol L

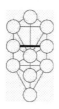

This Path between Mercy and Severity is the unequivocal one of plain Justice. Not requital or revenge in any way whatever. Simply the rightings of wrongs and equalisation of energies throughout all cycles of Life. The Law of Cosmic Compensation in action. The "stick and carrot" method of controlling human behaviour. The good old primitive system of child psychiatry - "Do this and you get a sweetie, do that and you get a beating." Nothing in Nature is more effective for getting rapid and certain results. This is where we learn what to do or not to do in order to align ourselves with the Laws of Life. Reward and punishment may be old fashioned, but they still work best for humans unable to understand anything better. Not that we are ever punished by any offended Deity. We have to remember the adage: "We are not punished *for* our sins, but *by* them." In other words we punish ourselves by our own behaviour. This is the Path whereon we must come to terms with our self-made karma and sort out the compensatory mechanism of its cause-and-effect action in our lives. It is a more than important Path, for it comes centrally across the Tree-Plan this side of the Abyss and is the only Path crossing three others of equal importance. Those of Grace, Obligation and Immortality. The connection of these with the Principle of Justice should be fairly obvious. On Path L we may expect to encounter:

People: Those concerned with the processes of Justice in the sense of recompense and wrong-righting. Knights of the Holy Grail. Peace keeping military governors and soldiers of their forces. Nurses and medicals trying to deal with wounds and injuries inflicted by wars and disasters. Those trying to cope with trouble-makers in an ordered society. Defenders of the weak and helpless.

Places: The Justice Hall of the Grail Castle. Courts of Justice anywhere. Opposites of action such as battlefields and peace conference chambers. Hospitals for the injured and pleasure grounds for the fit. Deserts and gardens. Scenes of contrast convertible to each other, providing one represents Mercy, and the other Severity or Economy.

Things: Mars-Jupiter symbolism, Scales of Justice and blunt Sword thereof. Thunderbolt and Cornucopia. Anything bitter-sweet. Fire and Water. Iron and tin. Battleships and pleasure cruisers. Bombers and airliners. As we descend the Tree so we can allow our imagery to become more modern. We could contrast unearned wealth and deprived poverty here. Or income versus Income Tax!

Thotol M

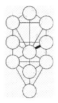

This Path connects Mercy with Beauty. A truly powerful combination. Not force in the form of explosive or violent energy, but the firm quiet power which pervades everything and in the end overcomes all opposition or antagonism. Hence the Tarot symbol of Strength, not to be taken in the sense of "brute force and ignorance," but sheer spiritual endurance and indomitable courage which persists to the point of immortality. Well did Portia call Mercy "mighties in the mightiest," for that is indeed its underlying attribute. True Mercy can only come from Strength, for it implies forbearance from the strong towards the weak. Beauty has its own strength too, which is directly of the Spirit, and therefore indestructible. The most beautiful objects in this world can be physically reduced to atoms, yet only the artifacts have been destroyed, not their beauty, which is and will remain within the minds of those who once beheld them. On this Path we have to learn the real power of Patience and what can be achieved with its aid, even if we must wait one lifetime after another until eventual accomplishment of aims. Perhaps not an easy lesson but an entirely essential one if we are to climb the Life-Tree to its summit with any success. Here we are liable to meet:

People: Those personifying the characteristic of this Path with quiet and dignified Inner strength and spiritual fortitude which prevails against all evil. This is a Sun-Jupiter Path, so we can expect very magnificent types of people thereon, not in appearance alone by any means, but especially in quality and behaviour. They have a radiance about them which is unmistakable. Magnanimous and strong, they are an infallible support of all who sincerely used their assistance to continue living in this world.

Places: Wherever we might meet instances of the patient and peaceful application of power in performance of purpose. That covers an enormous area. Examples could include construction sites, ocean liners, air liners, dams, power houses, atomic piles, engine rooms, waterfalls and so on. On intellectual levels there might be studies, reading rooms, meditation chambers, oratories, anywhere allowing quiet concentration of consciousness.

Things: Solar-Jupitarian symbolism. Tin and gold ornamentations. Could be dynamos, motors, power presses, the Masonic ashlar and hoist, the Rod as a lever. Protective clothing apart from military armour. Shelters. Stores and provisions, providing these are for some charitable purpose. A Solar power plant or equipment. Some quite new form of energy we have not discovered yet.

Thotol N

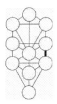

Another lovely Path connecting Mercy to Victory or Achievement. Not an ultimate achievement, but any in the long line which adds up to such a high level. Here the achievements may not be astounding, but they are at least worth making on our way to the top of the Tree. As we might expect with a Jupiter-Venus connection, the Tarot Empress links in here. That is because this is where we have to learn how to govern our emotions, which is a major achievement in a human life. Rule of emotions does not in the least mean their suppression or elimination, but full enjoyment of them under conscious control of their energies. "Love under Will." Uncontrolled emotions usually bring us terrible suffering and unhappiness, as most of us have learned the hard way. Once they can be governed to order they will bring only joy and tranquillity, making the best they can out of very sad situations. The Victory here is over our own faulty natures, and it is often a lifelong struggle. Balancing out sexual stresses might be the major achievement of a lifetime, or for that matter several incarnations, but sooner or later it has to be tackled on this Path, and successfully too. This is a Path of great activity and excitement, whereon our feelings have to be exercised and controlled, like young colts becoming gradually accustomed to harness and making a good relationship with humans who feed and care for them. On this Path we may find:

People: Rulers of their feelings and emotional impulses. No puritans or prudes of any kind whatever, but those who use their sensitivities instead of letting their emotions determine their conduct. Artists of the arts, master musicians, dramatists, painters, writers, all concerned with affairs of the soul and heart. Especially those of regal manner capable of grand gestures.

Places: Studios, theatres, gardens, temples, places of pageantry for the sake of joy and emotional expression under controlled circumstances. Could be sports stadiums. Could also be love-making environments. Anywhere where a sense of achievement in some cultural sense is possible.

Things: Jupiter-Venus symbolism. Bronze artifacts. Whatever supplies a feeling of comfort and satisfaction in living. There is something luxurious about the feeling of this Path, and an impression of entitlement to its advantages. Even so, it should be realised that all its wealth and wonders are only transitory and impermanent. They are there for the purpose of encouragement towards far higher standards of spiritual Life beyond bodily limitations.

Thotol P

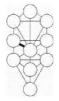

In even the finest lives there is always some element of trouble and disturbance while we live short of Perfection itself. This is where we meet one of its more dramatic forms on the Tree. The Path between Severity and Harmony, when Harmony can only be restored by some drastic or possibly desperate action. Maybe the sacrifice of one life for the sake of many, or the aversion of a major disaster by means of a minor one. Here it could mean the break-up of illusions in order to find Truth. The downfall of lies and deceits so that verity may come to light. A sort of safety-valve to relieve the pressures of living, or a blown fuse to protect delicate circuitry. This is the "overload cut-out" Path of Life, and the Blasted Tower makes a good Tarot symbol. Here we have to learn how to "blow off steam" safely and without wrecking our Life-structure or injuring others if possible, or at least with a minimum of damage if entirely unavoidable. We also have to learn that violence for its own sake or senseless destruction is never permissible, and nothing except restoration of seriously threatened Harmony and balance in Life ever justifies drastically energetic methods in dealing with situations. For example, the Great Fire of London was checked by blowing up houses in its path to create fire-gaps. This is definitely a Path of such emergency procedures, demanding rapid action when required. We can expect to encounter on it:

People: Reformers who might be considered a curse by many they disturb, but are necessary to the ecology of Existence. Sometimes these may be revolutionaries against utterly corrupt and oppressive governments which resist all other attempts at reformation. Demolition experts, but *never* deliberate wreckers. Exposers of evil everywhere. Attackers of untruths. Breakers out from bondage to anything bad or vicious. Could be those who have to force themselves out of their own bad habits or harmful attachments. Grail knights in action.

Places: Wherever circumstances demanding drastic reactions might apply. Might be a battle. A confrontation. A political meeting. An undersea wreck to be cleared by blasting. A fire to be extinguished. A dangerous ruin to destroy. Tangle of weeds to clear. Intellectual equivalents of these. Surgical removal of growth in operating theatre, or cutting off a gangrened limb. Burned off fields.

Things: Mars-Solar symbolism, Iron and gold. Sharp sword, scalpel. Feeling of discomfort in some rightful cause. Astringent smells. Antiseption. Cauteries. Uniforms and weapons. Rubbish-clearing equipment. Garden flame-guns. Excavators. Disinfectants and chemical cleaners. Bonfires. Lightning flashes.

Thotol Q

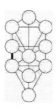

Here is another tiresome yet necessary Path between Severity and Glory or Honour. It is rightly symbolised by the Tarot Devil. He is not the "Author of Evil" taught by the Christian faith, but rather the Spirit of Opposition met with by everyone during the course of their lives when nothing seems to go right, and Life itself seems apparently against ones best efforts and schemes. The Tarot Devil is also the Tester, whose adverse actions determine how we face up to trials and difficulties. Either we outlast and overcome them, or they beat us down and leave us defeated until death on the other side of the sphere gives another chance to live and redeem our ruination. Here we have to balance Honour against Stringency and learn how to combine them so as to steer a course through the oppositions and troubles Life throws at us, and emerge with a sense of spiritual glory. We have to build up resistance to temptation into stupid, time-wasting, and false activities which only retard real spiritual progress. Many of these connect with the pseudo-glories of snobbery, social distinctions, wealth-worship, and the like limitations. Here is where we should learn to distinguish between genuine Glory, and what human society usually substitutes for it. On this Path we must literally deal with the Devil and put him in his proper place, which is not any kind of Hell, but a position in our own estimation. We should see him as Provoker and Challenger whom we shall have to outwit in our struggles against the adversities we encounter in Life. It may be significant that in the old Mystery-plays demons were always tricked or outwitted by inspired humans. This is a Mars-Mercury Path, and who should know how to baffle demons better than Hermes of the silver speech? Between the iron discipline of Mars, and the intelligent guile of Hermes, what Devil should stand much chance against anyone who has mastered the secrets of this Path, on which we are likely to meet some very interesting types:

People: These are what Jung would have called the "Trickster-Figure" kinds. In old initiations they acted as testers of character by contrived situations calculated to fool candidates if possible, yet provide clues to arouse suspicion and lead to discovery of truth by intelligent investigation. "Perception through provokation" as the adage went. The aim was to stimulate original thinking in order to deal with difficult and unexpected problems. Possibly a good motto for this Path would be that of the Boy Scouts - Be Prepared - for almost anything.

Places: Could be anywhere that trying and deceptive circumstances might be encountered. Homes, offices, public places, hospitals, everywhere humans foregather and are likely to impose on each other. Ancient initiation caverns, Old time Masonic Lodges, Universities, colleges, political gatherings, there is almost no end of likelihoods on this Path..

Things: Mars-Mercury symbolism. Iron and quicksilver. False items of appearance such as artificial limbs, teeth, etc. Make-up. Masks. Forged papers and money. Dud cheques and credit cards. Practical jokes. Unfulfilled promises. Blind alleys and bogus schemes. Fake jewellery. Inaccurate instruments. Anything to hinder or annoy.

Thotol R

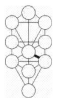

This Path makes a delightful change from the last two. It joins Victory to Beauty and is pleasantly personified in the Tarots by the Lovers. What in Life is more triumphantly beautiful than love? This is the Path where we should experience the wonders of real love between human souls. Not simply sex between bodies without anything else, but the almost unbelievable beauty and sense of an immortal achievement in conjoining Life-consciousness shared by souls of complementary polarity who find in each other what they need in themselves for the sake of progress toward Perfection. In other words the spiritual equivalent of a physical sex-act, which may or may not be coincidental with that experience. It is true that many humans may never find this Path in a lifetime as an actuality, but this is no reason why they should not explore it imaginatively. Maybe their visit here is only momentary, but even that would make an unforgettable memory for the remainder of an incarnation. Love is indeed immortal, and if we only came back to birth through the Gates of Love alone, what a wonderful world this could be. On this Path we have an opportunity to learn how Love triumphs over Death, and conquers by the power of its Beauty alone. "*Amor omnia Vincit*" is a good motto here. This is a radiantly warm and lovely Path, difficult to tear oneself away from, yet again it is a transitory experience of Life at our present levels. Apart from love between sexes, this Path can include other loves in Life. A love of Nature, a love of music, the arts, all that we describe as lovable in a broad sense. A love of children, gardening, animals, whatever we consider worth loving in this world. On this Path we should meet:

People: Lover-Archetypes from Adam and Eve right down to Abelard and Heloise. Beautiful and lovely beings rejoicing in their attachment to each other. Also those who truly love Life in one form or another. Musicians, dancers, and those who love the Orphic Tradition. Romanticists.

Places: Beautiful gardens and parks. Lagoons and soft sandy beaches. This is rather a luxury Path, so everything should be seen as pleasantly as possible. Richly furnished bedrooms and other apartments. Art galleries, concert halls. Anywhere that one might imagine being accompanied by a truly beloved Life-partner. A first-class restaurant for instance. A medieval Court of Love. This Path is one of real enjoyment everywhere, yet it should not be given undue preference before others equally important to living experience.

Things: Sun-Venus symbology. Gold and Copper. Lamps and girdles. Palm branches, anything associated with romantic settings. Playgrounds. Soft and beautiful clothing of a sensuous nature. Jewels. Nice perfumes. Intimate whispers, accessories of the amatory arts. Aphrodisiacs.

Thotol S

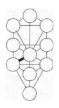

This Path is a Sun-Mercury one, connecting Glory with Beauty, another splendid Lifeway. The Tarot symbol is the Chariot, which has so much meaning in the sense of spiritual travel throughout the whole Universe in search of Truth. Sky-chariots were very old Sun-symbols bearing important Gods across the heavens. Nowadays they symbolise spacecraft carrying other than human forms of Life on conscious missions connected with Mankind. There is no reason why we should not see the Chariot-symbol in this modern light.

The chariot wheel has always been a Solar sign, and Hermes the patron of travel, especially flight. If spaceships are Solar powered and piloted by intelligent beings with extremely advanced technology, their connection with this Path is surely unmistakable. Here is where we have to develop all the skills under the Sun in order to advance ourselves along the Line of Light leading to Divinity. Everything which comes from an illuminated intelligence and the glory of a human mind at its best belongs here. This is the Path of technical ability in every field, scientific, mechanical, mathematical, electronic, and the crafts in general. Also of occult interests in the Hermetic way, such as ceremonial magic, Rosicrucianism, Masonry, and so forth. Scholarly and philosophic literature belongs to this Path, and so does academic humour. Whatever moves the mind to make definite journeys in pursuit of specific purposes is connected with this Path, which is for the investigator, not the dreamer. On it we shall probably meet:

People: Time-Space travellers. Seekers of intelligence along any lines. Questers of the Grail. Agents of Inner authorities. Telepaths. Also communication workers, detectives, transport specialists, not forgetting aviators and mariners. Possibly telekineticists from the future. Hero-figures from the past. A few Qabalists engaged on "The Work of the Chariot."

Places: Too varied to specify. Could be absolutely anywhere reachable by imagination in past, present, or future. Might be too blurred to focus properly, but there might be impressions of vehicle interiors, traffic termini, roads, rails, vapour trails, or anything suggesting travel and activated movements.

Things: Sun-Mercury symbolism. Gold and quicksilver. Alchemical equipment, scientific scenes, spacecraft, flying carpets, golden horses. All forms of transport. Wings, balloons, flying gear. Could be sub-aqua too. Anything to do with mind-mobility and Quests.

Thotol T

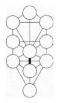

This is an extremely important Path, being the middle section of the Middle Pillar conjoining Sun and Moon by the Beauty-Foundation connection. Since it is central to the Tree of Life scheme, it is well represented by the Solar Tarot Symbol. Between the Luminaries, it carries an intensity of Light beyond the ability of ordinary mortals to bear. Human survival here is purely on spiritual levels, and only possible through a process of purification sometimes called "Self-sacrifice," which has to be very accurately interpreted, and certainly does not mean letting everyone impose ill-treatment on some masochistic victim. This is part of the Middle Pillar which is the Mystical Way directly to Divinity which so few humans can follow. It demands an absolute and unequivocal sacrifice of all pseudo-self interests, and so unhesitating acceptance of the Supreme Self intention behind the individual being. No token gestures or symbolic substitutes are of the slightest value here. The sacrifice has to be an actuality on all Life-levels. This seldom proves possible to the overwhelming majority of mortals, and moreover is usually impractical, because alternative routes along the Orphic and Hermetic Ways are always available, though of course considerably slower and much more tortuous. Nevertheless we need to appreciate this Path theoretically and imaginatively, for despite its difficulties for humans, quite a number have attempted it before falling away in search of easier tracks to Truth. On this Path from a human standpoint everything is intensely brilliant and blindingly beautiful, and on it we might meet the appearances of:

People: Avatars and supersouls seeking to link Humanity and Divinity. Those who have risen beyond necessity of re-embodiment except in the cause of

Cosmic Love for creation. Apparently angelic beings who are Life-forms of other worlds. A few humans attempting the Way of At-One-Ment through sacrifices of self-interests.

Places: This word scarcely applies to Path T. There is certainly a sense of environment, but that describes a condition here rather than a location of any kind. It may be best to work with ideas of a Heaven-state on sub-Eternal levels. A sort of paradisial place having a limited duration and extension.

Things: Sun-Moon symbolism. Gold and silver ornamentation. Splendours of every sort. A sacrificial altar with glowing fire and incense. Wonderful music. Glowing colours.

Thotol V

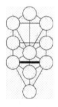

Here are linked the Principles of Victory and Glory, a Venus-Mercury combination. Emotion and intelligence joined. On this Path there is a constant swing between the heart and head directives of our lives, where facts and feelings are often in opposition as we try to strike a balance between them. Sometimes we come to surprising if not very accurate conclusions, which serve us for a while until we supersede them with whatever looks more likely at the time. This makes for what we call the "ups and downs" of Life, so the Path is truly shown as the Wheel of Fortune Tarot Trump. On these lower levels of the Tree it is mostly the unevenness of Life which constitutes the interesting phenomena. This is where we take chances with everything and frequently rely on "Lady luck" or the Goddess Fortuna to help us along. We also learn that a lot of Life is a matter of cycles, where periods of good and bad fortune chase themselves round and round in a ceaseless chain of events which Buddhists deplore and seek eternal freedom from. Here we have to learn as much as we can about the workings of this "wheel," and how to level out the inequalities and eventually emancipate ourselves from its fascinations. Learning to cope with Love and Luck is one of Life's most difficult lessons, but this is the Path whereon we have to start sorting ourselves out along those lines. This is also where human men and women must learn to live with each other both intelligently and affectionately, for that makes the best bet for success in the lottery of marriage. Altogether a tricky Path, as one might expect of anything connected with Hermes, but it is traversed by many millions of humans for most of their lives, so it could be called a well-beaten one. On it we will find:

People:	All kinds of folk taking chances with Life. Rich and poor changing places. Alternating sadness and gladness everywhere. Show people of every kind. Husband and wife partnerships. Witty and winsome types in contrast and combination. Gamblers. Fortune tellers. Hermes being patron of thieves and market-places could place some old characters on this Path. So could Venus in her Aphrodite-aspect.
Places:	Wherever fortunes change. Stockmarkets, racetracks, etc. Also where lovelife may alter drastically, and that is open to wide interpretation. An ordinary home, a palace, a theater, circumstances have to decide the place. A mortuary would *not* be apposite for this path for instance, yet a prison might, depending on supporting story.
Things:	Venus-Mercury symbolism. Copper and quicksilver. Anything associated with chance. Dice, cards, roulette wheels, lottery tickets, even Government Bonds or stocks and shares. All signs of Love and Luck, such as horseshoes, wedding rings, lovers knots, etc.

Thotol W

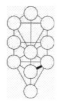

Here we are between Victory and the Foundation. Venus and Luna. A difficult Path, because we have to learn how to handle not only our sex-fantasies, but our dreams, beliefs, ideals connected with religion from the devotional aspect, romantic aspirations, and similar ideology. Moreover we have to do this not by any direct contacts with Inner sources, but reflectively by inferential processes. It is as if we were working through a mirror to guide our movements and impressions. This is where we must find out how to live by instincts rather than reason. Since it is characteristic of a feminine nature to rely on emotional and instinctive reactions more than calculated considerations and cold logic, the Tarot Priestess symbolises this Path very accurately. Many a life has been saved by some woman's instinctual findings, providing these are directed by the Divine Intention within her, and not her own personal inclinations. Hence the Priestess significance. On this Path we must discover how to be "God-guided" by means of our feelings and reflective reactions with whatever we encounter in Life. This calls for great skill in mediation and meditation, especially of an Orphic nature, which is definitely a "Priestess" faculty notwithstanding the physical sex of any Path-traveller. Esoterically men must learn to be women, and women learn to be men, while both discover how to become neither on the Paths to Perfection. On this particular Path we are supposed to develop the art of devotion to whatever Deity we desire close contact with through intense feeling for Its image. Here we have to deal with the basics of our Life-beliefs from the point of view—"I don't know whether it is or not, but I feel it must be, and that decides the issue for me now." Faith based on feeling. Millions run their lives on that alone and get along well enough with it. We should meet on this Path:

People:	Nuns and religious dedicants. Nurses. Those devoting their lives to good causes. Probably mostly females, though there could be males of a sensitive, possibly poetic nature. Introspective types given to brooding. Religious artists. Temple flower arrangers and sacristans.
Places:	Temples, cathedrals, cloisters, Lady chapels and oratories dedicated to Goddesses. Hospitals, nurseries, but could be anywhere the atmosphere of this Path is encountered. Beautiful gardens and natural scenery is likely. So is moonlight and calm water with reflections.
Things:	Pleasing devotional objects. Copper and silver. Prayer beads, illuminated psalters. Embroidery. Rich vestments, soft fabrics. Religious artwork. Children's toys of a gentle kind. Flowers. All sorts of Venus-Lunar symbology.

Thotol X

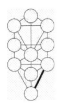

This Path links Victory to the Kingdom, or Venus-Earth. A direct and positive Path on which humans have to sort out their sex needs and come to terms with sex as a Life-urge in this world so as to make the best relationship with it that they can. Here we should learn that sex as a purely biological impulse is only the very bottom of the ladder, and we have to climb from there until we can see it as an activity which is capable of enlarging our spiritual experience in far wider fields than this world can offer. This is the Path on which we have to decide whether we shall accept sex as something purely concerned with this world, take what we can get out of it and leave things at that, or look for something bigger and better from sex on higher and finer levels of living. That is to say do we limit sex relations to bodies only, or do we seek them with our souls too? Whichever we do, this Path is where that decision must be made. Its Tarot Trump is the World, because this is where we must make up our minds whether we confine our consciousness purely to mundane affairs and not bother with esoteric investigations, or start looking for Life along lines leading out of earthly environments. We can please ourselves as to which we do. There are only three Ways out of this world toward Divinity. The Hermetic, the Orphic, or the Mystical. This Path is the first step along the Orphic Way if we want to take it. The enjoyment of emotions and fulfilment of feelings. It is true that many experiences here may be ephemeral, and not of profound significance, but they are necessary to Life, and are part of our Perfection-process once we know how to evaluate and employ them properly. Without them we should not be proportionate examples of humanity. We are in this world to experience it and evolve until we learn how to live otherwise and emancipate ourselves from embodiment. On this Path we are fairly certain to meet up with:

People: Those we love, or feel strongly about as attractive fellow beings. People we admire or would want to know. Companionable and amusing folk of an ordinary kind in whose company we could feel happy and relaxed. Good friends and nice neighbours. Perhaps not on a permanent basis, but definitely welcome while acquaintance lasts maybe an incarnation.

Places: Almost anywhere that happy human relationships are possible. Pleasure places, social scenes, intimate surroundings, etc. Certainly nowhere evoking sad or bitter feelings. Could be quite ordinary environs like homes, shops, offices, workplaces, and so forth.

Things: Venus-Earth symbolism. Copper and clay combinations. Erotica. Anything connected with friends and families. Culinary equipment. Sports gear. Domestic stuff of all varieties. Clothes, fashions, adornments. Whatever suggests the atmosphere of this Path.

Thotol Y

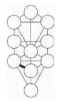

This Path is really the masculine equivalent of W, and joins Glory to the Foundation, or Hermes to Luna. It is essentially a magical and ceremonial Path concerned with mind and reasoning processes. A Magician is a "Transformation Image," and therefore that is the Tarot Trump here. This is where we must reckon with reason in a magical manner, and learn how to make our minds serve our wills in our search for Truth. Again we have the reflective element of Luna here, which means the use of inference and deduction rather than direct encounter. Still, the Magic Mirror is a good investigative tool if we remember to reverse meanings in our minds. Occult pageantry and psychodrama is very much part of this Path, and both ritual and rubric of religious practice are closely connected with it. For those who find mysterious performances and customs a fascinating study, this is where expertise in those subjects is gained. It is also a scientific Path in the sense that metaphysics are tackled more from a logical and reasonable angle than some high-flown and far fetched approach by fantasy alone. Those travelling this Path often have a fondness for elaborate apparatus such as "psionic" equipment, and they favour solid symbolism of a mechanical or electronic nature. Especially if this is liable to bewilder or impress others because of its alleged importance. Hermes does love his little tricks. This is the Path where we have to employ our creative talents inventively, so as to extend and expand our minds, also to improve our skills in mind-management. The practical use of psychology is essential here too. As a general rule, this Path is rather too active for much meditation or contemplative work. Thought is translated into experimental action with the rapidity one would expect of Hermes, though often with the off-mark one associates with Luna. Here we learn truth by inference from our errors, which is quite a normal human procedure, though inadvisable to repeat *ad nauseam*. Expect to meet on this Path:

People: Ceremonialists of every kind. Priests, magicians, members of Masonic and Occult Orders, psychiatrists, doctors, actors, all brilliant thinkers and speakers. Writers of occult and allied literature such as Science-fiction. Composers of classical music connected with such themes. Anyone associated with the "Inner Arts."

Places: Occult Temples, Lodges, anywhere secret ceremonies are held. Also stages, consulting rooms, laboratories. Anywhere that activities are conducted in connection with mindworkings and investigation of Inner affairs.

Things: All sorts of Hermetic apparatus. Mercury-Lunar symbolism. Silver and quicksilver. Ceremonial robes. Lodge regalia. Ritual books. Electro-chemical equipment or musical instruments used in occult or psychological activities. Hypno-mechanisms. Anything likely to be linked with this line of human behaviour.

Thotol Z

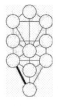

This penultimate Path between Glory and the Kingdom, or Mercury and Earth, is that of Man the Scientific Seeker. Here we know nothing while we ask for everything, and go in search of secrets to make us successful in Life. Hence the Fool Tarot symbol, which really means the "Innocent," or non-knower at the start of a Quest. Man rushes in where angels fear to tread, and demands that Deity answers whatever he asks. He does not realise that he is insisting on obtaining the means of his own destruction if his foolishness cannot be held in check. Here is the Path where we have to learn how to control the natural madness in mankind by means of earthly commonsense and Hermetic rationality. Otherwise we are living on the edge of an Abyss like the Fool in the picture. It is an apt symbol in many ways here, for Man is truly mad in many ways. Mad for money, power, sex, fame, admiration, and a million other seeds of self-destruction. Fools are not idiots though, and they can come to their senses if they sincerely want to, which is what this Path is all about. There is an old truism that only a fool can be made wise, which of course signifies a needed state of non-knowledge before a process of imparting wisdom can commence. It is also a truism that a specialist in knowledge of some particular sort may be an absolute fool in other directions. We often find brilliant scientists or scholars in specialised subjects are complete innocents in other areas quite well known to ordinary people. So here is the Path whereon we are supposed to convert our natural foolishness into caution, and our innocence into experience. Simplicity and sophistry have to be blended in order to produce a reasonably intelligent human being who can get by in most of the ways we are likely to enter in this world. On this particular Path, we shall surely come across:

People: Average mortals of all sorts, but mostly those with some aim in Life, or ambition to pursue in search of some distinction or other. This is most probable in scientific, literary, engineering, medical, or professional fields. Business, political, and commercial activities are also prominent here. Not, on the whole, very spiritual types. The fool has said in his heart: "There is no God."

Places: Shops, offices, factories, ships, aircraft. People of this Path are found almost anywhere in this world, but very seldom in churches or Temples, unless they are as victims of fraud or imposition on the part of "religious racketeers."

Things: Mercury-Earth symbolism. Quicksilver and clay. Ordinary clothing for profession or job represented. Objects of this Path are more probably connected with technology than arts or religion. Could be theatrical in character. Musical gear unlikely, but mathematical equipment quite probable. Educational equipment too.

Thotol Th

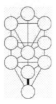

At last the final Path on the Tree connecting Luna to Earth. An interesting factor here is that this Path is the first one to be accomplished as a physical actuality by Mankind. Human feet have literally travelled to the Moon. Nevertheless human minds and souls must still make progress along this Path in their own way if we are to gain any spiritual stature in our Universe. The Tarot symbol is the Moon, and it represents our first struggles to lift our Inner selves away from earth-levels towards the Light of Truth behind our beings. Initial human efforts to adapt with the spiritual structure underlying Creation are as uncertain, shaky, and often as pathetic or comic as a baby trying to toddle its wobbly way towards a trusted elder relative. Yet without those wavering steps it would never learn to walk at all. Here we are faced with the Inner equivalents of those first footsteps up the Middle Pillar of the Way to Light. Looking over human history, we can see most of our past mistakes and failures together with our partial successes along this section of our Truth-trail. Moreover we can also see how we have translated these into our own times. Weird cults of every kind, "way-out" costumes and customs, bygone beliefs twisted into pseudo-modern appearances. "Spirit-guides" of the last century turned into "Spacemen" for this one. On the other hand there is a very genuine and deep sincerity shown by the heartfelt human need for contact with spiritual realities however faintly grasped they may be. This is the Path whereon we "see in a glass darkly," by the weaker Lunar Light, rather than risk being blinded by staring at the Sun directly. It is spiritually much safer to see things by reflection instead of losing our insight altogether by unwise exposure to radiation. So here is where we struggle and fumble to find almost any sort of foothold on the first rung up the Ladder of Life towards Ultimate Light. This Path holds both gladness and sadness along its strange byways. We shall meet some very odd people, and have some queer adventures while we are on it, for it is a mixed and muddly Path, with many twists and turns, none leading to Truth, but all affording clues about where to look next. On this Path we should find it difficult to avoid:

People: Religious, mystical, and idealistic enthusiasts of every conceivable variety. Eccentrics, eclectics, and individualistic approachers of the Absolute and Its Aspects under any form. Priests and pastors of all faiths. Cultists and followers of every creed, no matter how peculiar. In our times, Neo-Pagans, spiritualists, occultists, and anyone at all with Innerworld ideas who are looking for even a glimmer of reflected Light above Earthly levels of living.

Places: Churches, Temples, Lodges, Circles, Sacred sites, Homes, Underground caverns. Mountain tops. Hermitages, arenas, convokation rooms, anywhere that meetings with the people of this Path are likely. Could be a telephone kiosk, a library, or wherever a prearranged meeting might be kept.

Things: Moon-Earth symbols. Silver and clay. Items here are too impossibly numerous to specify. Religious and mystical gear of every imaginable variety, including books, pictures, musical instruments, and all art/craft work connected therewith. Mirrors, screens, crystals, dowsing rods, and so forth. Colourful costumes or uniforms and habits reflecting every human effort at spiritual evolution. The whole of our "Outer Court" in fact, together with all its toys and trappings.

All the foregoing is just the barest outline of what might be expected on each of the Paths as very general guidelines. Merely a few suggestions to act as starting points from which to develop the far broader and deeper channels of consciousness which are waiting to be explored by enquiring minds and souls. No matter how much Pathworking may be done however, the purpose of it must never be lost sight of or there is no use doing it at all. This purpose is packing a maximum amount of categorized consciousness behind the minimal focal point of a single summative symbol. That one consideration needs to be dwelt on and reiterated as often as necessary to make it a directive of every Inner adventure on the Tree. The process is symbolised in esoteric lore as the relationship of the Macrocosm with the Microcosm, or put another way, the connection between God and man. This is illustrated schematically by the well-known Hexagram of interlaced triangles. The descending triangle shows the focalisation of Divine consciousness to contact Man as a "micro-miniaturised" likeness of God. The ascending triangle indicates humanity concentrating virtually the whole of its history into a single point aimed at the Absolute. That is how mutual contact is established.

This is what is meant by the commandment to: "Love God with *all* thy mind and soul." We need to aim our entire Selves at our "Image of the Infinite." Not just a few random thoughts and passing feelings, but all we were, are now, and ever will be. The whole of us. Our past incarnations, present ones, and every future life needed to reach that Ultimate Reality. That is what we should be learning on all Paths of Life, whether by the Tree system, or however else we try to tread them.

At any rate, now that we have learned how to load an ordinary alphabet with a whole mass of Life-meaning, we shall have to find out the use of this for telecommunication with "Inworlders" who are willing to work the same system for contacting our consciousness with theirs. This could be both an interesting and agreeable experience.

G. Thotolese: Conversing With "Gods"

Learning to use "Thotolese" is not altogether unlike learning to communicate in Morse code. In order to learn Morse, an operator must be able to count at very high speed, estimating time-lengths of signals and silences at the same rate, while associating letters of the alphabet and numerals or punctuation with each distinctive combination of code-units. This is entirely an automatic mental action needing no knowledge of the actual meaning conveyed by the signals themselves.

To illustrate this point, an instance from the Camel Corps practice in Egypt during the second World War will serve beautifully. Their signal operators were then mainly Sudanese who neither spoke nor wrote English, yet received and sent radio messages in English at considerable speed. They were so trained that they knew when hearing Morse signals in their headphones, they had to make distinctive marks on paper which they were told were characters of the English alphabet, yet the language itself was not taught them. Conversely, they were trained when seeing an English character on paper, to translate this into finger movements on a Morse key. Thus the men were communicating with each other in a language which was unintelligible to them, though of course known to their officers. So the human mind is quite capable of coping with meaning on a purely mechanistic level, while unable to understand its intellectual or spiritual significance on higher levels of expression.

While reading ordinary script, we have to interpret the spaces between letters and words just as much as we follow the lines of each letter. In fact, what we actually read is the difference between the two. The negative of the space and the positive of the letter, becomes the neutral line of language we turn into meaning within our minds. In the case of Thotolese, we have to combine two fundamental Life-values to see a single consonant of our language. So the communication system we shall work with is roughly as follows. We must "think at the Gods" consciously through alphabetical symbols our subconsciousness has associated with specific experiences of Life. The "God-Beings" who are constantly in touch with our deep awareness, interpret those impressions into terms of their own consciousness. They return their reactions with us by "thinking at us" through variants of Life, which our minds translate as alphabetical combinations linked with our language. This may sound an elaborate way of communicating with ones own subconscious mind, but it is really a method of communicating with other agencies of awareness *through* ones subconscious mind, by means of an agreed code of consciousness.

In point of fact, all we are really doing is reorganise and bring to intelligent recognition levels a perfectly natural process of instinctive reaction with Life-forces normally beyond reach of our rational minds. Since our lives in this world are largely directed and controlled from those focal points, it is a great advantage to link them through our underlying connections with Life, by literate and understandable terms of expression we use amongst each other while conducting our Living-affairs on this Earth. At the same time it has to be fully realised that the limits of this scheme are determined entirely by individual abilities of literacy and concept-constructing in terms of formalised thinking. Unless people are actually capable of working with words and making meanings with them, they cannot translate subconsciously received messages into any human language. Assuming a fair to good average degree of intelligent literacy however, this is how first practical steps in Thotolese are suggested.

When proficiency in Pathworking is gained to the point where concentration on a single letter will simultaneously call up Path conditions into the worker's consciousness, whole words may be sent to subconscious levels and beyond in this way. First think of some very brief, impactive and significant sentence, calculated to attract attention from Inner sources of intelligence. Such as: "Awake and answer." Write this on paper in capitals. Transmit them one by one to the subconsciousness by filling the focal area of awareness completely, and exclusively, with the Thotol meaning of the letters for a brief moment per letter, allowing pauses between words. Cross out the letters on paper as they are sent. If it helps, the Path numbers may be written above and below each letter at first, though the message on paper is only for preliminary exercises, and has to be dropped altogether when practice makes it unnecessary. Eventually everything must be done in and by the mind alone.

In becoming conscious of each Path, it is important that this be done, so far as possible, with the whole of ones awareness for maybe the split fraction of a second. It is actually an entire Pathworking compressed into the smallest Time-Space unit appreciable to human intelligence. We must do more than flicker a thought casually from Path to Path as we go past them,. We should live each Path momentarily as we change consciousness from one to another. That is to say, we must "switch on" a Path, experience it, "switch it off," and then proceed to the next Path in less than a minisecond. At first this may be thought impossible or unlikely, but it is only a matter of practice and perseverance before quite a reasonable speed can be worked up. A good opportunity for such an exercise is while doing ordinary typing. With fingers poised over the keys, let the mind dwell on each single letter as a

Thotol value before striking them. Identify every letter according to its place on the Tree as it is struck. This will slow typing speed down considerably at first, but it will also speed up Path recognition to a comparible extent. It can help here to begin with a Path-letter plan easily visible, then put this on one side for occasional reference if needed, then turn it face down or cover it so that only desperation demands a glance at it.

To practice reception it is only necessary to reverse this process by quietly contemplating ones own Instate, and allowing spelled-out messages to arise naturally in the focal point of awareness. Although this sounds uncomplicated when described in such a way, it is actually an extremely intricate process. Theoretically the letters and words should come to the surface unimpeded by interference from subconscious directives concerned with pure self-interest and personal desires. We are only too liable to twist and translate our deep sources of informative intelligences into what we want to hear, rather than what they really mean. Moreover, we are virtually driven into doing this for the sake of self-protection, and quite often in order to maintain the balance of sanity against sheer adversities of Life in this world. Few indeed could stand the strain of being exposed to naked Truth all the time. So we have to adapt and compromise with our Life-consciousness in such a way, that we can relate with Truth obliquely through carefully constructed screens, rather than face its raw forces in our states of defenceless Inner exposure. Therefore we can expect our contacts with "The Gods" of our Inner Life to be coloured and presented according to our personal patterns of perception, and due allowance must be made for this factor.

For such reasons, it is far the best course before seriously starting to "Thotolise," to make a solemn compact with ones own sources of inner awareness, that leading questions of Life beyond ones actual ability to cope with independantly, will never be asked. For example, it would be foolish to enquire something like: "When and how will I die?", "How many planets are there in the whole Universe?", "Is there a God, and if so what is Its Name?", "What am I going to be in my next incarnation?". Such questions will never be answered factually in any case, but only through ones preconceptions of their purport which are usually very far off even good guesswork. On the whole, it is not a good idea to treat the

Tree solely as a fortune-telling machine or a curiosity satisfie r. The finest and most natural use of the Tree is for guidance of Life in the right direction towards Perfection. That is, after all, its primal purpose and normal function, so it might as well be employed according to its designer's intentions and specifications. If it is treated otherwise in some manner contrary to its maker's instructions, we shall only have ourselves to blame for any failures or breakdowns.

Therefore the wisest way to work with the Tree-system is to commence with short sessions preferably at set times of the day. Obviously the early morning after rising would be a good time, because of recent repose in contact with states of subconsciousness. Before bedtime is another obvious occasion, because of intended approach to the same levels. About a half-way period between the two for a few moments should be another "Thotol-break" if possible. This links the active mind concerned with full details of worldly occupation, with an underlying awareness of spiritual self-significance. About thee to five minutes is quite enough to start with, and at first a pen and paper, or possibly a pocket recorder, is useful as a thought-focussing mechanism. With practice, the brain-mind will do everything for itself perfectly well, though it is a sensible idea to make notes of what "comes through," for the sake of keeping records and giving some kind of continuity to the process.

One useful way of working is to begin by making the entire Tree a sort of background occupying the area of ones body. There is no need to focus it in sharp detail so long as awareness of its ambience exists, something like an awareness of whatever is behind ones back. The letters of the Paths are then summoned singly at speed to make words. If a question is asked, the query is indicated by sweeping consciousness rapidly up the Tree, then pushing it to Zero and beyond with one releasing stroke, after which relax and await any reply. It is best during initial sessions to keep contacts on very broad and general levels, being content to take what comes uncritically and undemandingly, simply noting that a sense of contact with other than ones own intelligence exists, and if so, any general impressions in connection therewith. For instance, does the contact seem sexed or merely neutral, is it close or distant, does it have emotional content, or is it disinterested, can it be identified, or is it entirely anonymous? Anything at all to establish some recognisable relationship. There is no point whatever trying to force or invent a fictitious reply. If none comes by the end of an agreed sessional time, then note N/C (No Contact) on the record sheet and leave it at that until next time. It is important not to feel annoyed, put out, or in any way bothered by a blank wall confronting ones consciousness, which has been hopefully extended for some friendly remarks from Inner intimates. Better to see a non-committal plain surface, than read a lot of rubbish flung there for nothing more than foolishness. One singe word of sense is worth more than a million words of stupidity.

The exact form of responses received through the Thotol system from Inner sources varies a great deal, depending on the mental make-up of recipients. Some tend to see words as if written almost immediately in front of their eyes in various styles. Others hear them spoken in differing voices or dialects. Others again only sense replies, or get the gist of them more or less instinctively. Everything depends on how we translate subconsciously received intelligence, into terms understandable by our ordinary abilities of awareness. This is really the case with normal human conversation. Our ears do not really hear other people speaking words. They hear specific noises which our minds turn into words, because they are already in our mental stock of understandings, arranged into categories, ready to be matched against anything our ears receive. The understanding of words is made by our minds alone through agreement amongst each other, about significance attached to sonics which are also represented by visual symbols, or in the case of blind people by tactile ones. Our senses receive signals which our minds match from their stores. Here, we have to receive signals from sources outside human origination altogether, and match these against our mental stock of words by means of the Thotol system, so that they make sense and have rational meanings.

It has to be realized right from the start that quality and content of communication does depend entirely on individual linkages with Inner living intelligences. Some people are liable to get miles of "messages" which could seem most remarkable or even fantastic, yet have extremely little solid significance behind them, being purely fictional in character. Others might get only a few laconic words or phrases holding keys of vital importance for their lives. In general it pays to keep a firm censorship control over incoming intelligence, and remain in contact only with reasonable and reliable sources of supply. This may take perhaps many months of careful checking and evaluation, but not a moment spent on such work will ever be wasted. Again and again the mind has to be trained so that it will translate inwardly received impulses into terms of thought comprehensible by normal consciousness. This means establishing firm disciplines of procedure which should suggest themselves to anyone with plain consciousness.

For example, incoming intelligence must be made to observe the simple rules of clarity, precision, and coherent construction. From the first a communicator should firmly refuse to accept rambling, vague, unclear, or dubious receptions. Repeatedly such meanderings have to be stopped and thrown back into the subconsciousness with the curt command in Thotolese: "Rephrase." Eventually this will have the effect of bringing communications into more satisfactory shape. The last thing an operator should do is allow himself to become negative and indifferent, permitting anything at all to suggest itself randomly and haphazardly. Like a radio operator receiving Morse, his attention should be keenly focussed and alerted all the while, supervising incoming signals with scrupulous care and concern. Only after writing them down in final form can he afford to relax and examine them critically.

As a sense of contact increases, it is necessary to become more and more selectively critical concerning what is received. Especially as regards predictive or specifically informative communications. Nothing whatever should be taken as accurate until either proven by events or strongly supported by rational thought. If a communication is obviously wrong, the reason should be sought. Say a predictive statement has been made that something will happen which in fact does not. Inaccuracy here is most often due to mistranslation by the mind of the receptor which formulates a possibility either feared or desired. The only sensible thing to do is make memoranda of what comes through, assess them later for accuracy or otherwise, then decide whether the percentage of correctness gives grounds for reliability or not. At least fifty per cent accuracy is necessary before commonsense can afford to take chances of action on "Inner information received."

Even then there will be need for continuous caution and checking over a long period before real reliance is placed in communications obtained from Inner sources by this, or any other means.

Once dependable contacts have been made and developed with Inner intelligences through this Thotol system, they themselves should instruct each individual how to proceed from that point. In all probability, each operator will be given some definite "code-call" which might consist of a name or a number-series. There is no use whatever trying to invent one of these codes for oneself. They have to come through Inner channels directly, and, like "magical names" should never be written down or used for any other purpose than communication with their point of Inner origination. Numbers of course are signalled by concentration on appropriate Spheres of the Tree. So the correct combination of numbers and letters properly signalled can be the keys to communication channels linking human consciousness with Inner levels of living intelligence. This was certainly discovered by old-time workers in Qabalah during their number-letter experiments, but whether or not they realized the prior necessity for subconscious associative symbolism before the system would work at all, is uncertain.

These old-timers assumed that the magic lay in the letters and numbers by themselves. Put them together rightly, and all secrets of the Universe could be disclosed. It did not seem to dawn on those early mystics that the magic lay in the chains of categorised consciousness formed by their own efforts to link these with literate symbols for units of intelligent awareness. The secrets of our Universe and Knowledge of the Gods do lie somewhere beyond easy reach of human minds, though not beyond our eventual range of evolutionary extension. That is what every twig of the Tree tries to tell us through the language of its leaves if we will take the trouble to learn it.

Anyone supposing that familiarity with the Tree language might result in instant answers to everything and consequent advantages over everyone else, will meet with nothing but disappointment. Reliable operators of the system "on the Inside" are not working for the sake of satisfying human curiosity and cupidity, but solely in order to help humans evolve into higher types of Life altogether. Therefore, somewhat like security agencies on Earth, they work on a "need to know" basis, which also seems to apply within their circles of consciousness. The tree-language will not put us in direct touch with Divine Omniscience, but it links us with those who mediate this all-awareness according to their degrees of ability, and our degrees of contact with their consciousness. Whether we call these entities Angels, Spirit Guides, or anything else makes no difference to their intrinsic natures. We and they alike are both distinctive species of intelligent Life, co-existing in the same Creative Cosmos on separative levels of expression.

In this world alone, for instance, we have many orders of Life existing entirely apart from each other's awareness, yet connected together by the "Overall Order" of Earth existence as a whole. Consider the worlds of fishes and birds, so similar in some ways, yet different in others. Both creatures fly around their environments, lay eggs, prey on supportive species, and have many habits in common, including communicative noises. Problem—how could a fish and a bird share intelligence with each other? More importantly, why should they and what mutual benefits might there be? Could birds warn fishes of approachable fishing fleets, or fishes caution birds against oil-slicks? Similar problems occur in the case of incarnate humans and those existing in connectable states of consciousness divided by dimensional incompatibilities.

Looking at Life as represented by its orders on our Earth, it would not seem that they are very anxious to communicate with each other, unless there is something to be gained by the exchange. Much the same could be said for the "Inner orders" also. Their close contacts with humanity are mainly governed by mutual interests. Where these coincide, will be the most likely contact-poits to explore or exploit. Hence the development of the Thotol system between human and other orders of Life, sharing similar spiritual aims and concepts of consciousness in connection with Cosmos.

To some extent we have been using the principle s of "Thotolism" for many ages past by the use of "God-Names," which were really code-calls for linking humans more closely with higher forms of intelligent Life, which are concerned with our evolutionary progress as potentially spiritual creatures. The

Christian church encouraged its members to communicate in the name of "*JESUS*," which had the coded significance in Greek of "*GE-ZEUS*," or Earth-Mother and Sky-Father. It could be said perhaps that Earth-mortals were instinctively calling their primal progenitors on other planets. A sort of general appeal back along ancestral lines of Life. Later on the name "*MARY*" (*MARI*) came into Christian usage as a "blanket-call" to the great Sea Mother from whose mysterious womb our bodily forms were born to Earthlife. So the "*JESUS-MARY*" call was esoterically an invokation to three of our Life elements, Earth, Air, and Water. It is possible that Christians had a fear of invoking Fire which suggested their Hell, or had a dislike of doing so because most Pagans were Solar worshippers.

One way or another humans have realised for a very long time past, that specific words were "magical," because these had the effect of putting their focal points of consciousness in touch with their Inner identities, and awakening degrees of awareness not normally accessible to their matter-concerned minds. Such words were seldom universal, but applied mainly through ethnic and other localised forms of understanding. The more we become word-thinking people, the more specialised was our "magical language," yet it was not until relatively late in human history that the sophisticated system of the literate Tree-Path-Plan became possible. Nor was it until our century that Key-word associations for unlocking secrets of the subconscious mind, was made into a scientific study. Early Qabalistic scholars believed they were contacting important Angels, who would inform them advantageously about the workings of the Universe. Modern psychologists believe they might uncover secrets of the human mind, which will enable them, or their paymasters, to control and manipulate mankind for quite a variety of reasons, all favourable to personal profits. Possibly very few souls indeed have sincerely tried to learn the "Language of the Gods," purely for the sake of learning how to live as a better than human species of Life on Earth and elsewhere.

The chances of an average person discovering much about Cosmic secrets through the use of Thotolese, are as remote as if they sought classified information from earthly human authorities. Probably less. They can always learn whatever their consciousness is capable of comprehending to the extent of expansion it will reach through the Tree-system, and no more than that. Inner communication have their own rules of Life to observe, their own hierarchy to obey, and their own obligations to fulfil. They are not a spy-service, nor may they intervene with the workings of natural laws in this world to a greater extent, than allowed by the exigencies of Existence Itself as limited by the control of Cosmic Consciousness. Moreover it takes a very highly specialised and competent Inner Intelligence to influence even slightly the course of human conduct and living on Earth. Direct contact with such beings is rarely possible to humans, and then only for some very significant reason. Grandiose claims by humans to have direct contact with, or special authority from High Gods or other Divine Beings are usually born of wishful thinking and ego-aggrandisement. Or possibly the humans concerned may have been maliciously misinformed by "Inner-Lifers," who are indifferent to human spiritual welfare, and possibly antipathic to our species of creature.

A major point in favour of the Thotol system is that it cannot very well be misused by seriously anti-human Inner intelligences, because its terms of reference are meaningless to them. Concepts such as Beauty, Discipline, Mercy, etc., are quite outside their normal scope of comprehension or behaviour. To them, the ideology of the Tree would seem insane and valueless, therefore beyond bothering with as a means of anti-human activity. Put bluntly, *the Tree system does not encourage humanity to destroy itself*, so it is of no help to those with such an aim in view. The risk of the Tree-system being deliberately perverted by anti-human minds is more than remote. Besides which,. they have already adequate means of reaching our consciousness through other channels. Therefore Thotolese is likely to remain more or less a "private line" between humans anxious to develop their spiritual potentialities, and those on the "other side of Life" who are concerned with assisting this process.

There is a specially important thing to bear in mind when making these communications. Inner intelligences are not embodied entities looking at Life on our levels as an experience which is happening to them. Therefore they do not have our points of view about Earth-events happening to us as pain-pleasure causations. They would not see death per se as anything very terrible for instance, though human inflictions of cruelty and malice on our own species would seem shocking and reprehensible. Our lives and theirs are so utterly different, it is virtually impossible to share experiences except to whatever degrees mutual symbology allows. Physical pain is not appreciable to those without human bodies, but the facts of grief and unhappiness because of illness can be appreciated as disturbances of balance, inharmonious distribution of energies and so forth. A lot of things causing us anxieties and problems seem relatively trivial from Inner angles of view, something like the mountains of nursery life being very small molehills to attendant adults. On the other hand many things we ignore or can barely be bothered with, cause a great deal of concern and serious thinking among Inners aware of their significance as factors affecting our mutual Cosmic relationships. Prominently among these are human hostilities among each other, exploitative treatment of other Life-species regardless of their evolutionary entitlements, mismanagement of natural energies, and irresponsibility of behaviour which could cripple this planet's part in a Life-perfection programme so far as our Solar system is concerned.

Humanity as such, has a function to fulfil on this Earth in the "Ecology of Existence" scheme applying to our corner of Cosmos. If we fail in this, then we begin to upset the balance of Life on other levels than our own, which calls for compensatory Cosmic action in consequence. Centuries ago this could usually be confined to relatively mild corrections, through individual and collective channels capable of bearing them by human readjustments to Earthlife. In recent history however, we have been growing dangerously near the outside edge of this procedure, because of our ability to alter the atomic structure of matter, and we have invaded Space beyond the confines of this planet. We are not only becoming a danger to ourselves, but a menace to other worlds as well, including the spiritual sub-structure of our own Life-order.

If the worst comes to the worst, and we cannot be controlled by consciousness, we could be controlled by catastrophe instead, and our species reduced to insignificance or even extinction. That, however, would mean a loss to Macrocosmic Life of quite a serious kind, and a set-back to the Perfection-Plan which would be very unwelcome to those most concerned—including our own most evolved members of mankind. Although spiritual survival would certainly continue, its quality would be diminished by the destruction of humanity, just as ours would be diminished by the disappearance of other animal life than our own in this world. Without humans, the "life of the Gods" would be so much the less. Even though we are but one small planetful in the whole Cosmos of Creation, we should still be missed, until we might be replaced by some more advanced species, which could scarcely be done without incalculable expenditure of Creative energy.

So pro-human orders of Inner intelligence have reasons to be concerned about our future, since this involves their conditions of consciousness as well. Hence the attempts at communication along literate lines, since humans are becoming more and more resistant to other approaches. How long this will take before it emerges from experimental stages into something acceptable by more than a minimum of human minds, depends entirely on the extent of human practice and performance, which is likely to be neither rapid, nor sustained. Even if the impossible happened and the process were perfected tomorrow, the mass of mankind would continue ignoring its import, as most of us have always ignored everything outside immediate cravings for "creature-comfort" and the satisfaction thereof.

The likelihood is that "Thotolese" will remain the study of dedicated specialists for quite a while to come, yet it is a good idea for the general principles of the system to be appreciated outside such select circles. Only a few years ago, the ideas of communication with other than mortals were confined to prayer and meditation by Churches, and spiritualistic trivia by the less orthodox. Now transcendentalism has taken a modern twist in terms of telepathy with people on other planets, and there are paperbacks on Qabalah to be had in most bookstores. Therefore Thotolese should scarcely be much of a surprise for many moderns, though not many are likely to push it past the printed page very far. However, if it gets into some kind of conscious circulation especially among Western thoughtways, that should serve the purpose behind it until further developments make its meanings more prominent.

Then, why should anyone with limited time to spend on

esoteric activities devote any of it to "Thotolising" his consciousness, in hopes of contacting intelligences living in different Life-dimensions than his own? First, for the same reasons that mountaineers run incredible risks. "Because it is *there*." It is an achievement much above anything that ordinary folk can do with their minds. Mountaineers have probably added much less to the stock of human knowledge and experience than other skilled activities, but they have demonstrated degrees of endurance and amazing ingenuity with survival gear invented to serve their needs. More than anything, they have shown the intense individualistic human desire to "overoutstand" their fellow mortals, by accomplishing something quite beyond any average ability. The thrill of touching earth which no human has ever set foot on till then, places them on an Inner pinnacle higher than the mountain itself. So does the sense of being one of an elite brotherhood, every life among which is in the hands of the others. Though maybe few mountaineers would admit it, their exercise gives them a feeling of virtual "God-hood," which they would not exchange for anything else Earth could offer.

Possibly most of all, Thotolisers might seek for convincing signs that there really are other forms of intelligent Life than humanity in existence, and that many of these do concern themselves with our development into more interesting beings than entities embodied in masses of moving meat. Once they learn how to listen intelligently within themselves, they may perhaps discern more meaning to their lives than moneymaking, and something more significant than social status. They might even get an inkling of where they are bound for as souls seeking their Source across the Ocean of Infinity. Anybody can read the theories of others and their opinions on these topics in books, but how many are willing to work at finding out their own Inner facts from resources freely available within themselves at the cost of some disciplined concentration? That is all Thotolese takes, yet the price is much too high for the majority of humans.

Of course there are difficulties of communication with Thotolese, as occur with any form of speech or writing. Our problem was well expressed by Shakespeare in his famously succinct lines: "I can call spirits from the vasty deep!", to which brag was retorted: "Why so can I, or so may any man, but - will they answer?" We can indeed call at length in Thotolese, or any magical language of the mind, yet would we recognise a reply if we received one? In the case of Thotolese the answer is most likely yes, though possibly not immediately, nor perhaps very clearly at first. The chances are that replies are likely to be obscurely oracular, until communicators at each end of the line become more accustomed to thinking in terms of each others values rather than expect identical viewpoints on life at the different levels concerned.

Then again, there is bound to be a good deal of "testing out" by operators of the Thotol system on Inner levels. They naturally need to know what type of human they are dealing with, before they commit themselves to any lasting contacts. The sort of human they seem most anxious to avoid, are those who expect their "spirit friends" to tell them everything they are supposed to do, want detailed instructions and information about daily events, and would contentedly let themselves be controlled like puppets, so long as nothing nasty ever happened to them. One of the quickest ways of shutting down communication by the Thotol system, is to keep demanding prophecies, privileges, and other wish-want information through it. All that happens when closure from the inside occurs, is that querant's enquiries are reflected back at them like echoes in an empty cavern, or from a blank wall.

This does not mean that no personal matters whatever may be mentioned via the Thotol system. It is rather a question of how they are presented and from which angle an approach is made. For instance, a pre-emptory order to change some purely personal circumstances, would most likely meet an ambiguous answer or none at all. Phrased as: "I am in great difficulties trying to make any Inner progress, because of such and such a situation. Can you help me solve my problems and assist my consciousness to deal with them please?", stands a much better chance of a reasonable reply. Thotol communications are largely governed by making right relationships in the first place. Get these sorted out as a priority, and the rest is mostly a matter of practice. If a wrong or inharmonious relationship is attempted in the beginning, nothing of any value will follow until this is corrected.

So what do? Thotol communications mainly consist of, and how should anyone know they really have a conscious contact with

Inner intelligence? As a rule because the formulated thoughts "beamed back" at the human end of the link have a strangely original quality about them, which differs from the human operator's ordinary methods of thinking, and seem as if someone else were speaking inside him. Perhaps the phraseology is somewhat other than his usual style of speaking and writing. Ideas or information may come to him which are quite outside his normal range of knowledge. By and large, there will be an unmistakable sense of "otherness" more than difficult to describe, but entirely recognisable by anyone who has once experienced it.

It is most unlikely that Thotol contacts will consist only of prophecies, long lectures in sermonising style, amazing revelations, exhortations to incite extravagant behaviour, or unreasonable demands of any kind. Words may in fact be very few, and often quite casual or just plain commonplace. Friendly humour and amusement is very probable. Sometimes it may scarcely seem worth the effort of making the contact, except for the feeling of relationship with other orders of Life in interconnected states of dimensional consciousness. Yet always deep down inside oneself is an instinct that whatever helps a realisation of individual linkage with the Spirit of Life, through chains of consciousness leading thereto, is very worthwhile having.

Something which has to be taken into account with all psychic communications, Thotol or otherwise, is the physical age of the operator. Middle age at the height of Intellectual capacity is probably the most reliable period. In youth there can be brilliant flashes, unsurpassed at any later date, and in latter life there is a tendency to non-reaction with Inner stimuli, which would evoke considerable response from younger people. It is largely a question of inspiration, a word implying the influx of "Spirit" absorbed by human organisms, as their bodies breathe the Element of Air. In youth we are inspired by hopes of making some kind of mark in this world. In age, nothing can inspire us, except prospects of being something better in another state of self elsewhere. In midlife we see our main chances of correcting youthful mistakes in time to accomplish what age is unlikely to achieve. This is when our contacts with Inner Life are usually of maximum value from the viewpoint of significance and importance. In order to take full advantage of it however, we should have to spend some of our youth-time setting up the mental mechanism enabling us to make the most of this productive period ahead. At the same time it will initiate an intellectual investment calculated to make the end-period of incarnation an interesting and spiritually stimulating experience.

However early or late in earthlife we set up the Thotol system, in the end every soul must make its individual contacts through it, and be guided by those according to communications received. One thing is certain. The system will not work at all without the necessary amounts of association exercises being faithfully carried out. For some people this may take quite a time, and for others it can be fairly fast, but only patience and perseverance will produce any results at all, and those may not be spectacular to start with. Nor could anybody except, actual practitioners themselves, form any fair opinions as to the scope and possibilities of Thotolese, and those could only comment on their own cases.

As a general ruling from hard experience, it would seem most unwise to divulge the contents of Thotol communications to others, except maybe when small intimate groups share a common contact for some specific work. Inner intelligences imparted to individuals is normally intended for them alone, and if they pass this along to other humans indiscriminately or thoughtlessly, contact-lineage is liable to be cut off from Inside for possibly quite a long time. That was why old-time practitioners made such strict rules of secrecy about their contact-rituals. It was not that their rites *per se* had anything very amazing in them, but connections with incompatible types of consciousness caused technical trouble leading to breakdowns in the mental and spiritual circuitry concerned, and subsequent loss of contacts which might have taken years of trouble and effort in building up. Our spiritual technology has not yet reached a point where this is a negligible risk, so while we are still forced to use old methods pending developments for the future, it would be advisable to observe procedures which have served us so well in the past. Archaic advice to tree-climbers holds good today: "Never let go of one branch before you have firm grip of the next." This certainly applies to the Holy Tree of Life if we want to avoid a fall. Here that means keeping Inner communications entirely confidential, unless there are very clear and consistent instructions which seem fully authorised to suggest another course of action.

H. Terminals for "Inner Intelligence"

Orthodox psychiatry would undoubtedly claim that the Thotol system connected no further than the operator's subconscious mind, and those using it were merely talking to themselves. Supposing this were indeed the case, it would still be worthwhile learning Thotolese, purely for the sake of communication with an area of awareness normally unavailable to our ordinary fields of consciousness. Nowadays however, even the most hidebound psychiatrists are grudgingly admitting that human subconsciousness might be in some sort of contact with unknown sources of intelligence, probably emanating from similar forms of Life elsewhere in our Universe. No matter how much they play this down, or sweep it under convenient carpets, they cannot very well deny the possibility altogether. Apart from anything else, it would be utterly ridiculous to affirm that a conscious mind cannot communicate with any other in existence, except through the physical senses using material media designed by humans for such a purpose. To say that every human mind is limited to an organic brain alone and cannot work beyond it, apart from natural or invented mechanisms, is just as absurd in this century as expecting people to believe the sun moves round the earth every twenty-four hours.

Probably few humans fully realise just how dependent we are on "superhuman" consciousness for making any evolutionary progress at all. In past ages primitive man had little contact with each other's minds, apart from immediate urges and needs. They relied mainly on their God-Concepts as a means of extending their lives into unknown areas. However inadequate those Deity-images may have been, they were at least some kind of vehicle for higher than human awareness to focus through and make contact with our forefathers. Wherever man went, he took his Gods with him to encounter other humans and their Gods, either in conflict or concord. Every experience added fractionally to the sum total of our advancement, until we began to grow beyond the scope of God-image for supplying our Inner intelligence, and consequently began to seek this on increasingly abstract levels. Philosophies arose to replace religion, and then science pushed philosophy aside as the latest lead toward enlightenment on our human path to "Heaven," however we interpret that term for perfection of our species.

We may have outgrown our cruder God-concepts which served the childhood of our civilization very faithfully, but we will never outgrow our essential need of contact with the Superconsciousness behind them, which reaches us in this world from yet undiscovered Cosmic origins. Perhaps we think we have become so clever that there is no necessity for anything outside our own minds whatever. Alone and unaided, are we capable of advancing constantly along all lines of consciousness, making more and more of our technical skills until - yes, until *what* ? Exactly what has Science to offer us as an Ultimate we may reach by our own resources? Nothing whatever except extinction to support a purely physical theory of the Universe. Scarcely a proposition likely to satisfy the questing spirit within humanity as a whole, which has consistently sought survival above and beyond every physical form of Life. Only a consciousness operating from those exalted conditions could possibly assure, or inform us concerning a Lifestate really worth living and working for, as human souls with hope of something better than this world's bargains. So if Science has no helpful suggestions on how to contact a consciousness of that kind, who can be blamed for asking elsewhere?

Religion, mysticism, magic, every unorthodox avenue of approach to Inner Life, has some tentative suggestions or standard practices to offer sincere seekers. Though their methods vary through almost the entire gamut of human behaviour, they all depend on precisely the same basic procedures. Intentional projection of consciousness through some type of associated focus, accompanied by hopes of invoking responsive currents of consciousness from intelligent Inner agencies, capable of translating such telepathy into common terms of comprehension. In some ways this is similar to radio researchers who beam mathematical codes into Outer Space on various frequencies, hoping to receive replies from anyone operating compatible equipment elsewhere in the Universe. As yet, communication on all fronts seems more subjective than otherwise, though no one aware of what is happening could justly deny the effects of this on mankind.

No human mind can increase its capacity or capability entirely out of its own contents. That would be like lifting oneself by ones own bootstraps. A mind will only develop its potentials or extend its abilities because of adequate contact with supplies of consciousness from other sources. In this world a great percentage of these are attributable to fellow-human stores of information made available by every sort of invented media. At the same time there is a very important amount of awareness converted to consciousness, through closure of its open circuits by direct contact with non-human intelligence. It is this type of thinking in particular which steadily evolves our consciousness and lifts our lives a little closer towards whatever truth we are trying to touch.

Let us say for example, that someone is struggling to reach comprehension about any point. Maybe an inventor is pushing his perceptive faculties along a specific line as far as he can go, yet cannot reach required results. He has a large amount of associated information to utilise, but none of this is enough to provide him with the answer he seeks. Eventually he starts projecting a polarised stream of awareness in which there is no actual force-flow, because its unconnected ends are reaching beyond the limits of his total reach of consciousness. If an obliging and capable agent of Inner intelligence closes that open circuit with exactly the right type of connection, there will follow a surge of energy through it and the mental mechanism then fulfils its function accordingly. The human concerned will be "inspired" by a vision of his objective and realise how to attain it. Whether or not he acts on this, or translates it into anything useful, is quite another matter. This is a considerable simplification of the process, but it should illustrate how human minds may be enriched by outside contacts completing their open-circuit enquiries, if these are effectively set up.

The "metaphysical mechanism" of the Thotol system working along these lines should not be too difficult to grasp. On our side we "push out" a double stream of consciousness, each channel of which represents a distinct type of Life-quality. We can think of these like the two wires in an electrical conductor, or the twin tracks of a stereo recording if this helps. If we can but extend this within range of some Inner intelligence willing to contact us, it will match up with something recognisable in those spheres of consciousness, and therefore make meaning within their terms of reference. They, on the other hand, can signal back with another polarised stream which translates into alphabetical signs at our end, because we have set up the mental machinery for that purpose. It is just a question of adjustment through a mutual medium.

All we are really doing, is construct terminals for Inner intelligence to reach our normal minds through units of our Earth-language. That is to say, we are making brains into cypher machines capable of decoding messages from other than human minds. Cypher machines are based on exactly this principle. They receive an unintelligible jumble of signals which are fed through a special device that "combs them out" into a pattern making straightforward sense in English, or whatever language the machine was set for. Sophisticated machines have a wide choice of such devices, so they can be preset for any code-system required. As yet, the Thotol system has only its single programme-pattern.

An early prototype of Thotolese using the Hebrew alphabet, linked its letters with natural phenomena on one side and bodily functions on the other. This connected the Macrocosm, or Body of God, with a correspondence in the Microcosm or Body of Man. Since man was said to be made in the image and likeness of his Divine Creator, a relationship between the two types of Life by means of a consciousness-symbol, in the shape of an alphabet letter, should theoretically make one Lifestate aware of the other. For instance, it was necessary to concentrate simultaneously on the palate, the West, wealth, the Sun, Wednesday, and the left ear, in order to isolate the letter K. An internal part of the head, a direction (Space), a human status (Event), a Cosmic power, a day of the week (Time), and an external part of the head. Thus concepts of Inner and Outer, Heaven and Earth, Time and Place, were all connected behind the single letter K. That was its code-combination according to the Book of Formation (*Sepher Yetzirah*).

This may seem a rather odd linkage, but the real purpose was to encourage human minds into thinking a little more like Inner Beings, and a little less like ordinary mortals. It is not easy even now for humans to deal with multiconcepts *en bloc*, and centuries ago it was much more difficult. Somehow or other human awareness had to be expanded by exercises in this art, because it will be normal thinking for future times. That describes the use of Thotolese very nicely. Exercises in practical multi-consciousness, or a step by step course in over-thinking. If we ever hope to speak with the Gods, we shall have to start thinking like Them sometime, and the Thotol system is a good way to begin this.

By way of contrast a mention may be made of the "Enochian Tongue" invented as a "Divine Language" by Dr John Dee, Queen Elizabeth the First's pet astrologer and secret agent. He was an expert cryptographer, and with the aid of his medium, Edward Kelly, devised a private code to communicate with his "spirit guides." This system still fascinates some occult students who attempt to use it for ritual invocations, which it was never designed for in the first place. From what records Dee left, his "spirits" did not seem any brighter, or more reliable, than their modern counterparts, but no doubt Dee found a lot of comfort in the sense of personal contact he felt with them.

Surviving Enochian shows a very limited language amounting to a vocabulary of only between six and seven hundred words spelled with an alphabet of twenty-one letters. If we can believe their translations, every word was connected with the current mysticism of Dee's time, and there are no references at all outside that field. The language did not seem to deal with human relationships in this world, or ordinary circumstances experienced by most mortals. That is to say, it was only capable of expressing what Dee seemed to think were proper topics of conversation among angelic circles. There were no words for "Devil" or even "wicked" in Enochian. The most abusive term was "*BABALON*," which was translated "Wicked harlot." At that time this word signified the Roman Papacy among English Protestants. God is "*IAD*" from the first initial of Yahweh. "Gods Mercy" is *YEHUSOZ* (Jesus), brightness is *LUCIFTIAS* (Lucia = Light), and "Mightier" is *MICALP*, from Michael the archangel whose name signifies "Like God." Enochian may have worked well enough for Dr Dee, but it is scarcely a practical system for our times. Nevertheless there is no reason why anyone determined to construct their own spiritual shorthand system should not do so, provided they are already in contact with an Inner intelligence prepared to share it with them.

We have to remember that the Thotol system developed among Judeo-Christian Europeans associated with educated Moslems, who were looking for unorthodox methods of making intelligent relationships with an Inner Life they believed was linking them together in their common search for Cosmic secrets. This effort was strongly discouraged by their respective religions, and in the case of Christians could cost them their lives under heresy laws. In such an oppressive political and social climate, their only hope was to associate by means of secret societies with all their elaborate security precautions and safeguards. Thinking and working with other than Establishment allowed topics, is always a dangerous process in many human groups on this Earth. Since most of these pioneers were university graduates with Latin as a common language, it seemed to them that Hebrew would make an excellent medium for communication with Cosmic companions, especially since the Hebrew scriptures were regarded as holy by their different cultures. So the Tree of Life arrangement was slowly assembled among these secret circles, remaining unknown outside them until relatively recently. That meant very few human minds were engaged on working with it, and a fair proportion of those for no particularly good purpose.

The regrettable reason for this was that so many people are attracted to secret societies for one-upmanship motives. In earlier days a number of students concerned with Qabalah were firmly convinced that their subject concealed a special code in which words might be found which gave immediate power over demons or spirits, which were then obliged to work for their new masters and bring these all they demanded in the way of fame, money, and every material advantage. Heaven alone knows how much time and trouble was wasted in search of those non-existent words. Perhaps a minority of seekers discovered after many years that they were actually contacting higher orders of living intelligence, which were not concerned with gratifying human greeds, but were truly interested in advancing our evolution through natural channels. Whether this consoled them for poverty-stricken lives spent in contemplative study is uncertain.

Oddly enough there is a background of truth behind the theory that magic words might enable mankind to make "Spirits" work for those knowing such wonderful secrets. To "speak with the Gods and Angels" means putting ourselves in some kind of touch with a considerably superior order of intelligence and culture than our own. Sooner or later we are bound to absorb enough from that Life-level to raise our living standards, because we are inspired by "information received" from what seems to us like Heaven. Those are the Gods who help us help ourselves by encouraging us to develop potentials within our depths, which they are aware of and we have not realised. Maybe they have had to do the same things in their far past, and are now remembering us from our remote future. Whoever they are, we need them. They are neither our servants nor masters, but simply our Leaders in Light.

The "Gods" connected with the Thotol system are evidently extremely interested in human capabilities and activities, almost as if they were studying us closely for some Cosmic reason of their own. They tend to communicate concerning our specialist skills whenever concentrations of consciousness are involved beyond our normal limits. That is to say, they will contact an artist about his painting, a composer about his music, or a craftsman about his handiwork. This is the main reason why occult training schools which knew what they were doing, always encouraged their initiates to take up handicrafts, especially in making their own magical equipment. The currents of consciousness involved with most craft procedures, particularly while learning them, make energy-patterns likely to attract the attention of intelligent and sympathetic Inner entities. When this is coupled to Thotolised thinking, the attraction is naturally very much increased. Old time monks who adopted the motto: "Work and Pray," had discovered the very close connection between those two activities, and how to combine them in a way that related the worker with the Inner Spheres his prayers were directed towards. That is probably why the Rosary became a popular devotion, since it linked contemplative praying with manual exercise in a minimum scale.

This close concern of our Inners with human occupations is especially noticeable while trying to tackle some craft problem, which needs original thinking or fresh ideas for finding a solution. Not infrequently an "Inner voice" will suggest something like: "Have you thought about so and so?" or, "Why not try this and that?" or again, "Ask so and so." Very often some extremely simple and practical way out of difficulty, which might not otherwise have been realised. Some of such ideas come from no further than our own subconsciousness, but there remains a highly significant percentage which cannot be accounted for, except by mental stimuli arriving from an unknown extraneous source. This seldom happens until someone has reached the absolute end of their own resources, and is pushing a concentration of consciousness past those limits in an attempt to break beyond such bounds. Perhaps it is significant that we call major incidents of this kind "breakthroughs" in modern parlance. Many years ago when connections between craftsmanship and Inner consciousness had been firstly established, the semi-religious cult of Free-Masonry came into being. This utilised ordinary craft tools and procedures as symbols for communicating with Inner instructors of Cosmic craftsmanship. Initiates were taught how to employ the normal instruments of their trade, in order to divine what the Life Spirit intended them to do with themselves in this world. This was only a sophisticated step from earlier customs of using sticks, stones, string, sieves, and humble items of cottage equipment to find out what the Gods were thinking about human situations.

Divination as a practice goes back to the depths of antiquity and stays with us today in quite a number of ways. It still depends on much the same motivation, which mostly boils down to personal advantage curiosity. However it is described, it amounts to this single drive in human nature which is not necessarily bad, but is very limited from a Cosmic viewpoint. It can be quite a hindrance to sincere metaphysicians attempting to study the Inner Universe from first-hand experience. The difference is not unlike a commercial interest in figures purely from a profit-and-loss angle, and the study of mathematics for the sake of understanding the meaning of relationships among Life-values per se. The commercialist is only interested in enriching his external personality for a single incarnation, while the genuine mathematician is concerned with enhancement of his Inner Identity, which extends toward Infinity. Both have their own special "language" based on figures, which could be incomprehensible to the other party.

The original meaning of the term "to divine" in its accurate sense, had nothing to do with foretelling the future only. It means specifically to discern the intentions of the Gods in any given human circumstances. That is to say, find out what the Divine Will acting through human beings meant them to do in specified conditions. The situation itself was already known to the enquiring humans, but the "Will of the Gods" therein was not. Hence the attempt to "divine" this vital factor by almost any means suggesting itself. It was not a case of: "Tell me what is going to happen so that I can do what I want about it," but: "Tell me what You would do if You were me in this earthly situation and difficulty." A Christian might describe this as asking the Lord's will to be done on earth as it is in heaven. That was divination in the serious sense of the word. Prediction, or forecasting events was only an arising side-issue, which assumed that if the Will of the Gods was duly done by humans, then such and such would most probably eventuate, but if not, then so and so was likely to happen instead. Human nature being what it is, people much prefered listening to favourable predictions rather than uncompromising directions from Divinities. So professional soothsayers predicted whatever their hearers would pay most for, while prophets proclaimed what no audience enjoys hearing about itself. Result? Rich fortune tellers and poor prophets.

From the flip of a coin to the full spread of a Tarot deck, most of us rely on divination to decide issues at some time of our lives, but how many of us do so from motivations of needing to know consciously what Divinity intends us to do in specific circumstances? Almost everyone wants to know events in advance without reference to Divinity in any way. It is about time we began to rediscover the true meaning of the divinatory art, and listened for the Language of the Gods spoken through our symbols, whether these are coins, cards, stones, words, or anything else. Only in this way are we likely to learn a meaning behind our lives which not only makes them more worth living, but also makes them worth continuing beyond bodily limits into better conditions of consciousness altogether.

It may be a new experience for many to lay out a Tarot spread from the viewpoint of asking Divine guidance concerning our human problems, but this would be a valuable and a valid practice. Who but the narrowest mind would dogmatise that Divine consciousness can only be contacted through official scriptures and teachings? Is not the Voice of God to be heard in every noise of Nature? No matter how remarkable or venerated the scriptures of any religion may be, they were all received and processed into literary form through the minds of men. Not one of them recorded themselves by any other magical means. Surely the same channels of communication remain open today, and are still available to whoever applies along the right lines. Thotolese is one such line suitable for workers of the Western Inner Tradition, much as the I Ching comes more naturally to those following the Oriental Approach. Both in common are legitimate lines, developed mainly for use by intellectual and educated people seeking thoughtful communion with Cosmic companions through mutual mental contacts.

Eventualy somebody is bound to wonder why a Thotol system was developed at all, when so many mediums and interpreters of "spirit messages" are already pouring out an almost endless spate of words in ever accumulating quantities. If it is possible for non-human entities to contact us through the minds of sensitive people, why should anyone bother with something we elaborate as Thotolese? A very sensible and pertinent query indeed. There is a good if somewhat disconcerting answer. Thotolese is a specialised method of communication, originally designed for minds approaching Inner Intelligence on what might be termed academic levels. In other words, it was intended to become a scholastic and technical language, dealing mostly with conditions of consciousness rather distantly removed from purely personal affairs of earthlife. Something like "Special-speak" or terminology used by experts on highly specialised subjects among themselves only.

This could explain why so many Qabalistic expressions seemed unpronounceable and obscure. They were not words in the ordinary sense at all, but whole concept-combinations based on Life-energies which had to be invoked by consciousness rather than cacophony. Strictly speaking, these so-called "words" were more like mathematical formulae represented by literary symbols. Their meaning lay in appreciation of their values rather than descriptions of their contents. There must have been many medieval, and maybe some modern magicians, who became very weary of roaring and wheezing away at these aphonics with no more results than relaxed throats or laryngitis. Had they used their minds instead of their mouths, they might have come to happier conclusions. There was an old warning once given to ceremonialists, that they should never use words in their rituals which they did not understand. A valuable injunction all too frequently ignored. It does not mean there is no value in sonics as such, when designed for specific ceremonial occasions where these are applicable. Very ancient and primitive sounds are often acoustically evokative of profound Inner contents. Thotolistic combinations meant for mental comprehension are of much later derivation.

We shall probably need every Inner system of communication there is to support us through the crisis of consciousness approaching our world. Our beliefs, outlooks, ideas, and almost everything will have to change very considerably, in order to cope with the advances of awareness ahead of us. Like the White Queen in Alyce, we shall have to move at our greatest speed so as to stay in the same spot. This means that our minds must move at enormously increased rates, so that the blurred background we are living against seems to remain steady. Adaptable as the human mind is, it will be strained to its utmost capacity by the impact of intelligence reaching us from remote ranges of Cosmos, which are coming a lot closer to us than we realised.

Probably for this very reason, many moderns are instinctively attempting to tackle all the various techniques which claim to extend or expand awareness in almost any Inner direction. Drugs and disciplines of every description are being employed for this purpose. So are much simpler and straightforward methods such as communion with nature itself by doing no more than settling in wild environs, and trying to make conscious contact with the animals, plants, insects, and every reachable element. Those trying to work this way are liable to feel a little self conscious at first perhaps. It might seem very silly or childish for an urban adult to attempt making friends with a tree, or listening to what the grass is whispering. Yet sometimes the humblest approaches to Truth may obtain results which are unachievable by extremely complicated methods. It is never wise to underestimate or ignore the penetrating power of sheer simplicity.

Perhaps it might be supposed that considerable psychic abilities are needed to work the Thotol system. On the contrary, there are no more psychic faculties involved than those posessed by quite ordinary folk. In fact, it was mainly evolved by people with considerable intellectual gifts, yet no particular aptitude for spectacular spiritual performances. It is something which has to be built up brick by brick as it were, until it rises into an edifice worth entering. To quote from the *Book of Formation*:

> Two stones build two houses,
> Three stones build six houses,
> Four stones build twenty-four houses,
> Five stones build one hundred and twenty houses,
> Six stones build seven hundred and twenty houses,
> Seven stones build five thousand and forty houses.
> From here on go out and think what the mouth is unable to speak
> and the ear is unable to hear.

What the mouth cannot say nor the ear detect is where all the extra material comes from in order to make such a rate of multiplication possible. The implication is that if we will but set one mental stone on another by our own efforts, the Great Architect will surely design something worth living in with them, and provide us with a supply to quarry our fresh ashlars from.

In general usage the Thotol system is for those who think with words, and construct the castles of their consciousness out of mind-formed materials. Yet words are only human conveniences for mentalities to deal with each other and adapt to living in this world. They are foci for our forces here, and do not have validity in other conditions of Life. We begin our incarnations in a wordless womb, and we finish them in the dumbness of death. Before birth and after liberation we have to communicate ourselves with others by non verbal means. To incarnate humans this may seem a very unsatisfactory process, but it is actually far superior to our slow, cumbersome, and limited way of exchanging consciousness with our species on this planet. By learning to think through the Thotol system here, we shall be reconverting our words back to the language we used while out of incarnation. This makes much more spiritual sense than the biggest book of philosophies ever written by hand.

All we learn in each separate earthlife, has to be specially packed into a compaction of consciousness we can carry through the doors of death. If and when we return to this world, that "sense-seed" becomes built into our genetics, from which it steadily grows with us as a guide to Life under another persona. By practising the art of "consciousness-compression," as we must when tackling Thotolese, we gain considerable advantages in the way of "laying up treasure in Heaven," which will stand us in very good stead when it comes to bargaining for best terms of rebirth. A valuable pre-birth legacy to ourselves from a past life, is worth a great deal more than any money legacy from someone else's death after we incarnate here again. Why worry unduly about what we have on earth to leave others when we die? It is much more important what we leave ourselves to begin our next births with. The most recent international studies have shown that human intelligence is eighty percent inherited. Any future inheritance must come from what we bequeath our reborn selves beforehand in the now, which is our past-to-be. When this is properly realised, we can truly begin to become WHAT WE WILL.

What are we? The central value of any religious or metaphysical system is no more than the assurances it can supply its followers of their individual significance. People belong to creeds, cults, or alternative arrangements of Inner Awareness purely in hopes of finding their Real Selves somewhere at the other end of the adventure. Whether they call this unity with God, Nirvana, or anything else, it amounts to the same ultimate objective. Christians believe that if Jesus could survive crucifixion, and live immortally afterwards, then so can they. Modern spiritualist believe that if they can communicate with defunct friends and relatives through a human medium, there are hopes for their spiritual survival also. All systems have their own methods of approach to the Infinite. The entire issue turns on one single point. Is an immortal identity possible for human beings, or not? If the answer is yes, then every form of faith has something valuable in it. If not, then the whole lot are the biggest and cruellest time wasting lie that ever became believed on Earth. The outcome is as simple as that.

It is really not so very difficult to find and place an unthinking, unreasoning, unquestioning, and absolutely unintelligent faith in Life Itself. Primitive people do this quite easily and have no particular fear of death, because it never occurs to them *that* might be the end of their lives. Change means something to them, but extinction has no meaning at all. The instinct they rely on so much for survival tells them they will go on living somehow or other, no matter what happens, unless they get really tired of existing and just "let go of themselves" altogether. Life leaves the choice entirely up to them. An interesting instance in point was the case some years ago of an aboriginal due to be hanged for murder. He was so delightedly cheerful at the scaffold, that the shocked chaplain held up proceedings while he tried to make the man see the gravity and meaning of his situation. The aboriginal grinned the solemnity cheerfully away, telling the chaplain he knew quite well what was happening. He would fall down dead at the end of that rope as a poor and unlucky man, after which he would eventually get up again as a white man with plenty of sixpences in his pocket. He could hardly wait for the trap to drop. His faith in Life outmatched the chaplain's by a long way. An educated intellect makes a considerable barrier against blind belief.

Qabalistic practice and the Thotol system both belong to intellect and education within the Western Inner Tradition, being more a product of enquiring minds rather than soaring souls. Mind is more or less the Middle Pillar between Body and Soul in search of Spirit, and is a development of evolving experience within Existence. Its aim at the top of that Pillar is not the Summit or Crown, but the Eternal Question of "*En na?*" ("what now" or "then what") above and beyond everything. Its message to man is: "Do not accept anything without question. Question the whole of Life, and especially question Divinity, which alone knows the answers. Become a Living Question Mark yourself." There is no guarantee that our queries will receive satisfactory replies by any instant response, but only an indication that if we are intelligent enough to ask them properly, we shall at least be given the chance of finding out for ourselves eventually. An old proverb says that whatever the mind of man can conceive must exist somewhere in the Universe, or we could not have thought about it in the first place. We can only imagine whatever is possible for us to attain somehow or other if we continue seeking it enough on all levels of Life.

Practitioners have reason for believing that the Thotol

system holds the Keys of their continuity in very convenient forms of consciousness. Certainly no other system on earth links a decanate conception of Divinity with an alphabet of human speech, so as to make literate sense with the combination. The nearest alternative is the *I Ching*, which has no alphabetic connections, being purely a mathematical arrangement wherein pre-coded symbols are chance selected by the casting of yarrow-stalk lots. There is of course the Nordic custom of casting rune-stones to decide what the Gods intend, and letter-formation by cast lots is indeed an ancient practice persisting to this day. The Halloween game of peeling an apple in one long strip, and then throwing this over the left shoulder in the hopes of it forming the initial of a future love, is an instance of this. Girdle cords are also whirled during incantations, and then released to form letter-like lines where they fall. All these and similar behaviours can be classified as appeals to the Gods for guidance by letters, but nothing else has even come close to the Thotol system for literary interpretations of spiritual communications by direct mental mediation.

The practice of automatic writing or Xenoglossy would not be a fair comparison with Thotolism at all. In those instances writing and speech have to be produced by the action of the subconscious mind influencing the muscular activities of hand or throat. The subconscious is assumed to have accepted direction by another intelligence than its usual operator. Whether this is so or not, there is no clear agreement between the mind of the medium and that of the communicator concerning the value and significance of not only every word, but each single letter of any words used. The result depends entirely on what one mind-level can get out of the other. This could be anything at all from Amazing to Zanyistic. In the case of Thotolism, there is a pre-agreed and practised standard of spiritual significances, through which both communicants must work in order to understand each other. The code of the Life-Tree is in itself the medium of communication among mentalities concerned. Results depend on how far a human mind is able to interpret consciousness directed at it from higher levels, via this common instrument of intelligence. This again depends on factors like individuality, practice, application, and a lot of similar variables. The end-product is liable to seem somewhat commonplace or average, compared with sensational and maybe startling "messages" received by other means, yet years of experience leave no doubt that it is definitely the steady and constant stream of "step-by-step" enlightenment, which leads us best from one stage of Life to another with the least casualties on the way.

So those who will be satisfied with nothing less than fantastic revelations from the "Great Beyond," and personal assurances from God Himself (preferably in writing of course) as to their unique importance in His estimation, might as well save themselves the work and trouble involved with the Thotol system, and settle for something a lot more showy if less reliable. For those contented to live and learn the lessons of Life quietly and steadily, in company with higher orders of consciousness which speak with "still, small voices" of spiritual commonsense, there is a great deal to be gained from studying Thotolese. If only a single word of real significance were comprehended every day, that would make more in a year than many learn in a whole incarnation. A question answered very slowly with the truth, is of greater value than one immediately responded to with a lie. This does not mean that all Thotol communications must needs be tedious or ambiguous. They are much more often quite terse and unequivocal, or else a refusal of reply is made plain enough. It used to be said that there were only three answers to prayer. Yes, No, and Wait. With Thotolese this could sound like "We will speak," "We will not speak," and "We will talk later." All are communications in themselves.

It must never be lost sight of that the act of communion with Divinity *per se* is always wordless. Words, especially on our side, may accompany the act or engage with it to any extent, but the actual contact itself is quite apart from any human verbalisation. In point of fact, no human being could ever be entirely out of contact with Divinity and continue existing. What we have come to call "communion," is a mutual recognition of ourselves in each others identity through some shared stream of consciousness. Divinity and Humanity meeting in a mutual act of acceptance. Christians claim this takes place through Eucharistic symbology, but none of them would expect the bread and wine to preach a sermon from the pulpit afterwards. If they are conscious of any verbalised communication during their contact-meditations, they usually regard this as a private matter between themselves and their Deity, and keeping close confidence about it subsequently. That makes very sound spiritual sense, and is recommendable to those seeking contacts of the same kind through Thotolistic means.

Just as the Eucharistic elements are physical symbols with which Christians hope for conscious contact with Deity through their Christ-Concept, so is the Tree of Life a mental symbol intended to accomplish a parallel end-result for Thotolists. Their symbol is meant to be received by their minds, in much the same spirit as a Christian receives the sacrament bodily. What should matter most in either case, is an actual experience of close relationship between the human and the higher Life-order approached. That in itself *is* the communion. Any accompaniment of verbal intelligence should be regarded as an addition to be taken in the light of its conscious content. So contact should always be the primary objective of Thotolists, and literary linguistics a secondary issue, no matter how much hoped for. Theoretically there is nothing to stop sincere Thotolists from designing ceremonies about their contact-practices, or treating them sacramentally with formalised psychodramas much in the style of a Mass.

Therefore the most sensible way to set up a workable Thotal system, is to regard its central Tree-symbol as a mediative means of making contact with Divinity to at least some degree, and act accordingly. The main thing is not to be concerned or worried if words do not immediately start pouring out on each occasion. In fact if they do, it might be well to suspect ones own subconscious, and check up carefully. There is normally a pause before any response through the Tree is received, during which the "sense of Presence" should somewhat intensify. It is far better to experience this "Presence" without any words following, than release a flood of words from the subconscious which cuts off or interferes with the orginal sense of contact. A good way of authenticating an Inner contact, is to estimate whether any accompanying verbalism increases or decreases ones awareness of it. If the former, then the contact is most likely a genuine one, but if the latter, most of the words are probably evoked purely from ones own subconscious. Even at that, they should serve some useful purpose. It takes a great deal of disciplined practice to prevent interference, while at the same time allowing the mind to permit the passage of whatever words are selected by the spiritual influence concerned.

Some while ago among the stricter schools of esoteric disciplines, the only "teachings" permitted were those which might instruct an intelligent mind how to make its own Inner contacts through methods which members of those schools had found practical from their combined experience. Initiates were taught *how* to learn from spiritual sources, then left entirely alone to decide for themselves *what* to learn, where to learn it from, and what to do if and when they ever learned anything. Having once been given the keys, they were expected to unlock every Inner door by their individual efforts. Nobody else was going to open another thing for them. From then on it was entirely a self-service affair. To some extent this was like teaching a clever child to read and write, then letting it loose in a library to learn everything else for itself, guided by inspiration alone. Such schools were indeed tough and uncompromising, offering nothing but hard work, out of which students would have to earn rewards as best they could. As might be expected, they were not overwhelmed by applications for admission, nor were they even accessible to ordinary people. No entrants would be accepted unless they showed great promise of survival through at least a good deal of the training. Western schools of this nature generally came to adopt the Thotol system as a basis of curriculum.

This "sink or swim" type of school may sound somewhat stringent, but they certainly got results out of their graduates. They worked rather on the lines of "health farms" which make patients deserve better health by accepting disciplines they would never agree to, if they were not frightened of possible consequences otherwise. As anyone might realise, there is nothing especial to a health farm which patients could not do for themselves in their own house for a fraction of the cost, if they had enough will power. What they actually pay for is the individual attentions of experts, who see that they carry out the recommended regimes for regenerating their bodily tissues. They are really buying beneficent bullying. It is similar in the case of some esoteric concerns cultivating a Thotal-based scheme of spiritual training. Administrators do no more than see that students either carry out their disciplines or go elsewhere for guidance. The option is entirely theirs.

All such students are taught, is how to listen to the Language of the Gods in themselves by means of the Thotol system. Nothing more. Anything else they would have to get from whatever Gods they managed to meet on their own home ground. From one point of view this might seem unfriendly, indifferent, perhaps even a little un-human. Careful consideration should show that it is no more than an honest admission of human limitations. No living soul on this Earth had the right, or should be allowed the power, to inflict its opinions and encounters with Divinity upon others as an authoritative act. We are quite entitled to share our findings with each other, and combine in any way we please to recognise Divinity through all forms of consciousness, but no one is entitled to insist: "This alone is authentic, and the rest are only inferior imitations." No matter what claims are made, in the end everyone seeking a Divinity, must come thereto by their own individual conclusions however those are reached.

The masses of Mankind do not look for conscious contact with Divinities on any levels. They are content to live within their lower limits, and maybe share occasionally in generalised God-concepts broadly accepted by large numbers of humans. Moreover, they can get through many incarnations in this world well enough by that method, until they begin asking the fatal question: "Who am I, and where am I going?" The *Ain*, or *Eh na?* of the Life-Tree. From thenceforth nothing will satisfy them except questing through life for that No-Thing. From one incarnation to another they will continue searching with increasing disillusionment, and eventually must admit with Faust:

> "I've studied now Philosophy,
> Medicine and Jurisprudence too,
> And to my cost, Theology,
> With arduous labour through and through.
> Yet here I stand with all my lore,
> Poor fool! No wiser than before."

Perhaps at that vital point, the realisation of being a Divine Fool, or Absolute Innocent at the foot of the Life-Tree, will give an awakened soul the courage to glance up through the branches and try to guess how they can be climbed. It could also happen that encouraging calls are heard, in a strangely familiar yet uncomprehensible language from somewhere overhead. At that instant a single leaf from the Holy Tree might flutter earthwards into hands outheld with suppliant wonder. On it is to be found a Symbol which explains how would-be climbers might begin mounting, until hands from higher levels reach down to help, accompanied by voices speaking clear words of welcome. Holding only one such leaf apiece, many may tackle the Life-Tree with increased interest and a new perception of its purpose. If sincere prayers are ever to be answered, then let this work provide a leaf of that nature, for the benefit of all who seek to share it.

Made in the USA
Las Vegas, NV
07 January 2021